CHEMISTRY REVISION FOR LEAVING CERTIFICATE

SECOND EDITION

MICHAEL QUIRKE

GW00728804

Gill & Macmillan

Gill & Macmillan Ltd
Hume Avenue
Park West
Dublin 12
with associated companies throughout the world
www.gillmacmillan.ie

© Michael Quirke 2003, 2007

978 0 7171 4138 8

Print origination by Macmillan India

*The paper used in this book is made from the wood pulp of managed forests.
For every tree felled, at least one tree is planted, thereby renewing natural resources.*

Contents

Introduction

This book covers the complete Leaving Certificate Chemistry syllabus, introduced in 2000. The Higher level is in addition to all of the Ordinary level and it is clearly marked. It covers the four options (1A, 1B, 2A and 2B). You should check which options will be examined in the year you sit your Leaving Certificate exam.

All of the mandatory experiments are listed and described, with the expected outcomes. Examples of calculations are included and are worked through in steps.

The layout of the chapters is designed to bring together material of a similar nature. For instance, the organic sections are grouped into just two chapters – one for the hydrocarbons and chloroalkanes, and the other for the compounds that contain oxygen, namely the alcohols, aldehydes, ketones, acids and esters. Similarly, Chapter 1 contains elements, atomic structure and radioactivity. By grouping topics in one chapter it emphasises the common themes that connect them naturally. It also simplifies revision and it allows you to revise a complete section of the course in one sitting.

At the end of every chapter there is a wide range of questions to test your comprehension and recall of the material that has been learned. The answers to all of the questions can be found within the chapter. The examination papers for 2005 are also included to give practice at the examination layout.

The usual advice for revision applies – organise it in good time and revise more than once. This book is of such a size that you should be able to revise quickly and often. And remember, the best person to answer your questions and to help with revision is your teacher.

I would like to thank my students (present and past) at St. Joseph's Secondary School, Doon, Co. Limerick for their enthusiasm, my wife Teresa for her support, and the editorial staff at Gill & Macmillan for their quiet efficiency.

Michael Quirke

Mandatory experiments

indicates Higher level only.

1. Flame tests (Li, Na, K, Ba, Sr and Cu only) p. 10.

2. Redox reactions:

   (a) Displacement reactions of metals (Zn with Cu^{2+}, Mg with Cu^{2+}) p. 25.

   (b–c) Halogens as oxidising agents (reactions with sulfites and Fe^{2+}, bromides and iodides) p. 27–30.

3. Tests for anions in aqueous solutions: chloride, carbonate, nitrate, sulfate, phosphate*, sulfite*, hydrogencarbonate* p. 41.

4. Determination of the relative molecular mass of a volatile liquid p. 55.

5. Preparation of a standard solution of sodium carbonate p. 72.

6. (a) Standardisation of a hydrochloric acid solution using a standard solution of sodium carbonate p. 76.

   (b) (Ordinary level only) A hydrochloric acid/sodium hydroxide titration, and the use of this titration in making the salt sodium chloride p. 76.

7. *Determination of the concentration of ethanoic acid in vinegar p. 76.

8. *Determination of the amount of water of crystallisation in hydrated sodium carbonate p. 77.

9. *A potassium manganate(VII)/ammonium iron(II) sulfate titration p. 79.

10. *Determination of the amount of iron in an iron tablet p. 81.

11. *An iodine/thiosulfate titration p. 83.

12. *Determination of the percentage (w/v) of hypochlorite in bleach p. 85.

13. Determination of the heat of reaction of hydrochloric acid with sodium hydroxide p. 93.

14. Monitoring the rate of production of oxygen from hydrogen peroxide, using manganese dioxide as a catalyst p. 100.

15. Studying the effects on the reaction rate of (i) concentration and (ii) temperature, using sodium thiosulfate solution and hydrochloric acid p. 105.

16. Preparation and properties of ethene (combustion, tests for unsaturation using acidified potassium manganate(VII) solution, and bromine water) p. 115.

17. Preparation and properties of ethyne (combustion, tests for unsaturation using bromine water and acidified potassium manganate(VII) solution) p. 115.

Chapter 1 – The periodic table of elements. Atomic structure. The electronic structure of atoms. Radioactivity

1.1 THE PERIODIC TABLE OF THE ELEMENTS

What are elements?

To the ancient Greeks, the elements consisted of earth, fire, air and water, and everything else contained varying amounts of these elements.

Robert Boyle (son of the Earl of Cork) was the first scientist to consider elements in modern terms – **elements are substances that cannot be broken down into simpler substances by chemical means**.

Over many years and by various methods of analysis all of the elements of the earth were identified. For instance, **Humphry Davy**, a scientist who worked in the early nineteenth century, discovered many of the reactive metals by electrolysis of their salts. He discovered sodium, potassium, calcium, magnesium, barium and strontium.

There are 92 naturally occurring elements on earth (though a few more have been made artificially in nuclear reactors).

Each element has its own symbol by which it is recognised in every language. The symbol consists of one or two letters: if it has only one, this is always a capital letter; if the symbol has two letters, the first is always a capital and the second is always a small letter. For example, C is carbon, O is oxygen, Co is cobalt.

You must be familiar with the symbols for the first 36 elements, including Na for sodium, P for phosphorus, K for potassium, Fe for iron, Cu for copper, etc.

HIGHER LEVEL

Early in the nineteenth century (in 1829), **Dobereiner** found that when he arranged the elements in order of their atomic mass (atomic weight), there were some elements in **groups of three**; these had **similar chemical properties** and the **atomic mass of the middle one was the average of the other two**. He called these groups **triads**. Examples of triads include Li/Na/K, and Cl/Br/I.

Later in the nineteenth century (in 1864) after more elements had been discovered, **Newlands** found that when the elements were arranged in order of their atomic mass, similar **elements** occurred at **every eighth** position, or every **octave**.

In 1869 **Mendeleev** also arranged the elements in increasing atomic mass, and produced a table with elements with similar **chemical properties in groups**. To achieve this table he had to:

- leave gaps for elements that he predicted would be found
- **reverse the order** of the atomic masses for certain pairs of elements, (e.g. Te and I).

1

Figure 1.1   The periodic table.

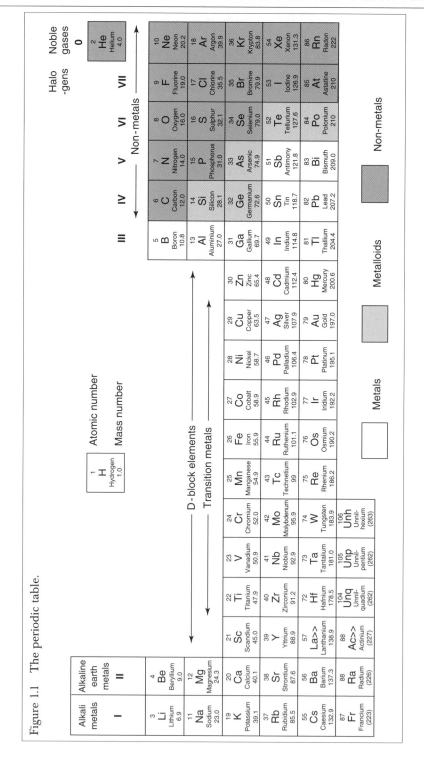

The **modern periodic table of the elements** is very similar to Mendeleev's table except that:

- It has no gaps.
- It includes the noble gases.
- It is based on the order of increasing **atomic number**.

In the periodic table the **groups of elements have similar chemical properties**. Some groups have names, for example:

- group I, the alkali metals
- group II, the alkaline earth metals
- group VII, the halogens
- group VIII, the noble gases.

See Figure 1.1.

1.2 ATOMIC STRUCTURE

What is matter made of?

The universe consists of energy and matter. Unlike energy, **matter occupies space** (it has volume) and **it has mass**.

John Dalton published the idea that **matter is made of atoms**. He believed, wrongly, that atoms were the smallest particles of matter and that they could not change. We now know that there are smaller particles – subatomic particles – within atoms, and that radioactive atoms do change into other atoms. Nevertheless, we can define an **atom** as **the smallest part of an element that has the chemical properties of that element**.

Substances may consist of the following particles:

- **uncombined atoms** (for example, metals and noble gases)
- **molecules** (groups of atoms that are chemically combined)
- **ions** (atoms that have acquired a charge by losing or gaining electrons).

The **law of conservation of mass** states that **in a chemical reaction there is no change in mass**; that is, the total mass of the reacting chemicals equals the total mass of the products. This means that in a chemical reaction **matter is not destroyed**. (In a nuclear reaction there is a loss of mass as some matter is converted to energy in accordance with Einstein's equation $e = mc^2$.)

Discovery of the electron

The first subatomic particle to be discovered (towards the end of the nineteenth century) was the electron.

HIGHER LEVEL

Crookes experimented with the conduction of electricity in vacuum tubes, from which the air had been removed. He discovered **cathode rays** emitted from the negative electrode and observed that they formed shadows and that they could spin very light paddles (see Figure 1.2). He concluded that cathode rays consist of very small particles coming off the negative electrode (called the cathode).

J. J. Thomson found that cathode rays consist of **negatively charged particles** by observing that they were attracted to a positively charged plate and, like an electric current, they were deflected in a magnetic field (see Figure 1.3).

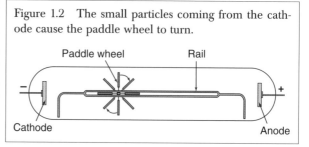

Figure 1.2   The small particles coming from the cathode cause the paddle wheel to turn.

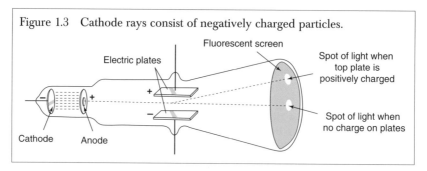

Figure 1.3   Cathode rays consist of negatively charged particles.

HIGHER LEVEL

By varying the strength of the magnetic field to match the force of the electric field Thomson calculated the ratio of the charge of an electron to its mass – the **e/m of an electron** (see Figure 1.4).

Electrons from all kinds of metals used as cathodes were found to behave in the same way, so they were assumed to be present in all atoms. Thomson proposed that atoms consisted of tiny electrons embedded in a sphere of positive charge, like a plum pudding.

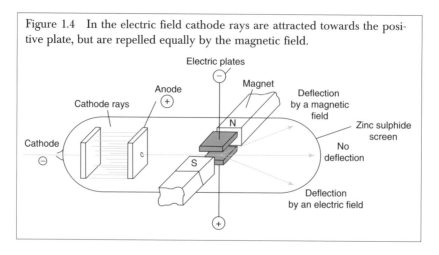

Figure 1.4   In the electric field cathode rays are attracted towards the positive plate, but are repelled equally by the magnetic field.

An Irish scientist, **George Stoney**, proposed the name **electron**.

Millikan measured the size of the charge and the mass of electrons. He experimented with charged **oil droplets** that he suspended between a positively and a negatively charged plate, and was able to measure the **size of the charge of an electron**. Thus using the e/m already known, the mass of an electron was also calculated.

Discovery of the nucleus

Rutherford observed that some **alpha particles** from a radioactive source were rebounded off a thin foil of **gold**, while most of them either passed straight through or were deflected by small angles (see Figures 1.5 and 1.6). Because alpha particles

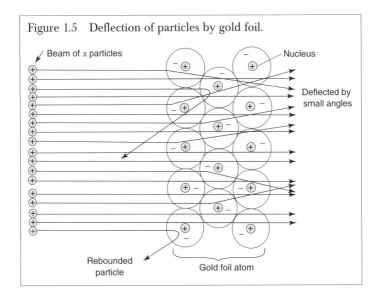

Figure 1.5   Deflection of particles by gold foil.

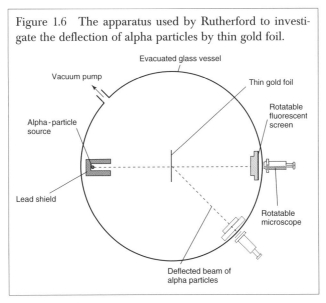

Figure 1.6   The apparatus used by Rutherford to investigate the deflection of alpha particles by thin gold foil.

have a positive charge (they consist of two protons and two neutrons, like the nucleus of helium), Rutherford concluded that the atom's positive charge is located in a small part of the atom and that most of the volume of the atom is empty. Rutherford's model of an atom therefore consisted of a **nucleus** of positive charge, surrounded by electrons a large distance from it.

HIGHER LEVEL

Rutherford also found that atoms of oxygen and nitrogen **emitted positively charged particles** when they were bombarded by **alpha particles**. He called the positive particles **protons**.

Chadwick (in 1932) bombarded beryllium atoms with **alpha particles** and found that they **emitted particles that had no charge** but had the same mass as protons. He called the particles **neutrons**.

In summary:

- **Crookes**. Cathode rays inside gas vacuum tubes consist of particles.
- **Thomson**. Discovered electrons – cathode rays consist of negative particles. He calculated the e/m of electrons.
- **Millikan**. Calculated the charge (e) and the mass (m) of an electron from his oil drops experiment.
- **Rutherford**. Discovered the nucleus – alpha particles rebounded off gold foil.
- **Rutherford**. Discovered protons – alpha particles ejected positive particles from oxygen and nitrogen atoms.
- **Chadwick**. Discovered neutrons – alpha particles ejected neutral particles from beryllium.

Table 1.1   The subatomic particles

	Relative charge	Relative mass	Location
Proton	+ 1	1	In the nucleus
Neutron	0	1	In the nucleus
Electron	− 1	1/1840	Around the nucleus

Atomic number and mass number

HIGHER LEVEL

Moseley discovered that the frequency of X-rays produced from any metal was proportional to the number of protons in its atoms. Thus, the **atomic number** could be calculated.

The numbers of protons, neutrons and electrons of an atom are found in two numbers that are provided for each element on the periodic table of the elements.

The **atomic number** (Z) of an atom is the **number of protons** that it has; and it always has the **same number of electrons**.

The **mass number** (A) of an atom is the **number of protons plus neutrons** that it has. Thus, the number of neutrons of an atom is found by subtracting Z from A.

Example

These sodium atoms have 11 protons, 11 electrons and 12 neutrons.

What are isotopes?

Isotopes are atoms of the same element with different mass number due to having a different number of neutrons.

Almost all elements have isotopes. For example, hydrogen has three isotopes, and unusually for isotopes, these different forms of hydrogen have different names:

- $_1^1H$ (protium) has 1 proton and no neutron
- $_1^2H$ (deuterium) has 1 proton and 1 neutron
- $_1^3H$ (tritium) has 1 proton and 2 neutrons.

Carbon also has three isotopes: $_6^{12}C$, $_6^{13}C$, $_6^{14}C$.

What is the relative atomic mass of an element?

The relative atomic mass of an element (A_r) is the average mass of an atom, relative to one-twelfth of the mass of a ^{12}C atom.

The relative mass of an element can be calculated from (a) the mass of its isotopes and (b) their relative abundance. These are measured in a **mass spectrometer** (see Figure 1.7).

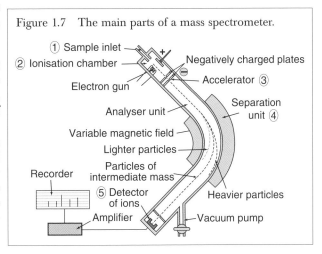

Figure 1.7 The main parts of a mass spectrometer.

HIGHER LEVEL

Example

A sample of chlorine has two isotopes and their normal abundance is as follows: 75% is ^{35}Cl and 25% is ^{37}Cl. Calculate the A_r (relative atomic mass) of chlorine.

Answer

In 100 atoms the weight of the 75 atoms is 75×35, i.e., 2,625, and the mass of 25 atoms is 25×37, i.e., 925. Thus the mass of 100 atoms equals $2625 + 925$, i.e., 3,550. Therefore the mass of an average atom (A_r) is 35.5.

The mass spectrometer

The mass spectrometer is an instrument that provides two measurements:

- the relative mass of the atoms (or molecules)
- their relative abundance.

HIGHER LEVEL

The processes that take place in the instrument are as follows:

1. **Vaporisation**. The sample is injected as a gas, or as a liquid that is heated to vaporise it.
2. **Ionisation**. An electron gun bombards the atoms with high-energy electrons which knock electrons off the atoms, forming positive ions.
3. **Acceleration**. A high-voltage negatively charged plate accelerates the positive ions towards it and they pass through a hole.
4. **Separation**. An electro-magnet produces a strong magnetic field in the separation unit and the ions are deflected towards the detector. The lighter ions are deflected most.
5. **Detection**. The detector responds to the ions that hit it and produces a signal that corresponds to the number of ions. The size of the magnetic field that sent the ions to the detector corresponds to the mass of the ions. A computer converts both measurements into a spectrum on a paper recorder. The result is a **mass spectrum**. The bottom axis records the mass and the vertical axis records the relative abundance (see Figure 1.8).

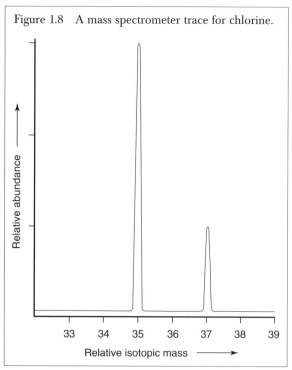

Figure 1.8   A mass spectrometer trace for chlorine.

1.3   THE ELECTRONIC STRUCTURE OF ATOMS

HIGHER LEVEL

Line emission spectrums

When a gas is heated or conducts electricity, it emits light (for example, the yellow light of sodium street lights). If the light is passed through a **spectroscope** or **spectrometer** (they contain a prism or diffraction grating) it is broken up ('dispersed') to form **series of lines of different colours** or frequencies (see Figure 1.9).

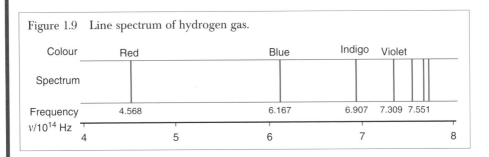

Figure 1.9   Line spectrum of hydrogen gas.

For instance, the **Balmer series** is a series of lines of different colours that is in the emission spectrum of **hydrogen**. (There are also invisible lines in the infra-red and ultra-violet (UV).)

The spectrum is characteristic (unique) for each element and it can be used to identify the presence of an element in a sample.

Absorption spectrums: the atomic absorption spectrometer (AAS)

When white light is passed through a hot gas the atoms absorb the same colours or frequencies of their emission spectrum to produce a corresponding series of black lines in the spectrum of white light – an absorption spectrum.

The **amount** of light that is absorbed is proportional to the concentration of the element and this principle is used in **quantitative** analysis in an AAS to **measure the concentration of a metal** in a solution.

What happens is that the sample is evaporated in a flame and light with the same frequencies as the absorption spectrum for a **particular metal** is passed into a sample (for example, light from a sodium lamp is used when the amount of sodium is being measured). The brightness of the light before and after is compared to measure the absorption. The absorption for a sample of unknown concentration is compared with the absorption of standard solutions.

Mandatory experiment 1: Flame tests (Li, Na, K, Ba, Sr and Cu only)
See Figure 1.10.

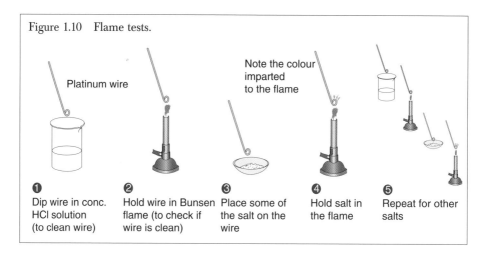

Figure 1.10   Flame tests.

① Dip wire in conc. HCl solution (to clean wire)

② Hold wire in Bunsen flame (to check if wire is clean)

③ Place some of the salt on the wire

④ Hold salt in the flame

⑤ Repeat for other salts

Note the colour imparted to the flame

Platinum wire

A flame test is conducted by placing a small amount of the pure compound containing the metal (usually a chloride because they are volatile), on a platinum wire in the edge of a blue flame of the Bunsen burner. The wire may be cleaned with concentrated HCl before it is used to pick up another sample.

The colour of the light from heated metals can be diagnostic as it depends on the particular energy levels of the electrons. Note the colour of these metals in a flame:

- Ba – green
- Cu – blue-green
- K – lilac
- Li – crimson
- Na – yellow
- Sr – red.

What are energy levels in atoms?

An energy level is the fixed amount of energy (quanta) that an electron can have. In the ground state the electrons occupy the lowest energy levels.

The evidence for energy levels came from the examination of the hydrogen emission spectrum by **Bohr**.

HIGHER LEVEL

The emission spectrum of hydrogen as evidence for energy levels

The emission spectrum of hydrogen consists of a series of coloured lines (Balmer series). The explanation for the lines is as follows: Hydrogen atoms have one electron. In the ground state the electron is in the lowest energy level.

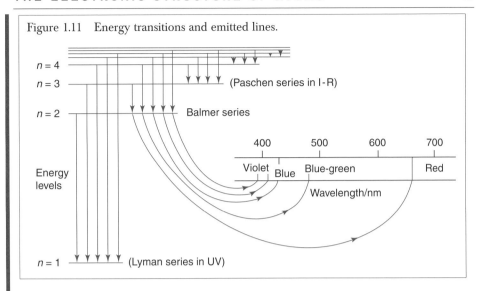

Figure 1.11   Energy transitions and emitted lines.

When the atom is heated the electron absorbs energy and rises to a higher energy level E_2. The excited electron falls down to a lower energy level E_1, and the loss of energy, $E_2 - E_1$, is emitted as a defined line of light, with a specific frequency, f. The energy of the emitted line is calculated as $h \times f$, where h = Planck's constant.

$$h \times f = E_2 - E_1$$

Because the frequency of each line is specific, this implies that the values of E are fixed. This means that the energy levels for the electron have fixed amounts of energy.

Each line in the Balmer series arises from electrons falling to the 2nd energy level from the 3rd, 4th, 5th and higher energy levels. (When the electrons fall to the 1st energy level, the lines are in the UV.) See Figure 1.11.

Energy sublevels

Magnification of the spectral lines revealed that the lines consisted of a small number of finer lines that were very close together. These were explained as being due to the subdivisions of the energy levels, and the energy sublevels were termed 's', 'p', 'd' and 'f'.

* The first energy level has one s sublevel.
* The second energy level has s and p sublevels.
* The third energy level has s, p and d sublevels.
* The fourth energy level has s, p, d, and f sublevels.

The Bohr model of the atom

The electrons move around the nucleus in **fixed orbits**, corresponding to the energy levels and sublevels.

The first energy level holds two electrons; the second level holds eight electrons. The third energy level can hold 18 electrons, though it appears to be full when it has eight electrons so that the next two electrons go in to the fourth energy level.

HIGHER LEVEL

Atomic orbitals

The Bohr model was modified by the work of physicists in the 1920s and 1930s.

* **De Broglie** demonstrated that electrons had a wave nature.
* **Heisenberg** stated his **uncertainty principle**: it is impossible to know simultaneously the position and the velocity of an electron. Therefore the location of an electron can only be given as a probability of it being within a certain space.

Thus, the notion of electrons having a fixed orbit around the nucleus was changed to that of the orbital:

* **An orbital is the space around a nucleus where there is a high probability of finding an electron**.
* An orbital can hold up to two electrons (of opposite spin).
* An s orbital has a spherical shape; a p orbital has the shape of a dumb-bell.

The s sublevel has **one** s orbital; the p sublevel has **three** p orbitals; the d sublevel has **five** d orbitals, and the f sublevel has **seven** f orbitals. See Figure 1.12.

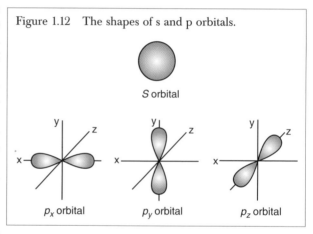

Figure 1.12   The shapes of s and p orbitals.

S orbital

p_x orbital p_y orbital p_z orbital

The electronic configuration of atoms

You are expected to use the periodic table to write down the electronic configuration (s, p) of the first 36 elements. Remember that the electrons do not enter the d sublevel after the p sublevel until they have first filled the next s sublevel (see Figure 1.13).

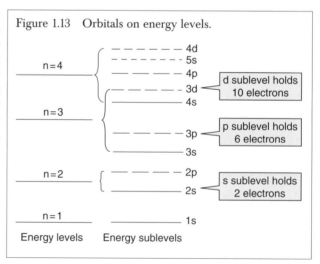

Figure 1.13   Orbitals on energy levels.

n=4   —————— 4d
           - - - - - - - - 5s
           —————— 4p
           - - - - - - 3d   d sublevel holds 10 electrons
           —————— 4s

n=3   - - - - - - 3p   p sublevel holds 6 electrons
           —————— 3s

n=2   - - - - - 2p
           —————— 2s   s sublevel holds 2 electrons

n=1   —————— 1s

Energy levels   Energy sublevels

Examples

H: $1s^1$
He: $1s^2$
Li: $1s^2, 2s^1$
C: $1s^2, 2s^2, 2p^2$
O: $1s^2, 2s^2, 2p^4$
Na: $1s^2, 2s^2, 2p^6, 3s^1$
Ar: $1s^2, 2s^2, 2p^6, 3s^2, 3p^6$
Ca: $1s^2, 2s^2, 2p^6, 3s^2, 3p^6, 4s^2$
Sc: $1s^2, 2s^2, 2p^6, 3s^2, 3p^6, 4s^2, 3d^1$
*Cr: $1s^2, 2s^2, 2p^6, 3s^2, 3p^6, 4s^1, 3d^5$
*Cu: $1s^2, 2s^2, 2p^6, 3s^2, 3p^6, 4s^1, 3d^{10}$
Ga: $1s^2, 2s^2, 2p^6, 3s^2, 3p^6, 4s^2, 3d^{10}, 4p^1$
Kr: $1s^2, 2s^2, 2p^6, 3s^2, 3p^6, 4s^2, 3d^{10}, 4p^6$.

*Note the promotion of an s electron in order to half-fill or fill the d sublevel.

The electronic configuration of ions

If the ion is **positive**, it has formed from an atom that has **lost** electrons, and the number of electrons it has lost is the size of the charge. For example, Na^+ ions have lost one electron, and Mg^{2+} have lost two electrons. Thus, the number of electrons in a Na^+ ion is the number of electrons in an Na atom **minus** one, i.e. $1s^2, 2s^2\ 2p^6$.

If the ion is **negative** it has formed from an atom that **gained** electrons, and the number of electrons it has gained is the size of the charge. For instance, F^- has one extra electron, O^{2-} has two extra electrons. Thus, the number of electrons in an F^- ion is the number of electrons in an F atom **plus** one, i.e. $1s^2, 2s^2\ 2p^6$.

Examples

- Na^+ has $11 - 1$ electrons, i.e., 10. Its electronic configuration is $1s^2, 2s^2, 2p^6$.
- Mg^{2+} has $12 - 2$ electrons, i.e., 10. Its electronic configuration is $1s^2, 2s^2, 2p^6$.
- F^- has $9 + 1$ electrons, i.e., 10. It has the same electronic configuration as the above ions.
- O^{2-} has $8 + 2$ electrons, i.e., 10. It also has the same electronic configuration.

All of the above ions have the same electron configuration as the noble gas Ne, which has 10 electrons.

The arrangement of the electrons in the p orbitals

There are three p orbitals of equal energy, p_x, p_y, and p_z. The electrons fill these orbitals according to this rule: **electrons occupy the orbitals on their own before filling them in pairs**.

See Figure 1.14.

Figure 1.14   The electron arrangement of oxygen showing the arrangement of electrons in the p orbitals.

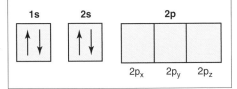

Examples

- C has two p electrons in the 2nd energy level: $2p_x^1$, $2p_y^1$.
- N has three p electrons in the 2nd energy level: $2p_x^1$, $2p_y^1$, $2p_z^1$.
- O has four p electrons in the 2nd energy level: $2p_x^2$, $2p_y^1$, $2p_z^1$.
- F has five p electrons in the 2nd energy level: $2p_x^2$, $2p_y^2$, $2p_z^1$.
- As has three p electrons in the 4th energy level: $4p_x^1$, $4p_y^1$, $4p_z^1$.

Atomic radius

Using X-rays, the distance between the nuclei of two atoms of the same element that are covalently bonded has been measured. **The atomic radius is half the distance between the nuclei of two covalently bonded atoms of an element** (see Figure 1.15).

Going down a **group** the atomic radius **increases** because the outer electrons are in higher energy levels (shells) and because they are shielded from the nucleus by the inner energy levels. Going across a **period** the atomic radius **decreases** because the nuclear charge is increasing and because the electrons are in the same energy level and thus no extra shielding results (see Figure 1.16).

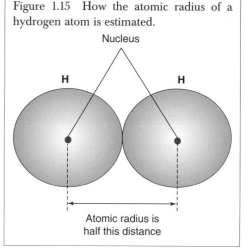

Figure 1.15   How the atomic radius of a hydrogen atom is estimated.

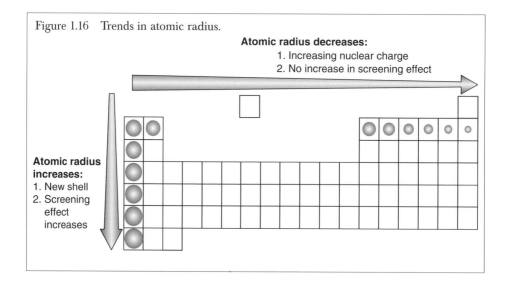

Figure 1.16   Trends in atomic radius.

HIGHER LEVEL

Ionisation energies

The first ionisation energy of an element is the minimum amount of energy that is needed to remove the most loosely held electron from an isolated atom in its ground state. It can be represented as:

$$A - e^- \rightarrow A^+$$

- Going down a **group** the ionisation energies **decrease** because (a) the atomic radius is increasing and (b) the extra shielding by the inner energy levels.
- Going across a **period** the ionisation energies **increase** because (a) the nuclear charge increases, and (b) the atomic radius decreases.
- Going across a period there are two exceptions to the general trend: (a) when the s sublevel is full; for example, Be is higher than expected (b) when the p sublevel is half-full; for example, N is higher than expected (see Figures 1.17 and 1.18).

The **second ionisation energy** is the amount of energy to remove an electron from a positive ion. It can be represented as $A^+ - e^- \rightarrow A^{2+}$.

The **third ionisation energy** is the amount of energy that is needed to remove an electron from a double positive ion. It can be represented as $A^{2+} - e^- \rightarrow A^{3+}$.

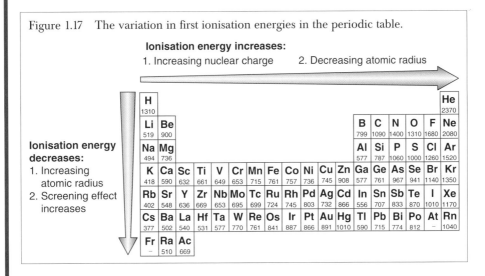

Figure 1.17   The variation in first ionisation energies in the periodic table.

The complete ionisation of an atom

When an atom is ionised by the removal of all of its electrons in turn, the ionisation energies increase because the size of the positive charge of the ion is increasing and because the atomic radius is decreasing. Thus, there is a **gradual increase** in ionisation energy as the electrons are removed from the same energy level, but there is a **large increase** when an electron is removed from an inner energy level (see Figure 1.19).

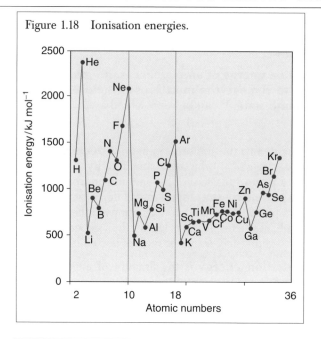

Figure 1.18   Ionisation energies.

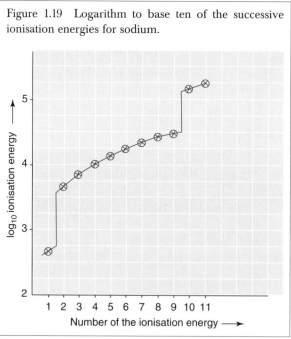

Figure 1.19   Logarithm to base ten of the successive ionisation energies for sodium.

For instance, Na has the electron arrangement $1s^2, 2s^2, 2p^6, 3s^1$. The ionisation energies for Na show a large increase after the 1st ionisation energy because the outer energy level (3s) has **one** electron. There is another large increase after the 9th when the 2nd energy level has been emptied and the next electron comes from the 1st energy level.

Chemical properties and electronic structure

The chemistry of each group of elements depends on the **number of outer electrons**. As you go across the table the number of outer electrons in each group increases from one to eight.

Noble gases, group VIII, have a full outer shell and consequently they are very stable, with almost no chemical reactions. Other elements need to lose or gain electrons to get the electron configuration of their nearest noble gas. This happens in chemical reactions. During a chemical reaction there is a transfer or sharing of electrons between atoms, to bring them to the electron configuration of noble gases, and then they stop reacting. This produces ions or molecules.

Metals are on the left of the periodic table. Their atoms tend to **lose** electrons to non-metals.

Non-metals are on the right of the periodic table. Their atoms tend to **gain** electrons from metals, or to share electrons with other non-metals.

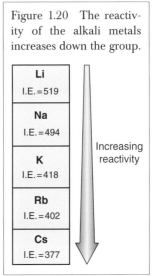

Figure 1.20 The reactivity of the alkali metals increases down the group.

Variation in the chemical properties in a group

Group I is the alkali metals (see Figure 1.20). They share the chemical properties of reacting easily with water and with oxygen. They react by **losing** their outer electron. As you go **down** the group the ease of reacting **increases**, because of:

- increasing atomic radius
- increased shielding of the nucleus from the outer electron by the inner energy levels.

Group VII is the halogens (see Figure 1.21). They share the chemical properties of reacting easily with the metals. They react by **gaining** an electron. As you go **down** the group the ease of reacting **decreases**, because of:

- increasing atomic radius
- increased shielding of the nucleus from the outer energy level by the inner energy levels.

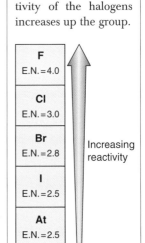

Figure 1.21 The reactivity of the halogens increases up the group.

1.4 RADIOACTIVITY

What is meant by radioactivity?

Radioactivity is the emission of alpha, beta or gamma radiation from the unstable nuclei of atoms.

These are **ionising radiations** that are able to interact with atoms, causing them to lose electrons, and thus form ions. They are normally detected by a **Geiger-Muller tube**, or by their effect on photographic film.

Radioactivity was discovered by **Becquerel** (in 1896), who found that a **uranium** salt had affected a photographic plate that was wrapped in black paper.

Pierre and Marie Curie found two new radioactive elements – **polonium** and **radium**.

Alpha (α) **radiation** consists of a stream of **positively charged** particles, and so are deflected towards a negative charged plate, and by a magnetic field. Alpha particles (see Figure 1.22) consist of two protons and two neutrons, which is the same as the **nucleus of He**. Thus an alpha particle is represented as $_2^4\text{He}$.

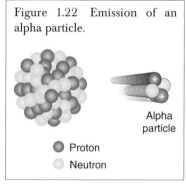

Figure 1.22 Emission of an alpha particle.

Alpha particles are ionising particles that can knock electrons from the atoms that they collide with, thus ionising the air or anything else that they pass through. Because of their relatively large size they quickly collide with so many atoms that their **penetrating distance**, before they lose their ionising energy, is **quite small** – just 4–6 cm of air, or a thin sheet of paper.

HIGHER LEVEL

When a nucleus emits an alpha particle the atom changes to a **new element** that is two behind it on the periodic table. **The atomic number is reduced by two and its mass number is reduced by four**.

Example

$$_{88}^{226}\text{Ra} \rightarrow {}_{86}^{222}\text{Rn} + {}_2^4\text{He}$$

$$_{95}^{241}\text{Am} \rightarrow {}_{93}^{237}\text{Np} + {}_2^4\text{He}$$

Beta (β) **radiation** consists of a stream of **negatively charged electrons** coming from the nucleus, and so they are deflected towards a positively charged plate, and by a magnetic field. A beta particle (see Figure 1.23) is represented in nuclear equations as $_{-1}^{0}\text{e}$.

Figure 1.23 Emission of a beta particle.

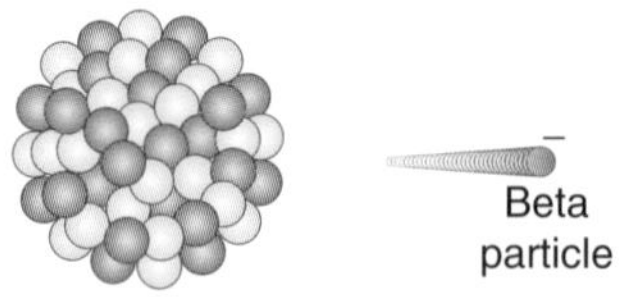

An electron is produced within the nucleus when a neutron changes to a proton and an electron.

Neutron → proton + electron

Beta particles are **less ionising** than alpha particles, (because of their smaller charge and because they are travelling faster), and so their **penetrating distance is**

greater (before they lose their ionising energy) – they can travel several metres through the air and through up to 5 mm of aluminium.

HIGHER LEVEL

When a nucleus emits a beta particle **the atom changes to the next element** on the periodic table. **Its atomic number increases by one and its mass stays the same**.

Example

$$^{14}_{6}C \rightarrow {}^{14}_{7}N + {}^{0}_{-1}e.$$

Note that in the case of either alpha or beta radiation there is a **nuclear reaction**, which produces a new element. In a **chemical reaction** the nucleus remains the same, and no new element is produced, although there is a change in the number of electrons around the nucleus.

Gamma (γ) rays are high-energy electromagnetic waves of very short wavelength (or high frequency). They are not deflected by magnetic or electric fields (see Figure 1.24). They are usually emitted after a nucleus has emitted an alpha or beta particle to lower the energy level of the nucleus to a more stable state.

Gamma rays are also ionising, but they have the **greatest penetrating power**, as they are more weakly ionising than beta or alpha particles. Gamma rays can travel great distances through the air and up to a few cm of lead.

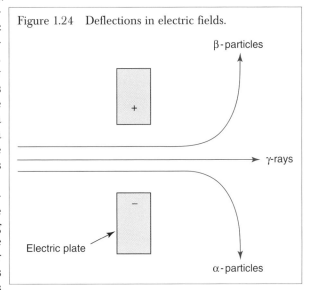

Figure 1.24   Deflections in electric fields.

Table 1.2   Summary of nuclear radiations

Radiations	Their nature	Penetrating power
alpha particles	+ particles (helium nucleus)	low – stopped by sheet of paper
beta particles	− particles (electrons)	medium – stopped by 5 mm of aluminium
gamma radiation	electromagnetic waves with high frequency	great – stopped by a few cm of lead

Uses for radioisotopes

Radioisotopes are radioactive isotopes of elements. They can be produced by bombarding normal atoms with neutrons in a nuclear reactor. They are **chemically identical** to the normal isotopes, but they can be detected by their effect on photographic film or by a Geiger-Muller tube.

- **Medicine**. Cobalt–60 emits gamma radiation that is used to kill cancer cells. The radiation is also used to sterilise surgical equipment. Radioactive tracers can be injected into the blood or inhaled to investigate the circulatory and breathing systems.
- **Food preservation**. Gamma rays kill microbes in food without affecting the food.
- **Industry**. Tracers can be added to liquids in leaking pipes to find the source of the leak. Radiation can also be used to check on the thickness of rubber tyres, and to examine welds.
- **Archaeology**. Carbon dating measures the ratio of carbon–14 to carbon–12 that still remains in biological material to calculate how old it is. Carbon–14 decays by beta emission at a fixed rate (its half-life). In living material there is a fixed ratio of carbon–14 to carbon–12. The greater the difference from this ratio, the older the materials is.

What is the half-life of a radioactive element?

The half-life of a radioactive element is the time it takes for half of its nuclei to decay. It is a fixed property that cannot be affected by temperature or other means.
Half-lives vary from fractions of seconds to thousands of years.

The occurrence of radioactivity

Radioactivity is part of nature. In Ireland there is concern over the build-up of radon, a naturally occurring radioactive gas that is released from the rocks in certain parts of the country. Measures are now adopted to prevent its entry through the floors of new houses by using a plastic barrier. Discharge of radioactive wastes to the Irish Sea from Sellafield has resulted in radioactive substances entering certain sea foods.
Radiation is of concern as it may cause genetic mutations, including mutations that cause cancer.

TEST YOURSELF

(* indicates Higher level)
1. (a) What are elements?
   (b) What was the role of each of the following in the discovery of elements?
      (i) Boyle
      (ii) Davy.
*2. What were the contributions of the following to the development of the periodic table?
   (a) Dobereiner
   (b) Newlands.

3. Compare Mendeleev's table with the modern periodic table.
4. What are the names of these groups of elements: I, II, VII, VIII (or 0)?
5. State the law of conservation of mass.
6. Define:
   (a) atom
   (b) molecule
   (c) ion.
7. What did Thomson discover about cathode rays?
*8. Outline the contributions of each of the following in the discovery of the electron:
   (a) Crookes
   (b) Thomson
   (c) Millikan
   (d) Stoney.
9. Outline the contribution of Rutherford in the discovery of the nucleus.
*10. Outline the roles of Rutherford, Chadwick and Mosely in the discovery of the proton, neutron and atomic number.
11. Compare the mass, charge and location of the proton, neutron and electron.
12. Define:
   (a) atomic number (Z)
   (b) mass number (A)
   (c) relative atomic mass (A_r).
13. What are isotopes?
14. Outline the role of the mass spectrometer in determining the relative atomic mass of an element.
*15. Explain the following processes in a mass spectrometer:
   (a) vaporisation of the sample
   (b) production of ions
   (c) acceleration of ions
   (d) separation of ions by mass
   (e) detection of ions.
*16. Use a mass spectrum to find the mass and relative abundance of the isotopes of an element, and hence to calculate the A_r of the element.
17. What are energy levels in an atom?
18. (a) Use Bohr-style diagrams to draw any atom of the first 20 elements.
   (b) What do the atoms of any group in the periodic table have in common?
19. What colours are the flames from the following metals when they are heated in a Bunsen flame? Why do they have different colours?
   (a) Li
   (b) Na
   (c) K
   (d) Ba
   (e) Sr
   (f) Cu.
*20. (a) Outline how to view the emission spectrum of an element.
   (b) Describe:
       (i) the emission spectrum of hydrogen
       (ii) the absorption spectrum of hydrogen.
   (c) What does an analytical chemist use an atomic absorption spectrometer for? Explain how this instrument works.

*21. Outline briefly how the emission spectrum of hydrogen provides evidence for energy levels in atoms.

*22. (a) How were energy sublevels discovered?
  (b) How many sublevels are in each of the first four energy levels?

*23. (a) Define 'orbital'.
  (b) Outline the contributions made by the following that changed the concept of electron orbit to electron orbital:
    (i) de Broglie
    (ii) Heisenberg.
  (c) Compare the shapes of s orbitals and p orbitals.

*24. (a) Write the s, p electron configuration of the first 36 elements.
  (b) Write the s, p electron configuration of the ions of the s and p block elements.
  (c) Write the electron configuration of the individual orbitals of the p block elements of (i) N, (ii) S.

25. (a) Define 'atomic radius'.
  (b) Describe and explain the changes in atomic radius going:
    (i) down a group
    (ii) across a period.

26. Explain in terms of atomic radius and the screening effect why
  (a) there is an increase in activity of the elements in group I going down the group
  (b) there is a decrease in activity of the elements in group VII going down the group.

*27. (a) Explain, or give an equation for the first ionisation energy of an atom.
  (b) Describe and explain the changes in ionisation energy going:
    (i) down a group
    (ii) across a period.
  (c) Why do the elements in the following groups have higher than expected ionisation energies?
    (i) group II
    (ii) group V.
  (d) When the successive ionisation energies of an element are graphed, explain why:
    (i) there a gradual increase in value
    (ii) occasionally there is a higher than expected increase in value.

28. (a) Define 'radioactivity'.
  (b) Compare the nature and penetrating ability of alpha, beta and gamma radiation.
  (c) State two uses for radioisotopes.
  (d) Define 'half-life'.

*29. (a) Compare nuclear and chemical reactions.
  (b) Use a periodic table of the elements to write equations for the following nuclear reactions:
    (i) the emission of an alpha particle from ^{241}Am
    (ii) the emission of a beta particle from ^{14}C.

Chapter 2 – Oxidation and reduction (redox). Electrolysis

2.1 OXIDATION AND REDUCTION

What is meant by an 'oxidation' reaction?

1. The simplest meaning of 'oxidation' is a reaction in which oxygen gas reacts with a substance, for example, in burning, rusting and respiration:

$$Mg + \tfrac{1}{2}O_2 \rightarrow MgO$$

The magnesium was oxidised.

2. Non-metals – for example, chlorine or sulfur – can also oxidise when they react with metals:

$$Na + \tfrac{1}{2}Cl_2 \rightarrow NaCl$$

The sodium was oxidised.

3. Oxidation is any reaction in which there is a loss of electrons:

$$Zn + Cu^{2+} \rightarrow Zn^{2+} + Cu$$

The zinc was oxidised.

What is meant by a 'reduction' reaction?

1. The simplest meaning of 'reduction' is a reaction in which oxygen is removed from a compound to release a metal:

$$CuO + H_2 \rightarrow Cu + H_2O$$

The copper oxide was reduced.

2. Reduction is any reaction in which there is a gain of electrons:

$$Zn + Cu^{2+} \rightarrow Zn^{2+} + Cu$$

The copper ion was reduced.

! *'OILRIG' is a useful reminder:* **oxidation is loss; reduction is gain (of electrons)**

Oxidation and reduction *always* happen simultaneously – a redox reaction. In a redox reaction there is a **transfer of electrons**. The substance that loses electrons is oxidised, and that which gains the electrons is reduced.

Oxidising and reducing agents

An oxidising agent causes another substance to become oxidised and, in the process, the oxidising agent is reduced.

Common oxidising agents include oxygen gas (O_2), chlorine gas (Cl_2), chlorine compounds in bleach, for example the hypochlorite ion (ClO^-), potassium manganateVII $(KMnO_4)$ and hydrogen peroxide (H_2O_2).

A reducing agent causes another substance to be reduced, and in the reaction it becomes oxidised.

Common reducing agents include carbon monoxide gas (CO), sulfur dioxide gas (SO_2), and the sulfite ion in solution (SO_3^{2-}).

Oxidising and reducing agents are useful for:

- **sterilising**, that is, to kill bacteria. For instance chlorine or hypochlorite is added to swimming pools, and sulphite is added to jams and fruit drinks.
- **bleaching** coloured substances. Paper that was bleached by a reducing agent, for example, SO_2, slowly becomes oxidised by the air and turns yellow, but when it is bleached with an oxidising agent, for example, NaClO, it remains white in the air.

The electrochemical series of metals

As a general rule, **metal atoms tend to lose electrons**, that is, they are oxidised, but the ease with which they are able to be oxidised varies. The most active metals are most easily oxidised.

The electrochemical series is a series of metals arranged in order of their ability to be oxidised. The most active (most easily oxidised) metal is first.

Table 2.1   The electrochemical series

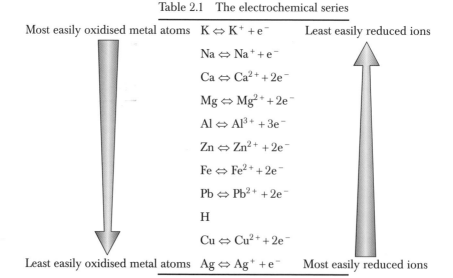

Most easily oxidised metal atoms	$K \Leftrightarrow K^+ + e^-$	Least easily reduced ions
	$Na \Leftrightarrow Na^+ + e^-$	
	$Ca \Leftrightarrow Ca^{2+} + 2e^-$	
	$Mg \Leftrightarrow Mg^{2+} + 2e^-$	
	$Al \Leftrightarrow Al^{3+} + 3e^-$	
	$Zn \Leftrightarrow Zn^{2+} + 2e^-$	
	$Fe \Leftrightarrow Fe^{2+} + 2e^-$	
	$Pb \Leftrightarrow Pb^{2+} + 2e^-$	
	H	
	$Cu \Leftrightarrow Cu^{2+} + 2e^-$	
Least easily oxidised metal atoms	$Ag \Leftrightarrow Ag^+ + e^-$	Most easily reduced ions

Displacement reactions of metals

When a metal atom is oxidised it becomes a + ion, but the + ion can be reduced to become an atom. Thus, these **redox reactions are reversible**, and whether an oxidation or reduction reaction happens depends on the strength of the oxidising or reducing agents. For instance, the atoms of the metals at the top of the list in Table 2.1 are very easily oxidised to form their ions; conversely, their ions are very stable and it is difficult to reduce them. The atoms at the bottom of the list are very difficult to oxidise but their ions are very easily reduced to their atoms.

What happens when an active metal is placed in a solution with the ion of a less active metal?

A redox reaction happens as follows:

- The atoms of the active metal are **oxidised** and change to ions and dissolve.
- The ions of the less active metal accept the electrons (and are thus reduced) and change to atoms, on top of the active metal.

The result is that the active metal dissolves, while at the same time the less active metal is formed from the solution of its salt. **The active metal has displaced the less active metal from the solution**.

An example of industrial use of metal displacement

Scrap iron is added to a solution of copper sulfate. The iron dissolves and copper metal forms on the iron.

Mandatory experiment 2(a). Displacement reactions of metals

See Figure 2.1.

1. Zinc in copper sulfate solution

Procedure
Add pieces of zinc to a solution of copper sulfate.

Result
Copper (red-brown) appears on the zinc (some of the zinc dissolves) and the blue colour of the solution fades.

Reactions

$$Zn \rightarrow Zn^{2+} + 2e^-$$
$$Cu^{2+} + 2e^- \rightarrow Cu$$

2. Magnesium in copper sulfate solution

Procedure
Add pieces of magnesium to a solution of copper sulfate.

Result

Copper (red-brown) appears on the magnesium (some of the magnesium dissolves) and the blue colour of the solution fades.

Reactions

$$Mg \rightarrow Mg^{2+} + 2e^-$$
$$Cu^{2+} + 2e^- \rightarrow Cu$$

Note: When a metal is placed in a solution of a metal salt that is higher up the series, no reaction occurs.

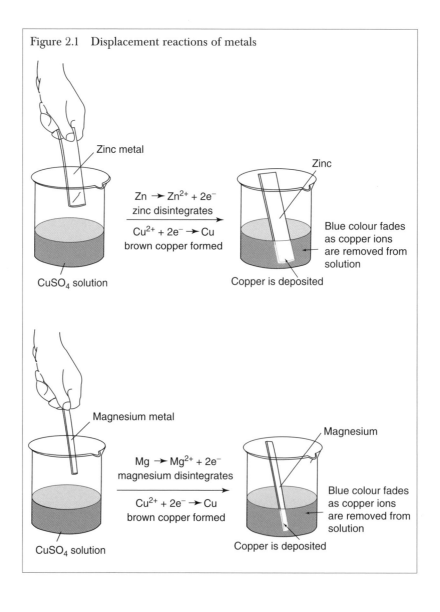

Figure 2.1   Displacement reactions of metals

Zinc metal

Zinc

$$Zn \rightarrow Zn^{2+} + 2e^-$$
zinc disintegrates

$$Cu^{2+} + 2e^- \rightarrow Cu$$
brown copper formed

Blue colour fades as copper ions are removed from solution

CuSO$_4$ solution

Copper is deposited

Magnesium metal

Magnesium

$$Mg \rightarrow Mg^{2+} + 2e^-$$
magnesium disintegrates

$$Cu^{2+} + 2e^- \rightarrow Cu$$
brown copper formed

Blue colour fades as copper ions are removed from solution

CuSO$_4$ solution

Copper is deposited

The halogens as oxidising agents

Chlorine, bromine and iodine are halogens. Their atoms react by gaining electrons, that is, they become reduced. This causes other atoms to lose electrons, thus the halogens are oxidising agents.

Mandatory experiment 2(b). Halogens as oxidising agents

1. The oxidation of sulfite (SO_3^{2-}) to sulfate (SO_4^{2-}) (see Figure 2.2).

Procedure

(a) Test a solution of sodium sulfite for the presence of sulfate by adding barium chloride solution to form a white precipitate. Add HCl and observe that the white precipitate dissolves in the HCl, showing the presence of sulfite but not sulfate.

(b) Add a solution of a halogen, for example, chlorine water, to a solution of sodium sulfite. Then test the solution for sulfate ions: add barium chloride to form a white precipitate. Add HCl and observe that the precipitate does *not* dissolve.

Reactions

(1) Oxidation of sulfite to sulfate:

$$SO_3^{2-} + H_2O \rightarrow SO_4^{2-} + 2H^+ + 2e^-$$

(2) Reduction of chlorine atoms to chlorine ions:

$$Cl_2 + 2e^- \rightarrow 2Cl^-$$

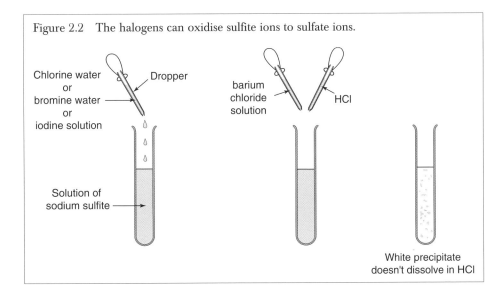

Figure 2.2 The halogens can oxidise sulfite ions to sulfate ions.

Chlorine water or bromine water or iodine solution

Dropper

barium chloride solution

HCl

Solution of sodium sulfite

White precipitate doesn't dissolve in HCl

2. The oxidation of Fe^{2+} to Fe^{3+} (see Figure 2.3).

Procedure

Add the halogen, for example, chlorine water, to an acidified solution of iron(II) sulfate (the acid prevents the oxidation by oxygen in the air). Test the solution for iron(III) by adding sodium hydroxide solution and observing the green/brown precipitate of iron(III) oxide.

Reactions

(1) Oxidation of Fe^{2+} to Fe^{3+}:

$$2Fe^{2+} \rightarrow 2Fe^{3+} + 2e^-$$

(2) Reduction of chlorine atoms to chlorine ions:

$$Cl_2 + 2e^- \rightarrow 2Cl^-$$

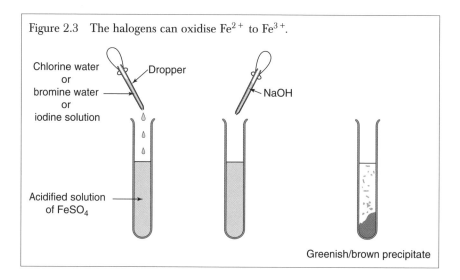

Figure 2.3   The halogens can oxidise Fe^{2+} to Fe^{3+}.

Chlorine water or bromine water or iodine solution

Dropper

NaOH

Acidified solution of FeSO$_4$

Greenish/brown precipitate

Comparison of the halogens as oxidising agents

Chlorine, bromine and iodine are oxidising agents, as they tend to gain electrons and become reduced to $-$ ions. This reaction is reversible; the ions can be oxidised to their atoms if a strong enough oxidising agent is present.

$$Cl_2 + 2e^- \Leftrightarrow 2Cl^-$$

$$Br_2 + 2e^- \Leftrightarrow 2Br^-$$

$$I_2 + 2e^- \Leftrightarrow 2I^-$$

Of the three elements, **chlorine is the strongest oxidising agent**, next is bromine, and then iodine. (This is due to the size of the atoms and the shielding of the nucleus from the outer electrons.)

Mandatory experiment 2(c). To compare the halogens as oxidising agents

See Figure 2.4.

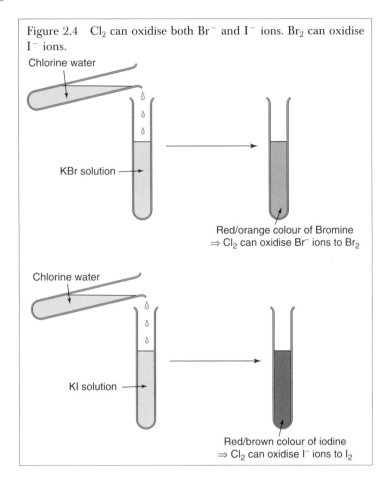

Figure 2.4 Cl_2 can oxidise both Br^- and I^- ions. Br_2 can oxidise I^- ions.

Chlorine water

KBr solution

Red/orange colour of Bromine
$\Rightarrow Cl_2$ can oxidise Br^- ions to Br_2

Chlorine water

KI solution

Red/brown colour of iodine
$\Rightarrow Cl_2$ can oxidise I^- ions to I_2

1. Chlorine is aded to a solution of (i) a bromide salt (ii) an iodide salt.

Procedure
Add chlorine water is added to a solution of (i) a bromide salt (ii) an iodide salt.

Result
The solutions change colour to (i) red/orange as bromine is formed and (ii) red/brown as iodine is formed.

Reactions
(i) $2Br^- - 2e^- \rightarrow Br_2$ (red/orange)

$Cl_2 + 2e^- \rightarrow 2Cl^-$

(ii) $2I^- - 2e^- \rightarrow I_2$ (red/brown)

$Cl_2 + 2e^- \rightarrow 2Cl^-$

Conclusions
Chlorine is a stronger oxidising agent than bromine or iodine.

2. Bromine is added to a solution of an iodide salt (see Figure 2.5).

Procedure
Add bromine water to a solution of an iodide salt.

Result
The solution changes colour to red/brown as iodine is formed.

Reactions
$2I^- - 2e^- \rightarrow I_2$ (red/brown)

$Br_2 + 2e^- \rightarrow 2Br^-$

Conclusions
Bromine is a stronger oxidising agent than iodine.

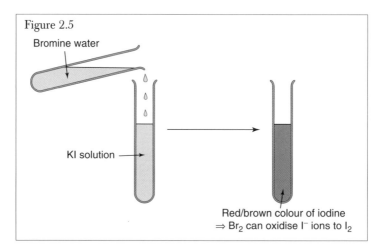

Figure 2.5
Bromine water
KI solution
Red/brown colour of iodine
$\Rightarrow Br_2$ can oxidise I^- ions to I_2

3. Bromine is added to a solution of a chloride salt.

Procedure
Add bromine water to a solution of a chloride salt.

Result
No reaction takes place, as the chlorine is a stronger oxidising agent.
Similarly, if iodine is added to a solution of a chloride salt or a bromide salt, no reactions occur, as iodine is a weaker oxidising agent than bromine or chlorine.

2.2   ELECTROLYSIS

Electrolysis causes a chemical change to a compound by passing an electric current through it when it is dissolved or when it is melted.
Redox reactions occur at the electrodes:

* At the **cathode** a **reduction** reaction occurs.
* At the **anode** an **oxidation** reaction occurs.

'CRAO' is a useful reminder of which reaction happens at each electrode: **cathode/**
! **reduction; anode/oxidation.**

Electrolysis of a solution of copper sulfate with copper electrodes

Industrial application: purification of copper by using impure copper at anode and collecting pure copper at cathode.
See Figure 2.6.

Results
Copper is deposited on the cathode ($-$), while the copper anode ($+$) dissolves.

Reactions
Cathode (reduction takes place):

$$Cu^{2+} + 2e^- \rightarrow Cu$$

Anode (oxidation takes place):

$$Cu - 2e^- \rightarrow Cu^{2+}$$

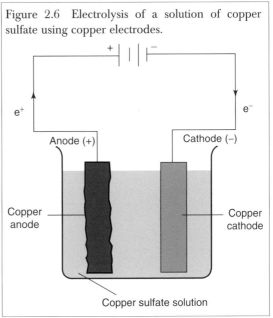

Figure 2.6   Electrolysis of a solution of copper sulfate using copper electrodes.

Industrial application to purify copper: use impure copper as anode and pure copper will be deposited on cathode.

Electrolysis of acidified water using inert electrodes

See Figure 2.7.

Results
Hydrogen gas is formed at the cathode ($-$), while oxygen gas is formed at the anode ($+$).

Reactions
Cathode (reduction takes place):

$$2H^+ + 2e^- \rightarrow H_2$$

or

$$2H_2O + 2e^- \rightarrow H_2 + 2OH^-$$

Anode (oxidation takes place):

$$H_2O - 2e^- \rightarrow \tfrac{1}{2}O_2 + 2H^+$$

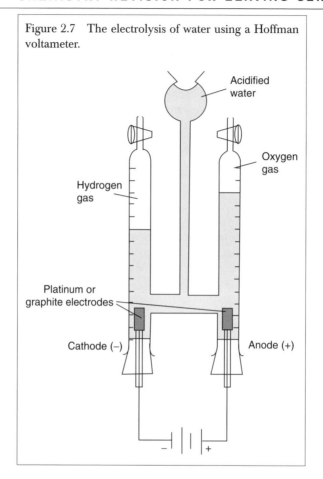

Figure 2.7   The electrolysis of water using a Hoffman voltameter.

HIGHER LEVEL

Electrolysis of sodium sulfate solution using inert electrodes

See Figure 2.8.
   A few drops of **universal indicator** are added to the solution. Platinum or graphite are suitable as electrodes.

Results

At the **cathode** ($-$) the solution becomes **blue** (alkaline) and a gas is produced.
At the **anode** ($+$) the solution becomes **red** (acidic) and a gas is produced.

Reactions

Universal indicator is green in a neutral solution, red in an acidic solution, and blue in an alkaline solution.

Cathode (reduction takes place):

$$2H_2O + 2e^- \rightarrow H_2 + 2OH^-$$

This makes the solution alkaline.

Anode (oxidation takes place):

$$H_2O - 2e^- \rightarrow \tfrac{1}{2}O_2 + 2H^+$$

This makes the solution acidic.

The H^+ and OH^- will combine to form H_2O.

Note: The sodium and the sulfate ions are very stable and are not oxidised or reduced. They are **spectator ions** to the reactions, and their function is to help conduct the current.

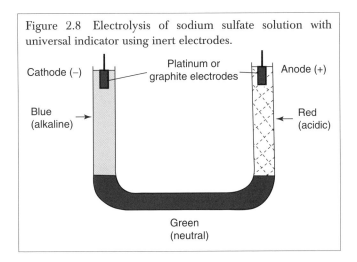

Figure 2.8 Electrolysis of sodium sulfate solution with universal indicator using inert electrodes.

Electrolysis of a solution of potassium iodide using inert electrodes

See Figure 2.9.

A few drops of **phenolphthalein indicator** are added to the solution. Platinum or graphite electrodes can be used.

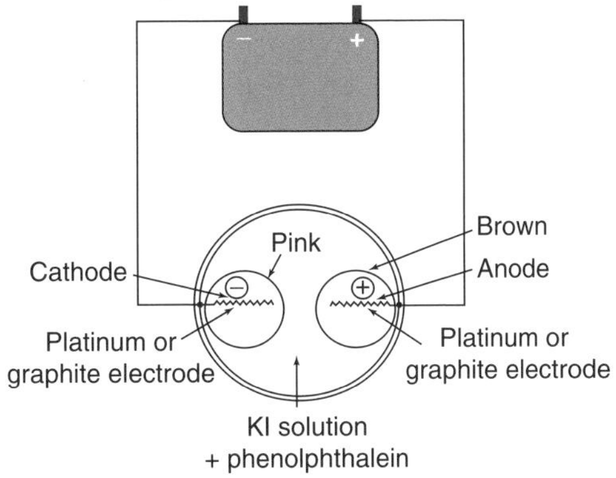

Results

At the **cathode** $(-)$ the solution becomes **pink** (alkaline) and a gas is produced.

At the **anode** $(+)$ a **brown** substance (iodine) is formed.

Reactions

Phenolphthalein is colourless in acidic solution and it is pink in an alkaline solution.

Figure 2.9 Electrolysis of potassium iodide solution with phenolphthalein using inert electrodes.

Cathode (reduction takes place):

$$2H_2O + 2e^- \rightarrow H_2 + 2OH^-$$

This makes the solution alkaline, i.e., pink, due to the alkaline ions, OH^-.

Anode (oxidation takes place):

$$2I^- - 2e^- \rightarrow I_2 \text{ (brown colour)}$$

Note: The potassium ion is very stable and it is not reduced. It is a spectator ion.

Oxidation numbers (ON)

The oxidation number of an atom or ion is the charge it has or appears to have if the bonds are assumed to be ionic.
Rules for assigning ONs:

- The ON of an element is 0.
- The ON of an ion is the charge that it has.
- The ON of F is always -1.
- The ON of O is -2, except when it is in OF_2 (its ON is $+2$) and in H_2O_2 (its ON is -1).
- The ON of H is -1 when it is with metals, and $+1$ when it is with non-metals.
- The ON of group I is 1 and the ON of group II is 2.
- The sum of the ONs of the atoms in a compound ion is equal to the charge that the ion has.

Transition elements and other elements can have a **variable ON**, depending on the nature of the other atoms that they are bonded to. The ON is included in the name of the compound, for example, manganeseIV, ironII, etc.

Why do we calculate an ON?

Using the above rules we can calculate the ON of an element that is present in a molecule or ion. This has two uses:

- **We can identify that a redox reaction has occurred when the reaction caused a change in the ON**, that is, the ON of an element in a reactant is different to its ON in one of the products. **If the reaction caused the ON to increase, then that element was oxidised; if its ON decreased, it was reduced.** If a reaction does not cause a change in the ON of any element, then it is not a redox reaction.
- We can use the change in the ON to **balance redox equations**. (See the section in chemical equations.)

Examples of calculating ONs
1. Calculate the ON of S in the following species:

    (a) SO_2
    (b) SO_3^{2-}
    (c) SO_4^{2-}
    (d) $S_2O_3^{2-}$

Answers

The ON of O is -2 in these species. (The ON of oxygen is always -2, except in OF_2 and H_2O_2).

(a) The molecule of SO_2 has no charge, therefore the sum of the ONs is 0.

$\Rightarrow$ ON of $S + 2(-2) = 0$
$\Rightarrow$ ON $-4 = 0$
$\Rightarrow$ ON $= 4$.

(b) The SO_3^{2-} ion has a charge of -2, therefore the sum of the ONs is -2.

$\Rightarrow$ ON of $S + 3(-2) = -2$
$\Rightarrow$ ON $-6 = -2$
$\Rightarrow$ ON $= -2 + 6$
$\Rightarrow$ ON $= +4$.

(c) The SO_4^{2-} ion has a charge of -2, therefore the sum of the ONs is -2.

$\Rightarrow$ ON of $S + 4(-2) = -2$
$\Rightarrow$ ON $-8 = -2$
$\Rightarrow$ ON $= -2 + 8$
$\Rightarrow$ ON $= +6$.

(d) The $S_2O_3^{2-}$ ion has a charge of -2, therefore the sum of the ONs is -2.

$\Rightarrow 2(\text{ON of S}) + 3(-2) = -2$
$\Rightarrow 2(\text{ON}) - 6 = -2$
$\Rightarrow 2(\text{ON}) = -2 + 6$
$\Rightarrow 2(\text{ON}) = +4$
$\Rightarrow$ ON $= 4/2 = +2$.

2. Calculate the ON of Mn in MnO_4^-.

Answer

The ON of O is -2. The MnO_4- ion has a charge of -1, therefore the sum of the ONs is -1.

$\Rightarrow$ ON of $Mn + 4(-2) = -1$
$\Rightarrow$ ON $-8 = -1$
$\Rightarrow$ ON $= -1 + 8$
$\Rightarrow$ ON $= +7$

3. Is a reaction that changes SO_3^{2-} to SO_4^{2-} a redox reaction? If so, is the S oxidised or reduced in the reaction?

Answer

The reaction is:

$SO_3^{2-} \rightarrow SO_4^{2-}$

The ON of S in SO_3^{2-} is $+4$ (see above example)

The ON of S in SO_4^{2-} is $+6$ (see above example)

The reaction changed the ON. It is therefore a redox reaction. The reaction increased the oxidation number, so the S was oxidised. (Thus, SO_3^{2-} is a reducing agent.)

TEST YOURSELF

(* indicates Higher level)
1. Give two meanings for 'oxidation' reactions.
2. (a) What is meant by 'oxidising agent'?
   (b) Name two oxidising agents.
3. (a) What is meant by 'reducing agent'?
   (b) Name two reducing agents.
   (c) State two uses for oxidising and reducing agents.
4. (a) What is meant by the 'electrochemical series' of metals?
   (b) Place these metals in order: calcium, copper, magnesium, and potassium.
   (c) Describe what happens when zinc is added to a solution of copper sulfate. Write half-equations for any reactions.
5. (a) Describe what happens when a halogen, for example, chlorine, is added to a solution of sodium sulfite. Write half-equations for any reactions.
   (b) Outline how to show that chlorine is a stronger oxidising agent than bromine or iodine.
6. (a) Describe what happens when a copper sulfate solution is electrolysed using copper electrodes.
   *(b) Write half-equations for any reactions.
7. (a) Describe what happens when acidified water is electrolysed using platinum electrodes.
   *(b) Write half-equations for any reactions.
*8. Universal indicator is blue in alkaline solutions and red in acidic solutions. In the electrolysis (using inert electrodes) of an aqueous solution of sodium sulfate that contained universal indicator, the solution around one electrode turned red and the other turned blue.
   (a) Explain, using half-equations.
   (b) State a suitable material for the electrodes.
*9. Phenolphthalein is colourless in acidic solutions and pink in alkaline solutions. The electrolysis (using inert electrodes) of an aqueous solution of potassium iodide that contained some phenolphthalein caused the area around one electrode to go pink, while the other turned brown. Explain, using half-equations.
*10. (a) Define 'oxidation number'.
   (b) What is the oxidation number of O in
       (i) H_2O?
       (ii) H_2O_2?
   (c) What is the oxidation number of S in
       (i) SO_2?
       (ii) SO_3^{2-}?
       (iii) SO_4^{2-}?
   (d) What is the oxidation number of Cr in
       (i) CrO_4^{2-}?
       (ii) $Cr_2O_7^{2-}$?
   (e) What happens to the oxidation number of an element when it is reduced in a reaction?

Chapter 3 – Formulas. Ionic and covalent bonding. Shapes of molecules. Intermolecular forces

3.1 FORMULAS

What is meant by valency?

The **valency** of an element is **the number of electrons that its atoms need to gain or lose in order to have a full outer shell**.

Atoms that have a full outer shell of electrons are stable. For example, **noble gases** do not react under normal circumstances as their atoms have a **full outer shell**. For instance, He has two outer electrons; the others have eight outer electrons. Their **inertness** is a useful property – helium is used in balloons instead of the lighter gas hydrogen as it does not burn; argon is used in light bulbs to prevent the filament from burning.

The atoms of the other elements can achieve a full outer shell in a chemical reaction by losing, gaining or sharing electrons. Thus, **the octet rule** states that elements react in order to achieve **eight outer electrons**. (However, the octet rule does not always apply to the transition metals, or to groups in the centre of the periodic table, for example, group III.)

The number of outer electrons in an atom is its group number. Therefore, the valency of an element is the group number if it loses electrons (i.e., a metal), or eight minus the group number if it gains electrons (i.e., it is a non-metal).

Thus, the valencies of the groups as you go across the periodic table are: 1, 2, 3, 4, 3, 2, 1, 0.

HIGHER LEVEL

Valency of the transition elements

Transition elements can have a variable valency, i.e., the valency depends on the nature of the other elements that it is bonded to. The valency of a transition element in a compound is given in the name of the compound.

For example, copper(I) oxide, copper(II) oxide, iron(II) oxide, iron(III) oxide, etc. Similarly for chromium and manganese – chromium(III), chromium(VI), manganese(II) and manganese(VII) are common valencies for these elements.

Simple formulas of binary compounds

To construct the formula of a compound, first use the periodic table of the elements to find the group number, and hence the valency. (Going across the table, the valencies are 1, 2, 3, 4, 3, 2, 1, 0.)

When both elements have the **same valency**, then **one atom of each** is present in the formula.

Examples

- NaCl (the valencies of Na and Cl are 1)
- MgO (the valencies of Mg and O are 2).

When the valencies are **unequal**, multiply the number of atoms until the valencies match.

Examples

- Na_2O (the valency of Na is 1 and the valency of O is 2)
- $MgCl_2$ (the valency of Mg is 2 and the valency of Cl is 1)
- $AlCl_3$ (the valency of Al is 3 and the valency of Cl is 1)
- Al_2O_3 (the valency of Al is 3 and the valency of O is 2).

Formulas of compounds that contain group ions

These valencies must be memorised:

(* indicates Higher level)

Valency of 1	Valency of 2
Hydroxide: OH^-	Carbonate: CO_3^{2-}
*Hydrogencarbonate: HCO_3^-	*Sulfite: SO_3^{2-}
*Nitrate: NO_3^-	*Sulfate: SO_4^{2-}

Examples

- NaOH
- Na_2CO_3
- $Mg(OH)_2$
- $MgCO_3$.

3.2   IONIC AND COVALENT BONDING

What is electronegativity (EN)?

See Figure 3.1.

EN measures the relative attraction of an atom for a shared pair of electrons. The scale was devised (in 1939) by **Linus Pauling** to explain the nature of bonds:

- When there is no difference in EN the bond is non-polar.
- When the difference is less than 1.7 the bond is a polar covalent bond.
- When the difference is greater than 1.7 the bond is ionic.

The electronegativity **decreases going down a group** because of:

- the shielding of the nucleus from the outer electrons by the inner energy levels
- the increasing atomic radius.

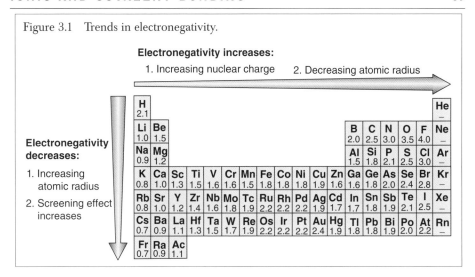

Figure 3.1   Trends in electronegativity.

The EN **increases going across a period** because of:

- the increasing nuclear charge
- the decreasing atomic radius

The most electronegative element is F. Next in value is O, then Cl and N.
Metals have low values of electronegativity – the least electronegative (sometimes called the most electropositive) element is at the bottom left of the periodic table.

Ionic bonding

The ionic bond is the electrostatic force of attraction between ions of opposite charge.

Ionic bonding is typical of compounds of metals with non-metals, (though some metal/non-metal compounds are covalent). In the reaction between a metal and a non-metal, the metal atoms **transfer electrons** to the non-metal atoms. Thus the metal atom becomes a positive ion and the non-metal atom becomes a negative ion.

The ions attract each other to build up an orderly array of alternating positive and negative ions, which is called a lattice. The internal structure of a crystal of sodium chloride is a cubic lattice. See Figures 3.2 and 3.3 for the formation and structure of sodium choride.

We can predict that the bonding between two elements is ionic if their **difference in electronegativity is greater than 1.7**.

Characteristic properties of ionic compounds

Ionic compounds:

- are solids with high melting points
- conduct an electric current when they are melted or dissolved
- tend to dissolve in water (although some of them are insoluble), but not in non-polar solvents such as cyclohexane.

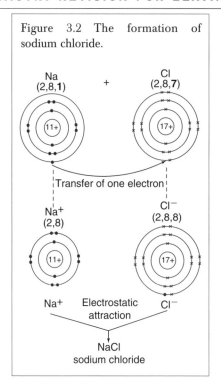

Figure 3.2 The formation of sodium chloride.

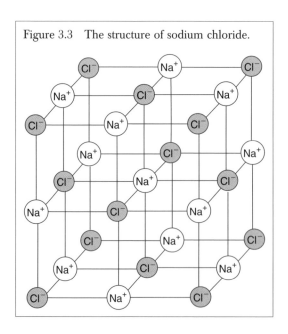

Figure 3.3   The structure of sodium chloride.

Note: Not all ionic compounds dissolve in water. It is useful to know that all nitrates and all sodium, potassium and ammonium salts are soluble.

Mandatory experiment 3: Tests for anions in aqueous solutions: chloride carbonate, nitrate, sulfate, phosphate*, sulfite*, hydrogen-carbonate*

(* indicates Higher level)

Chlorides (Cl)

See Figure 3.4.

Add a solution of silver nitrate $(AgNO_3)$. It forms a white precipitate (of AgCl).

$$(Ag^+ + Cl^- \rightarrow AgCl_{(s)})$$

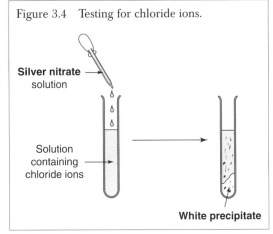

Figure 3.4   Testing for chloride ions.

Silver nitrate solution

Solution containing chloride ions

White precipitate

Nitrates (NO_3)

See Figure 3.5.

The brown ring test: Add fresh iron(II) sulfate solution. Slowly pour concentrated H_2SO_4 down the side of the test tube. A brown ring forms.

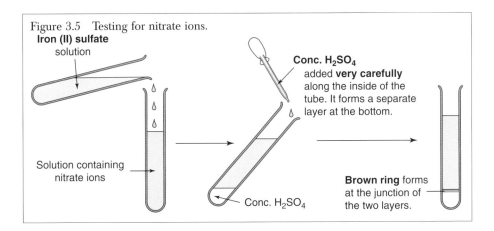

Figure 3.5   Testing for nitrate ions.

Iron (II) sulfate solution

Solution containing nitrate ions

Conc. H$_2$SO$_4$ added **very carefully** along the inside of the tube. It forms a separate layer at the bottom.

Conc. H$_2$SO$_4$

Brown ring forms at the junction of the two layers.

Carbonates and hydrogencarbonates

See Figure 3.6.

Add dilute HCl. It forms CO_2 gas, which makes limewater chalky white.

$$CaCO_3 + 2HCl \rightarrow CaCl_2 + H_2O + CO_2$$

$$CO_2 + Ca(OH)_2 \rightarrow CaCO_3 + H_2O$$

Figure 3.6   Testing for carbonate and hydrogencarbonate ions.

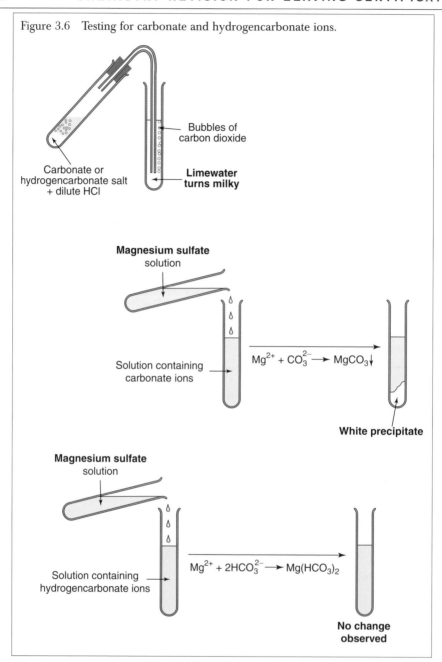

HIGHER LEVEL

To distinguish between solutions of carbonates and hydrogencarbonates, add a solution of magnesium sulfate ($MgSO_4$) or magnesium chloride ($MgCl_2$). The carbonate forms a white precipitate while the hydrogencarbonate remains dissolved.

Sulfates (SO₄) and sulfites (SO₃)

See Figure 3.7.

Add barium chloride (BaCl₂) solution. It forms a white precipitate.

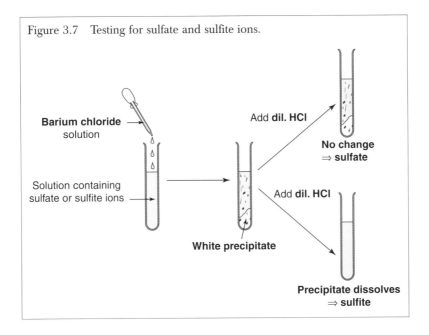

Figure 3.7   Testing for sulfate and sulfite ions.

Barium chloride solution

Solution containing sulfate or sulfite ions

White precipitate

Add **dil. HCl**

No change ⇒ **sulfate**

Add **dil. HCl**

Precipitate dissolves ⇒ **sulfite**

HIGHER LEVEL

To distinguish between sulfates and sulfites, add dilute HCl to the precipitates. The sulfite goes clear, while the sulfate remains white.

Phosphates (PO₄)

See Figure 3.8.

Add a solution of ammonium molybdate and a few drops of concentrated HNO₃. Heat to 60°C. A yellow precipitate forms.

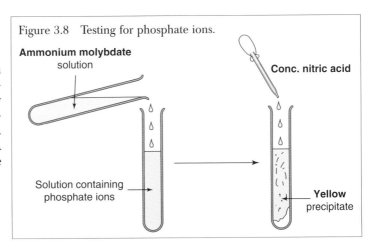

Figure 3.8   Testing for phosphate ions.

Ammonium molybdate solution

Conc. nitric acid

Solution containing phosphate ions

Yellow precipitate

Covalent bonding

A covalent bond is a shared pair of electrons. A single covalent bond has one pair of shared electrons; a double covalent has two pairs, and a triple covalent bond has three pairs of shared electrons.

Examples

- H–H
- O=O
- N≡N.

Covalent bonds are typical of the **non-metal elements** and the **compounds of non-metals**. (Metals do not form compounds together – they mix to form alloys.)

HIGHER LEVEL

A **sigma (δ) bond** (see Figure 3.9) is formed when the electrons are shared **in line with the nuclei**, i.e., a **head-on overlap** of orbitals; a **pi (π) bond** (see Figure 3.10) is formed when the shared orbitals overlap **side-on**, i.e., not in line with the nuclei.

Sigma bonds are stronger.

When there is a single bond it is a sigma bond. In a double or triple bond only one bond is a sigma bond; the others are pi bonds.

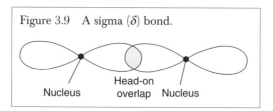

Figure 3.9   A sigma (δ) bond.

Nucleus   Head-on overlap   Nucleus

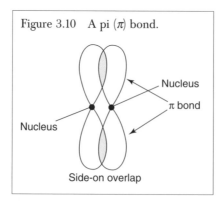

Figure 3.10   A pi (π) bond.

Nucleus

π bond

Nucleus

Side-on overlap

A **polar covalent bond** is a bond formed when the pair of electrons is shared unequally. It (see Figure 3.11) results when there is a **difference in electronegativity** (up to 1.7) between the elements, with the more electronegative element having a **partial negative charge**.

Examples of **polar solvents** include water and acetone. They can dissolve ionic compounds because the charged ends of the molecules are attracted to the oppositely charged ions and surround them, thus separating them.

Non-polar solvents, for example, cyclohexane and tetrachloromethane are used to dissolve non-polar substances, such as fats.

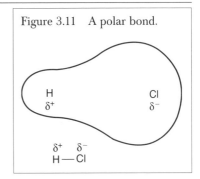

Figure 3.11   A polar bond.

Characteristic properties of covalent compounds

Covalent compounds:

- are either solids of low melting points, or liquids with low boiling points or gases
- do not conduct electricity when melted or dissolved
- tend to dissolve in non-polar solvents, for example, cyclohexane but not in water (there are some exceptions).

3.3   SHAPES OF MOLECULES

Small molecules can have the following shapes:

- linear
- triangular
- tetrahedral
- pyramidal
- V-shaped (bent).

HIGHER LEVEL

The electron pair repulsion theory

The shape of a molecule depends on the **number of pairs of electrons** that lie around the **central atom** of the molecule. The pairs of electrons repel each other to be as far apart as possible, with the following shapes resulting:

- One or two pairs of electrons around the central atom: **linear**. The bond angle is 180°.
- Three pairs of electrons: **triangular planar**. The bond angle is 120°.
- Four pairs of electrons: **tetrahedral**. The bond angle is 109½°.

To predict the shape of a module, first find the central atom in the periodic table and check its number of outer electrons.

Examples

BeH₂ (Figure 3.12). Be is in group II and so it has two outer electrons to bond with, consequently there are two pairs of electrons around the Be atom, and the shape of the molecule is linear.

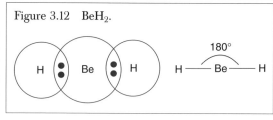

Figure 3.12 BeH_2.

BH₃ (Figure 3.13). B is in group III and so it has three outer electrons to bond with; consequently there are three pairs of electrons around the B atom, and the shape of the molecule is triangular planar.

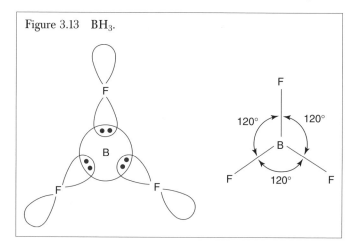

Figure 3.13 BH_3.

CH₄ (Figure 3.14). C is in group IV and so it has four outer electrons to bond with, consequently there are four pairs of electrons around the C atom, and the shape of the molecule is tetrahedral.

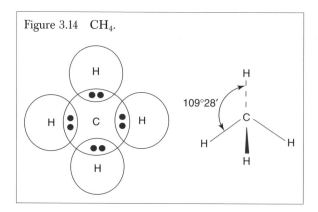

Figure 3.14 CH_4.

NH$_3$ (Figure 3.15). N is in group V and so it has five outer electrons, but it bonds only with three of them, keeping one pair of electrons as a non-bonding pair (a lone pair). The shape of the molecule is a kind of distorted tetrahedron, i.e., a pyramid, with the bond angle of 107°, due to the stronger repulsion from the lone pair.

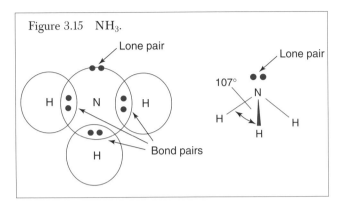

Figure 3.15   NH$_3$.

H$_2$O (Figure 3.16). O is in group VI and so it has six outer electrons, but it bonds only with two of them, keeping two pairs of electrons as non-bonding pairs. The shape of the molecule is a kind of distorted tetrahedron, i.e., V-shaped or bent, with the bond angle of 104°, due to the stronger repulsion of the two non-bonding pairs.

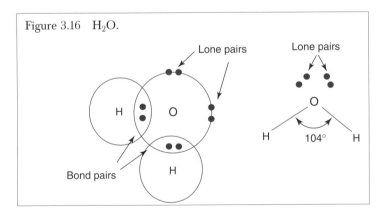

Figure 3.16   H$_2$O.

Polarity in molecules

Polar molecules have a centre of positive charge that is separated from the centre of negative charge. This separation of charge results in the molecule having a **dipole**.

Polar molecules have two requirements:

- polar bonds
- lack of symmetry.

CCl_4 is non-polar, even though the bonds are polar (there is a difference in EN between C and Cl), but the molecule is symmetrical (tetrahedral), and thus the centre of the negative ends of the four bonds is located in the centre of the molecule, with the centre of positive charge.

CO_2 is also a non-polar molecule, even though the bonds are polar. Because of the symmetry due to the linear shape of the molecule, the centre of negative charge is found at the centre of the molecule along with the centre of positive charge.

NH_3 and H_2O are polar molecules because they have polar bonds and molecular shapes that are non-symmetrical.

See Figure 3.17. Non-polar liquids are not attracted towards a charged rod; polar liquids are attracted.

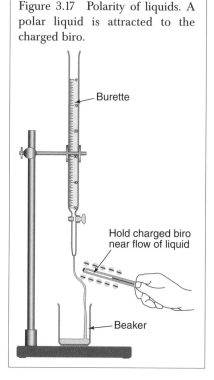

Figure 3.17   Polarity of liquids. A polar liquid is attracted to the charged biro.

Burette

Hold charged biro near flow of liquid

Beaker

3.4 INTERMOLECULAR FORCES

The force of attraction between ions is always stronger than forces of attraction between molecules.

There are three kinds of attractive forces that can attract molecules to each other. When these forces are strong, the molecules are pulled together to form a liquid or a solid.

- **Van der Waals** forces. These are the weakest forces that exist between neutral atoms. The force is strongest between atoms of largest mass (Ar), or between molecules of largest mass (Mr).
- **Dipole–dipole attraction**. The positively charged end of a polar bond is attracted to the negatively charged end of another molecule.
- **Hydrogen bonds**. When H is bonded to F, O or N, these elements are sufficiently electronegative to make the bond polar, and because the H atom has no other electron around the nucleus, a strong partial positive charge is revealed. Therefore, the H atoms are fairly strongly attracted to the negative parts of the other molecules. This results in H_2O being a liquid at room temperature with a fairly large boiling point.

Comparison of boiling points

The boiling point of a liquid is high when there are strong intermolecular forces.

- H_2: $-252°C$
- O_2: $-183°C$

- C_2H_4: – 104°C
- HCHO: – 21°C
- H_2O: 100°C
- H_2S: – 61°C.

H_2 compared with O_2. Both of these substances have non-polar bonds, and so the only intermolecular forces are **van der Waals**. Oxygen has a higher boiling point because its molecules have a greater mass (Mr of O_2 =32; Mr of H_2 =2).

C_2H_4 compared with HCHO. The C_2H_4 molecules are non-polar and so the intermolecular forces are the weak van der Waals forces. The HCHO molecule has a polar C=O bond and so there are **dipole–dipole** attractions between the molecules, which are stronger than van der Waals, and so it has a higher boiling point.

H_2O compared with H_2S. In H_2O molecules the H atoms bonded to the O atom create **hydrogen bonds** between the H_2O molecules. The H_2S molecules have polar bonds, and this creates dipole–dipole attractions between the molecules. However, the hydrogen bonds are stronger and so the boiling point of H_2O is higher.

TEST YOURSELF

1. (a) Define 'valency'.
   (b) What groups have a valency of:
      (i) 1
      (ii) 3?
   *(c) What group of elements have a variable valency?
2. What is the formula of the following compounds?
   (a) sodium oxide
   (b) magnesium chloride
   (c) iron(III) oxide
   (d) calcium hydroxide
   (e) sodium carbonate
   *(f) calcium hydrogencarbonate
   *(g) sodium sulfite
   *(h) magnesium sulfate.
3. Outline how to test a solution for the presence of:
   (a) chloride
   (b) nitrate
   (c) carbonate
   (d) sulfate.
*4. Outline how to test a solution for the presence of:
   (a) phosphate
   (b) sulfite
   (c) hydrogencarbonate.
5. Which ions are detected by the following reagents?
   (a) iron(II) sulfate and concentrated H_2SO_4
   (b) silver nitrate
   (c) HCl
   (d) barium chloride
   (e) ammonium molybdate.

6. (a) Define 'electronegativity'.
   (b) What difference in electronegativity indicates an ionic bond?
   (c) Outline and explain the change in electronegativity:
      (i) across a period
      (ii) down a group.
7. (a) What is an ionic bond?
   (b) List three characteristics of ionic compounds.
   (c) Outline how sodium chloride is formed and draw a diagram to show the arrangement of the outer electrons.
   (d) Describe the structure of a crystal of sodium chloride.
8. (a) What is a covalent bond?
   (b) What is a polar covalent bond?
   (c) List three characteristics of covalent compounds.
   *(d) Distinguish between a sigma and a pi bond.
*9. Describe the shape of the molecules of these compounds:
   (a) H_2O
   (b) CH_4
   (c) NH_3
   (d) BH_3.
*10. State two reasons why some molecules are polar.
*11. Describe:
   (a) van der Waals forces
   (b) hydrogen bonds.
*12. Say which of the following pairs of compounds has the higher boiling point and explain why:
   (a) C_2H_4/HCHO
   (b) H_2O/H_2S
   (c) H_2/O_2.

Chapter 4 – The gas laws. Moles.
Determination of formulas. Chemical equations

4.1   THE GAS LAWS

The kinetic theory of gases

Unlike liquids or solids, all gases have certain physical properties in common. There are **gas laws** that apply to all gases. This is because gas molecules are in rapid motion, are far apart, and are not attracted to each other. (Hence, the size of the molecules and the nature of their bonds have only a small effect on the gas laws.)

HIGHER LEVEL

An ideal gas is one that obeys the gas laws under all conditions of temperature and pressure. The properties of an ideal gas are based on the following assumptions:

- The volume of the molecules is insignificant to the volume that they occupy.
- The intermolecular forces of attraction are insignificant (because of their speed).
- The collisions between the molecules are perfectly elastic (so they do not lose energy when they collide).

However, **real gases deviate from the gas laws**, especially at **high pressures** and at **low temperatures**. Under those conditions the actual intermolecular forces and size of the molecules are most significant, and thus the gas deviates most from the ideal state.

  Also, the gases that are **least like the ideal gas** are those that have the **strongest intermolecular forces**.

Diffusion

Diffusion (see Figure 4.1) is the **spreading outwards of a gas** (or liquid). It happens because the molecules of a gas are in constant random motion. The lighter the molecules are (the smaller the M_r) the faster the molecules are moving, and thus the faster the gas diffuses. For instance, NH_3 diffuses faster than HCl. Also, the speed of

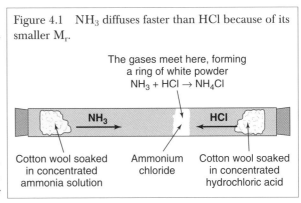

Figure 4.1 NH_3 diffuses faster than HCl because of its smaller M_r.

The gases meet here, forming a ring of white powder
$NH_3 + HCl \rightarrow NH_4Cl$

NH_3 HCl

Cotton wool soaked in concentrated ammonia solution   Ammonium chloride   Cotton wool soaked in concentrated hydrochloric acid

the molecules is faster at higher temperatures. (The average kinetic energy of the molecules is proportional to the Kelvin temperature.)

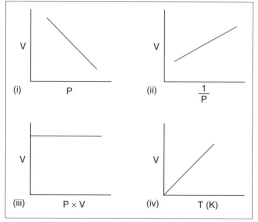

Boyle's law

Boyle's law states that the **volume** of a fixed mass of gas is **inversely proportional** to its **pressure**, when the temperature is kept constant. This means that if the pressure of a gas is doubled, its volume is reduced to half, and vice versa.

The law can be expressed mathematically as $P_1 \times V_1 = P_2 \times V_2$. (Calculations based on this law will not be examined.) The relationship between volume and pressure can be shown in graphs. See (i), (ii) and (iii) above.

Charles's law

Charles's law states that the **volume** of a fixed mass of gas is **directly proportional** to its **Kelvin temperature**, when the pressure is kept constant. (The Kelvin temperature is the Celsius temperature $+ 273$. For example, 20°C is $273 + 20$, i.e., 293K.) This means, that if the Kelvin temperature is doubled, its volume is also doubled.

The law can be expressed mathematically as $V_1/T_1 = V_2/T_2$. (Calculations based on this law will not be examined.) The relationship can be shown in graph (iv).

Combined gas law

$$\frac{P_1 \times V_1}{T_1} = \frac{P_2 \times V_2}{T_2}$$

Gas volumes at s.t.p.

Because the volume of a gas depends on the temperature and pressure, to compare volumes, they can be calculated at standard temperature and at standard pressure.

Standard temperature: 273K

Standard pressure: 1×10^5 Pa (100,000).

Question

Calculate the volume that 200 cm^3 of a gas at 27°C and at a pressure of 90,000 Pa would have at s.t.p.

Answer

$$\frac{P_1 \times V_1}{T_1} = \frac{P_2 \times V_2}{T_2}$$

Put the values for s.t.p. on the left side of the equation, and the other set of values on the right.

$$\frac{100,000 \times V_1}{273} = \frac{90,000 \times 200}{300}$$

$$\Rightarrow V_1 = \frac{90,000 \times 200 \times 273}{300 \times 100,000}$$

$$\Rightarrow V_1 = 163.8 \text{ cm}^3.$$

HIGHER LEVEL

Avogadro's law

Equal volumes of gases have an equal number of molecules (provided that the volumes are measured at the same temperature and pressure). This means that the volume of a gas is directly proportional to the number of molecules.

The law can also be stated on the basis of a mole of a substance having a definite number of molecules. Thus, **the volume of a gas is directly proportional to the number of moles (n).**

Gay–Lussac's law of combining volumes

The volumes of gases that react and are produced are in whole number ratios. This is because the volume of a gas is proportional to the number of molecules.

The volumes of gases can be deduced from a balanced equation.

For instance, $N_2 + 3H_2 \rightarrow 2NH_3$. Thus, if 100 cm^3 of nitrogen gas reacts, then 300 cm^3 of hydrogen has also reacted, and 200 cm^3 of ammonia gas was made.

Equation of state for an ideal gas

Putting together the above laws, we can see that the volume of a gas depends on three things:

$V \propto n$ (Avogadro's law)

$V \propto T$ (Charles's law)

$V \propto \dfrac{1}{P}$ (Boyle's law)

Which means that $V \propto \dfrac{nT}{P}$

Which means that $V = \dfrac{RnT}{P}$

where R is called the 'gas constant', and it has a value of 8.31 (when the other parameters are measured in standard units: Pa, m^3 and Kelvins).

This equation is usually written as follows:

$PV = nRT$

(P is pressure in Pa, V is volume in m^3, n is the number of moles, R is 8.31, T is the Kelvin temperature.)

Calculations based on the equation of state for an ideal gas

When the volume, temperature and pressure of a gas have been measured, the equation can be used to calculate the number of moles that are present.

Then, by measuring the mass of the gas, the mass of one mole, i.e., the M_r, can be calculated.

Question

A gas had a volume of 40 cm^3 at a temperature of 100°C and at a pressure of 100,000 Pa. Its mass was 0.2 g.

Calculate:

1. the number of moles of the gas that were present
2. the relative molecular mass (M_r).

Answer

1.
   (a) Convert the measurements into the standard units.

   (i) $40 \text{ cm}^3 = \dfrac{40}{1000 \times 1000} \text{ m}^3$

   $(1000 \text{ cm}^3 = 1 \text{ litre, and } 1000 \text{ litres} = 1 \text{ m}^3)$

   (ii) $100°C = 100 + 273$, i.e., 373K.

   (b) Use the equation of state for an ideal gas.

   $PV = nRT$

   $\Rightarrow n = \dfrac{PV}{RT}$

   $= \dfrac{100,000 \times 40}{1,000,000 \times 8.31 \times 373}$

   $= 0.0013$ mole.

2. Write an equation that links the number of moles and the mass.

   $0.0013 \text{ mole} = 0.2 \text{ g} \Rightarrow \text{one mole} = \dfrac{0.2}{0.0013} \text{ g}$

   1 mole = 153.85 g.

   $\Rightarrow M_r = 153.8$

Mandatory experiment 4: Determination of the relative molecular mass of a volatile liquid.

Procedure
See Figure 4.2.

1. Measure the mass of a clean dry flask, together with foil and rubber band to cover the mouth of the flask (m_1).
2. Place a small amount of the liquid (for example, propanone) in the flask, cover the mouth of the flask with the foil and make a tiny pinprick in it.
3. Hold the flask in a beaker of boiling water to completely surround it.
4. Measure the temperature of the water (T) and the atmospheric pressure (P).
5. When all of the liquid has evaporated, remove the flask from the boiling water and dry the outside of it.
6. Allow the flask to cool to let the vapour condense and to let the air back into it.
7. Measure the mass of the flask and the condensed vapour (m_2).
8. Fill the flask with water and measure its volume (V).

Calculations
1. Find the mass of the vapour $= m_2 - m_1$
2. Use the equation of state for an ideal gas to calculate the number of moles:

$$n = \frac{PV}{RT}$$

3. Calculate the mass of one mole.

4.2 MOLES

What kinds of particles are substances made of?

The particles that a substance is made of and which can react in chemical reactions are in some cases **atoms**, and in other cases **molecules** or **ions**.

For example, metals consist of a lattice of **uncombined atoms**. Their formulas are single atoms, for example, Na, Cu, etc. Carbon also consists of a giant lattice of atoms, and its formula is C.

Elements that are gases are usually **molecules**, for example, O_2, Cl_2, etc. Covalent compounds also contain molecules, for example, CO_2, etc.

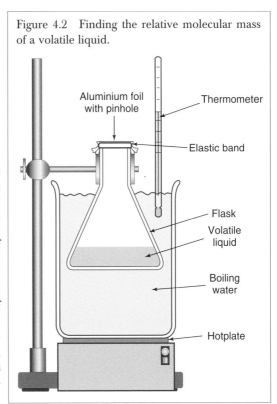

Figure 4.2   Finding the relative molecular mass of a volatile liquid.

Ionic compounds contain **pairs or small groups of ions**, for example: Na, Cl; Ca, CO_3; etc.

What is a mole?

A mole of a substance is the amount that contains Avogadro's number (6×10^{23}) of its particles.

A mole also contains the same number of particles as the number of atoms in 12 g of carbon–12. The number of moles of a substance can be found from its mass and, for gases only, from its volume.

Molar mass

The molar mass of a substance is the mass (weight) of it that contains one mole.

One mole of **atoms** is the relative atomic mass number (A_r) in grams. For example, one mole of C weighs 12 g, one mole of Ca is 40 g.

One mole of **molecules** is the relative molecular mass (M_r) in grams. For example, one mole of H_2O weighs $2(1) + 16$, i.e., 18 g. One mole of O_2 weighs $2(16)$, i.e., 32 g. One mole of $C_6H_{12}O_6$ weighs $6(12) + 12(1) + 6(16)$, i.e., $72 + 12 + 96$, i.e., 180 g.

Converting moles to grams

What is the mass of three moles of H_2O? Answer: 3×18 g, i.e., 54 g.

How many moles are present?

The number of moles can be found by dividing the mass of a substance by the mass of one mole.

$$\text{Moles} = \frac{\text{mass}}{A_r} \text{ or } \frac{\text{mass}}{M_r}$$

Question

How many moles of C are present in 72 g?

Answer

The A_r of C = 12.

Thus, moles $= \dfrac{72}{12}$

$= 6$ moles.

Question

How many moles of water (H_2O) are in 90 g?

Answer

M_r of $H_2O = 18$.

Thus, moles $= \dfrac{90}{18}$

$= 5$ moles.

Molar volume

One mole of **any gas** has the volume of 22.4 litres, when calculated at s.t.p.

Note: This only applies to gases. The volume of a liquid has to be converted to mass, using the value of its density.

Converting moles to litres

Question

What is the volume of three moles of any gas?

Answer

3×22.4 litres, i.e., 67.2 litres.

How many moles are present?

The number of moles can be calculated by dividing the volume in litres at s.t.p. by 22.4.

Question

How many moles are in 2 litres at s.t.p. of oxygen (or any gas)?

Answer

$$\text{Moles} = \frac{2}{22.4}$$

$$= 0.089 \text{ mole.}$$

Avogadro's constant

This is the number of particles that is in one mole. One mole contains 6×10^{23} particles.

HIGHER LEVEL

Converting moles to particles

Question

How many particles are in four moles?

Answer

$4 \times 6 \times 10^{23}$, i.e., 24×10^{23}.

Question

How many atoms are in two moles of CH_4?

Answer

Two moles $= 2 \times 6 \times 10^{23}$ particles $= 12 \times 10^{23}$ molecules of CH_4.
One molecule of CH_4 has 5 atoms
$\Rightarrow$ number of atoms $= 5 \times 12 \times 10^{23}$.

How many moles are present?
Divide the number of particles by Avogadro's number.

Question

How many moles are in 24×10^{23} particles?
Answer:

$$\text{Moles} = \frac{24 \times 10^{23}}{6 \times 10^{23}}$$

$= 4$ moles.

4.3   DETERMINATION OF FORMULAS

Different kinds of formulas

A compound is made when atoms of different elements combine, and they combine in definite ratios. For instance, one oxygen atom combines with two hydrogen atoms to form a molecule of water.

There are different kinds of chemical formulas to represent the atoms in the compound.

- The **empirical formula** is the simplest whole number ratio of atoms that are present in a substance.
- The **molecular formula** is the actual ratio of atoms that are present in one molecule (or set of ions).
- The **structural formula** is a diagram that shows the arrangement of the atoms in one molecule.

To calculate the empirical formula from the percentage composition

The formula of any substance is very important and they have been worked out by analysis of the relative weights of the elements that are present. This is known as the **percentage composition by mass**.

What to do

1. Assume there is 100 g of the compound, and calculate the number of moles of each element in 100 g.
2. Put the number of moles into the simplest ratio, by dividing each one by the smallest one. This usually brings all of the numbers to whole numbers.
3. Write the formula.

Example

A compound was broken down into its elements and their percentage masses were calculated. The compound consisted of 52.17% carbon, 13.04% hydrogen, and 34.79% oxygen. What is its empirical formula?

Answer

1. In 100 g of the compound there are 52.17 g of carbon, 13.04 g of hydrogen and 34.79 g of oxygen.

   Moles of C atoms: $\dfrac{52.17}{12}$

   $= 4.35$ moles.

   Moles of H atoms: $\dfrac{13.04}{1}$

   $= 13.04$ moles.

   Moles of O atoms: $\dfrac{34.79}{16}$

   $= 2.17$ moles.

2. Dividing by the smallest of these numbers (2.17):
   $C = 2$; $H = 6$; $O = 1$.

3. Empirical formula: C_2H_6O.

To calculate the molecular formula from the empirical formula

To calculate the molecular formula you need the **relative molecular mass, M_r.** The relative molecular mass can be found from a mass spectrometer or by other means (see mandatory experiment).

What to do

1. Calculate the mass of one unit of the empirical formula and divide it into the M_r.
2. Multiply the empirical formula by that number.

Example

A substance, whose empirical formula is C_2H_6O, has a relative molecular mass of 92. Calculate its molecular formula.

Answer

The mass of one unit is $2(12) + 6(1) + 1(16)$, which is $24 + 6 + 16$, i.e., 46.

The number of units in one molecule $= \dfrac{92}{46} = 2$

Thus, molecular formula is $2(C_2H_6O)$, i.e., $C_4H_{12}O_2$.

HIGHER LEVEL

Calculating the empirical formula from the masses of reactants and products

What to do

1. Calculate the mass of each element in the compound.
2. Divide by the A_r and calculate the number of moles of atoms.
3. Put the number of moles into the simplest ratio, by dividing by the smallest one.

Example

2 g of calcium was burned and formed 2.8 g of oxide. Calculate the empirical formula of the calcium oxide.

Answer

Mass of calcium = 2 g
A_r of Ca = 40

Moles of Ca atoms = $\dfrac{2}{40}$

= 0.05 mole.
Mass of oxygen in the compound = 2.8 − 2.0 = 0.8 g
A_r of O = 16

Moles of O atoms = $\dfrac{0.8}{16}$

= 0.05 mole.
Thus, empirical formula is CaO.

Getting the percentage mass from the formula

People who use chemicals may wish to compare the amount of an element in different substances in simple terms, not involving chemical formulas. One way of comparison is to provide the **% mass** of the element in a compound. For example, fertilisers are commonly compared by this method.

What to do

1. Use the molecular formula to calculate the relative mass of each element's atoms that are in one molecule.
2. Calculate the mass of one molecule by adding the masses of the elements.
3. Divide the mass of each element by the mass of the molecule, and multiply by 100.

Example

Ammonium phosphate, $(NH_4)_3PO_4$ is a fertiliser that provides nitrogen and phosphorus. Calculate the % mass of these two elements.

Answer

In one molecule the mass of N atoms $= 3(14) = 42$.
The mass of P atoms $= 1(31) = 31$.
The mass of one molecule $= 42 + 12(1) + 31 + 4(16)$, i.e. $42 + 12 + 31 + 64 = 149$.

% mass of $N = \dfrac{42 \times 100}{149}$

$= 28.2\%$.

% mass of $P = \dfrac{31 \times 100}{149}$

$= 20.8\%$.

4.4   CHEMICAL EQUATIONS

How to balance chemical equations

What to do

1. Write the equation in formulas. It is essential to realise that you **never change the formula of a substance**, and it is essential that you have the correct formulas.
2. To balance an equation **you can change the number in front of the formulas** of the reactants and products until the same numbers of atoms are in both sides of the equation.

Reactions involving combustion in air

When a substance burns, it reacts with the oxygen gas in the air. The formula for oxygen gas is O_2.

Example

Write a balanced equation for the combustion of magnesium.

Answer

Step 1. Write the equation in formulas.
The formula for any metal, or carbon or sulphur, is a single atom. The formula for oxygen gas is O_2. Check the valencies of Mg and O on the periodic table in order to decide on the formula of magnesium oxide – it is MgO.

$Mg + O_2 = MgO$

Step 2. Change the number in front of the formulas to get the same number of atoms on both sides.

$Mg + \frac{1}{2}O_2 = MgO$

or

$2Mg + O_2 = 2MgO$

Example

The combustion of natural gas, CH_4, produced CO_2 and H_2O. Write a balanced equation for the reaction.

Step 1. Write the equation in formulas.

$CH_4 + O_2 = CO_2 + H_2O$

Step 2. Change the number in front of the formulas to get the same number of atoms on both sides.

Because the CH_4 has only one C atom, it means that only one molecule of CO_2 can be formed. Because CH_4 has four H atoms, it means that two molecules of H_2O will be formed. Thus:

$CH_4 + O_2 = CO_2 + 2H_2O$

But the equation is not yet balanced because there are four atoms of O on the right and only two on the left. So, we must put 2 in front of O_2 to also have four atoms on the left side. Thus:

$CH_4 + 2O_2 = CO_2 + 2H_2O$

Example

The combustion of propane, C_3H_8 produces CO_2 and H_2O. Write a balanced equation.

Step 1.

$C_3H_8 + O_2 = CO_2 + H_2O.$

Step 2.

$C_3H_8 + O_2 = 3CO_2 + 4H_2O.$

Step 3.

$C_3H_8 + 5O_2 = 3CO_2 + 4H_2O.$

Using balanced equations to calculate the quantities of reactants and products

A balanced equation shows the ratio between the **number of molecules** of the reactants and products. It is the same ratio for the **number of moles** of the reactants and products. By using the number of moles you can calculate the mass, or volume (in the case of gases only), of the reactants and products.

Example

Limestone decomposes when it is heated according to the balanced equation $CaCO_3 \rightarrow CaO + CO_2$. Calculate (a) the mass of calcium oxide (b) the volume at s.t.p. of CO_2 that is produced, when 1000 g of limestone is decomposed.

Answer

Step 1. Change the mass of the reactant to the number of moles.
M_r of $CaCO_3 = 40 + 12 + 3(16)$, i.e., $40 + 12 + 48$, i.e., 100.
Thus, moles of $CaCO_3 = 1000/100 = 10$ moles.

(a) **Step 2**. Examine the balanced equation to find the ratio between the moles of reactant and products.
One mole of $CaCO_3$ = one mole of CaO
$\Rightarrow$ 10 moles of $CaCO_3$ = 10 moles of CaO.

(a) **Step 3**. Change the number of moles to mass.
M_r of $CaO = 40 + 16$, i.e., 56.
Thus, 10 moles of $CaO = 10 \times 56$ g
$= 560$ g.

(b) **Step 2**. Examine the balanced equation to find the ratio between the moles of reactant and products.
One mole of $CaCO_3$ = one mole of CO_2
$\Rightarrow$ 10 moles of $CaCO_3$ = 10 moles of CO_2.

(b) **Step 3**. Change the number of moles to the volume at s.t.p. (This can only be done for gases.)
One mole of a gas = 22.4 litres
$\Rightarrow$ 10 moles of $CO_2 = 10 \times 22.4 l = 224 l$.

HIGHER LEVEL

When reactants are in excess

A balanced equation tells us the ratio of the moles of the reactants as they react, but there is often an excess of one reactant, and so not all of it reacts. The reactant that is in short supply is the **limiting factor**. **All of the reactant that is in short supply can react**, and this determines how much of the other reactant (the reactant in excess) will react, and how much product will be made.

What to do

1. Calculate the number of moles of the reactants.
2. Check the balanced equation to find the ratio for the reaction, and deduce which is the limiting factor.
3. Calculate the number of moles of the reactant in excess that will react, and the number of moles of product that will be produced.
4. Convert the number of moles to mass or volume, as required.

Example

Limestone reacts with hydrochloric acid according to the balanced equation:

$$CaCO_3 + 2HCl \rightarrow CaCl_2 + H_2O + CO_2.$$

10 g of limestone was placed in a solution that contained 6 g of HCl. Calculate the mass of $CaCl_2$ that was produced and the volume of CO_2, at s.t.p.

Step 1. M_r of $CaCO_3 = 40 + 12 + 3(16)$, i.e. $40 + 12 + 48$, i.e., 100.
$\Rightarrow$ moles of $CaCO_3 = 10/100 = 0.1$ mole.
M_r of $HCl = 1 + 35.5$, i.e., 36.5.
$\Rightarrow$ moles of $HCl = 6/36.5 = 0.16$ mole

Step 2. Examine the equation to find the ratio of the reactants, and find the limiting factor:
One mole of $CaCO_3$ requires two moles of HCl.
Thus, 0.1 mole of $CaCO_3$ requires 0.2 mole of HCl.
As there is only 0.16 mole of HCl present, it means that HCl is the limiting factor.

Step 3. All of the 0.16 mole of HCl can react. From the balanced equation we deduce that only 0.08 mole of the $CaCO_3$ can react, and 0.08 mole of $CaCl_2$ and 0.08 mole of CO_2 will be formed.

Step 4. (a) M_r of $CaCl_2 = 40 + 2(35.5)$, i.e., $40 + 71$, i.e., 111.
$\Rightarrow 0.08$ mole of $CaCl_2 = 0.08 \times 111\,g = 8.88$ g.
(b) one mole of $CO_2 = 22.4 l$ (at s.t.p.)
$\Rightarrow 0.08$ mole $= 0.08 \times 22.4 l = 1.79 l$.

Calculation of the percentage yield

Some reactions, for example the oxidation of ethanol, produce more than one product. The percentage yield for the product is the ratio of the amount of product that the process produced relative to the maximum amount it could have produced if all of the reactant was converted to the desired product.

$$\% \text{ yield} = \frac{\text{mass of product that was produced} \times 100}{\text{maximum mass that could have been produced}}$$

An example based on mass of reactants and products is on page 126.
Percentage yield can also be calculated in the ratio of moles.

Example

The reaction between ethanol and ethanoic acid takes place according to this equation:

$$CH_3COOH + C_2H_5OH \rightarrow CH_3COOC_2H_5 + H_2O$$

If 0.1 mole of C_2H_5OH reacted to make 0.068 mole of $CH_3COOC_2H_5$, calculate the % yield.

Answer

According to the equation, one mole of C_2H_5OH produces one mole of $CH_3COOC_2H_5$. Thus, 0.1 mole could have produced 0.1 mole of product.

$$\Rightarrow \% \text{ yield} = \frac{\text{moles of product that was produced} \times 100}{\text{maximum number of moles possible}}$$

$$= \frac{0.068 \times 100}{0.1}$$

$$= 68\%$$

Balancing redox equations

What to do

1. Calculate the oxidation numbers (ON) and put the oxidation numbers of the elements that change under the elements in the equation. In general, the ON of O never changes, except for reactions involving OF_2 and H_2O_2.
2. Calculate the **change in ON** for each element, and then, if there is more than one atom in a molecule or ion, the **total change in ON for the molecule or ion**. Put this number above each molecule or ion.
3. Put a number in front of each molecule or ion that reacts in order to balance the changes in ON For example, if ion A changed by 1 and ion B changed by 2, then put 2 before A to balance the change in ON. Also, if ion A changed by 2 and ion B changed by 3, put 3 before ion A and 2 before ion B. Thus, the changes in ON (that is, the numbers of electrons transferred) are balanced.
4. Without changing the ratio of the reactants from step 3, adjust the number of ions and molecules that were produced.
   If H^+ ions are involved in making H_2O molecules, count the number of O atoms on the left and on the right, and the difference is the number of H_2O molecules. Then, the number of H^+ ions that react is twice the number of H_2O molecules that were produced.

Example

1. Balance the equation: $Fe^{2+} + Cl_2 \rightarrow Fe^{3+} + Cl^-$

Answer

Step 1. Assign ON to the elements.

$$Fe^{2+} + Cl_2 \rightarrow Fe^{3+} + Cl^-$$
$$+2 \quad\ 0 \quad\ +3 \quad -1$$

Step 2. Calculate the change in ON for each element and then each ion or molecule that reacts.

$$1 \qquad 2(1)$$
$$Fe^{2+} + Cl_2 \rightarrow Fe^{3+} + Cl^-$$

Step 3. Balance the change in ON.

$$2Fe^{2+} + Cl_2 \rightarrow Fe^{3+} + Cl^-$$

Step 4. Adjust the number of ions that were produced, without changing the ratio of the reacting species.

$$2Fe^{2+} + Cl_2 \rightarrow 2Fe^{3+} + 2Cl^-$$

Example

Balance the equation: $Fe^{2+} + MnO_4^- + H^+ \rightarrow Fe^{3+} + Mn^{2+} + H_2O$.

Answer

Step 1. Assign ON to the elements:

$$Fe^{2+} + MnO_4^- + H^+ \rightarrow Fe^{3+} + Mn^{2+} + H_2O$$

$$\phantom{Fe^{2}}+2 \quad\ +7 \qquad\qquad +3 \quad +2$$

Step 2. Calculate the change in ON for each element and then for each ion or molecule that reacts.

$$\phantom{Fe^{2+}}1 \qquad 5$$

$$Fe^{2+} + MnO_4^- + H^+ \rightarrow Fe^{3+} + Mn^{2+} + H_2O$$

Step 3. Balance the change in ON by placing the appropriate number in the equation:

$$5Fe^{2+} + MnO_4^- + H^+ \rightarrow Fe^{3+} + Mn^{2+} + H_2O$$

Step 4. Adjust the number of ions that were produced, without changing the ratio of the reaction species.

Count the number of O atoms on the left to calculate the number of H_2O molecules that will be made (that is, 4). Finally, double the number of H_2O molecules to find the number of H^+ ions that are needed in the reaction (that is, 8).

$$5Fe^{2+} + MnO_4^- + 8H^+ \rightarrow 5Fe^{3+} + Mn^{2+} + 4H_2O$$

TEST YOURSELF

*1. (a) What is meant by 'ideal' gas?
   (b) What are the assumptions about an ideal gas?
   (c) Under what conditions are real gases least like an ideal gas?
   (d) What kinds of gas are least like an ideal gas?

2. (a) Define 'diffusion'.
   (b) When comparing the rates of diffusion of gases, which one has the faster rate of diffusion?

3. (a) State, in words or by equation, Boyle's law.
   (b) State, in words or by equation, Charles's law.
   (c) Write an equation for the combined gas law.

4. Calculate the volume of a gas at s.t.p. when its volume at 20°C and at a pressure of 98,000 Pa is 2 litres.

*5. (a) State Avogadro's law.
   (b) $H_2 + \frac{1}{2}O_2 = H_2O$.
     (i) Use the equation to calculate the volume of oxygen gas that reacts with 500 cm^3 of hydrogen gas.
     (ii) Name the law that links the combining ratios of gases.

*6. (a) What is the equation of state for an ideal gas?
   (b) Use the equation of state to calculate the number of moles in 10 litres of gas that is measured at 100°C and at a pressure of 100,000 Pa, given that $R = 8.31$.

7. (a) Outline the procedure to measure the M_r of a volatile liquid.
   (b) If 0.12 g of a vapour has a volume of 84.5 cm^3 at a temperature of 100°C and at a pressure of 9.5×10^4 Pa, calculate its M_r.
8. (a) Define 'mole'.
   (b) What is the volume of one mole of a gas, measured at s.t.p.?
   (c) How many moles are present in 2 litres of gas (measured at s.t.p.)?
   (d) How many moles are present in
      (i) 2 g of oxygen gas
      (ii) 1000 g of carbon dioxide gas.
*9. (a) How many atoms are in 5 moles of ammonia (NH_3)?
   (b) How many moles are in a sample of gas that has 5×10^{20} particles?
10. Define:
   (a) empirical formula
   (b) molecular formula
   (c) structural formula.
11. (a) A compound consisted of 40% carbon, 6.6% hydrogen and 53.4% oxygen. Calculate its empirical formula.
   (b) If its M_r is 120, what is its molecular formula?
12. Calculate the empirical formula of a compound which consists of 46.66% nitrogen, 26.66% oxygen, 20% carbon and 6.66% hydrogen.
13. Calculate the percentage composition of nitrogen in these fertilisers:
   (a) NH_4NO_3
   (b) $CO(NH_2)_2$.
14. Write balanced equations for these reactions:
   (a) calcium hydroxide and carbon dioxide forms calcium carbonate and water
   (b) calcium carbonate and hydrochloric acid forms calcium chloride, carbon dioxide and water
   (c) the combustion of C_6H_{14} forms carbon dioxide and water.
15. $Fe_2O_3 + 3CO \rightarrow 2Fe + 3CO_2$
   Calculate the mass of iron that could be produced from 200 g of iron(III) oxide.
*16. $CH_3COOH + C_2H_5OH \rightarrow CH_3COOC_2H_5 + H_2O$
   10 g of CH_3COOH was reacted with 6.0 g of C_2H_5OH and 8 g of $CH_3COOC_2H_5$ was formed.
   (a) Calculate which of the reactants was in excess.
   (b) Calculate the percentage yield.
*17. Balance the following equations:
   (a) $MnO_4^- + Cl^- + H^+ \rightarrow Mn^{2+} + Cl_2 + H_2O$
   (b) $Fe^{2+} + H^+ + ClO_3^- \rightarrow Fe^{3+} + Cl^- + H_2O$
   (c) $Cr_2O_7^{2-} + Fe^{2+} + H^+ \rightarrow Cr^{3+} + Fe^{3+} + H_2O$

Chapter 5 – Acids, bases and salts. Volumetric analysis. Redox titrations

5.1   ACIDS, BASES AND SALTS

Acids are a group of compounds that have a number of features in common:

- They dissolve in water to release H^+ ions.
- They have a pH less than 7.
- They react with some metals, and with bases and carbonates to form salts.
- They change the colour of indicators; for example, they change blue litmus to red.
- **Strong acids** are fully dissociated in water. Examples include HCl, H_2SO_4 (in car batteries).
- **Weak acids** are only partly dissociated in water. Examples include ethanoic acid (in vinegar), citric acid (in lemons).

Bases are compounds that have the following features in common:

- They neutralise acids to form salts and water.
- If they dissolve in water they have a pH greater than 7.
- If they dissolve in water they change the colour of indicators, for example, they change red litmus to blue.

Bases that have been dissolved in water are called **alkalis**. They are caustic (corrosive). They cause the breakdown of fats to form soaps.

   Common bases include the oxides and hydroxides of metals, as well as ammonia. For example, NaOH (caustic soda, in oven cleaner), KOH (caustic potash), CaO (in cement), $Ca(OH)_2$ (in limewater), $Mg(OH)_2$ (in milk of magnesia) and NH_3 (in window cleaner).

What is a neutralisation reaction?

Neutralisation is the reaction between an acid and a base to produce a salt and water.

- **A salt is formed by replacing the H ion in the acid with a metal ion**.

When an acid reacts to donate its H^+ ions, the rest of the molecule becomes a negative ion, which becomes part of a salt, for example, a chloride or sulfate or ethanoate or citrate, etc.

Note: Not all salts are neutral. If a weak acid or a weak base is involved the salt may be acidic or alkaline, i.e., the pH at neutralisation may not be 7. The salts of weak acids are basic and the salts of weak bases are acidic. If both the acid and base are strong, then the salt solution has a pH of 7.

In biology, the neutralisation of excess stomach acid (HCl) is achieved with indigestion products, for example, milk of magnesia $(Mg(OH)_2)$; acids in soil are neutralised with quicklime (CaO), slaked lime $(Ca(OH)_2)$ and limestone $(CaCO_3)$.

Examples

- acid + base $\rightarrow$ salt + water
- $HCl + NaOH \rightarrow NaCl + H_2O$
- $H_2SO_4 + 2NaOH \rightarrow Na_2SO_4 + 2H_2O$.

Theories of acids

Arrhenius theory

Acids dissociate in water to produce H^+ ions. Bases dissociate in water to produce OH^- ions.

During neutralisation, the H^+ and OH^- combine to form H_2O ($H^+ + OH^- \rightarrow H_2O$), and the other ions combine to form the salt (for example, $Na^+ + Cl^- \rightarrow NaCl$).

HIGHER LEVEL

Bronsted–Lowry theory

Their theory expanded the concept of acids and bases to include all reactions where H^+ (protons) are transferred. Water is no longer considered necessary for a substance to have acidic or basic properties. Even water can be reacting as an acid or base.

An acid is a proton donor. A base is a proton acceptor.

Many acid/base reactions are reversible and the products of the reaction also act as acids and bases. When a proton is transferred between an acid and a base, the acid becomes a base and the base becomes an acid.

A conjugate acid-base pair are an acid and a base that differ by a proton.

Examples:

$$H_2SO_4 + NH_3 \rightleftharpoons NH_4{}^+ + HSO_4^-$$
$$\text{acid} \qquad \text{base} \qquad \text{acid} \qquad \text{base}$$

H_2SO_4 and NH_4^+ are acids because when they react they donate protons (H^+); NH_3 and HSO_4^- are bases because they accept the protons. When they react, the acid becomes its conjugate base, and the base becomes its conjugate acid.

The conjugate acid-base pairs are:

$$H_2SO_4/HSO_4^-$$

$$NH_4^+/NH_3$$

5.2   VOLUMETRIC ANALYSIS

How to express the concentration of a solution

A **solution** is made by dissolving a **solute** (usually a solid) in a **solvent**, usually distilled water.

A solution may be described as concentrated or dilute. A **concentrated solution** contains a lot of dissolved solute relative to the solvent, whereas a **dilute solution** either has less dissolved in the same amount of solution, or it has a similar amount dissolved in more of the solution. Thus, 'concentrated' and 'dilute' are vague terms, so precise methods of measuring concentration are required.

There are a number of ways to measure concentration.

- **g L^{-1}**: the number of grams in 1 litre of the solution
- **mol L^{-1}**: the number of moles in 1 litre of the solution. This is known as the molarity of a solution.
- **% (v/v)**: the number of cm^3 in 100 cm^3 of the solution. (v stands for volume).

HIGHER LEVEL

- **% (w/w)**: the number of grams in 100 grams of the solution. (w stands for weight)
- **% (w/v)**: the number of grams in 100 cm^3 of the solution

To calculate the % concentration

What to do
Calculate the amount that would be present in 100 cm^3 or 100 g of the solution.

Example 1
1. 4 g of glucose was dissolved in water and the solution was made up to 40 cm^3. Calculate the % w/v.

Answer
40 cm^3 of the solution contains 4 g of glucose

$\Rightarrow$ 1 cm^3 contains 4/40 g

$\Rightarrow$ 100 cm^3 contains $\dfrac{4 \times 100 \text{ g}}{40} = 10 \text{ g}$

i.e., 10% (w/v).

Example 2
2. 5 cm^3 of ethanol was dissolved in water and the solution was made up to 25 cm^3. Calculate the % v/v.

Answer
25 cm^3 of the solution contains 5 cm^3 of ethanol

$\Rightarrow 1$ cm^3 contains $5/25$ cm^3

$\Rightarrow 100$ cm^3 contains $\dfrac{5 \times 100 \text{ cm}^3}{25} = 20$

i.e., 20% (v/v).

Dilution of solutions

You can dilute a solution by a definite amount to change its concentration. For instance, adding 25 cm^3 of a solution to 75 cm^3 of water makes 100 cm^3 of a diluted solution. The original solution is now 25 cm^3 in 100 cm^3, i.e., it was diluted 1:4. The original solution is four times as concentrated as the diluted solution.

Similarly, by mixing 25 cm^3 of a solution with 225 cm^3 of water, the solution is diluted to 25 in 250, i.e., 1:10.

To calculate the molarity of a solution from grams per litre (g L^{-1})

What to do
Convert the mass to the number of moles.

Example
The concentration of an NaOH solution is 10 g L^{-1}. Calculate the concentration in moles per litre (i.e., mol L^{-1}, or M).

Answer
M_r of NaOH $= 23 + 16 + 1$, i.e., 40.

Moles of NaOH in 10 g $= 10/40$

$= 0.25$.

$\Rightarrow$ molarity of the solution is 0.25 M.

To calculate the number of moles from the molarity and the volume

A chemist keeps a stock of solutions of known concentration (known as standard solutions) and uses pipettes and burettes to accurately measure their volumes. Thus, the number of moles that are present in a reaction can be calculated.

The number of moles = volume (V) × molarity (M) (where the volume is in litres).

Example
How many moles are present in 25 cm^3 of a 2 M solution?

Answer
A 2 M solution contains 2 moles in 1000 cm^3:

i.e., 1000 cm$^3 = 2$ moles

$\Rightarrow 1$ cm$^3 = 2/1000$ moles

$$\Rightarrow 25 \text{ cm}^3 = \frac{2 \times 25}{1000} \text{ moles}$$

i.e., 0.05 mole.

Alternatively, use the equation:

moles = volume × molarity (when volume is measured in litres)

$$= 25/1000 \times 2$$

$$= 0.05 \text{ mole.}$$

Volumetric analysis in practice

For volumetric analysis a chemist needs standard solutions and accurate instruments to measure volume.

A standard solution is one whose concentration is known.

A primary standard is a substance that:

- is available in a pure state
- does not react with the air or its environment
- is very soluble in water.

Mandatory experiment 5: Preparation of a standard solution of sodium carbonate (see Figure 5.1).

The **primary standard in acid-base titrations** is anhydrous sodium carbonate, Na_2CO_3. It is available at 100% purity, it does not react with the oxygen or carbon dioxide of the air, and it has good solubility in water.

To prepare 1 litre of a 0.1 M solution:

M_r of $Na_2CO_3 = 2(23) + 12 + 3(16)$, i.e., $46 + 12 + 48$, i.e., 106.

Procedure

1. Weigh out 10.6 g (0.1 mole) of the sodium carbonate on a clean clock glass on a balance that is sensitive to two decimal places.
2. Using a fine brush, transfer it to a beaker containing $500/600 \text{ cm}^3$ of distilled or deionised water and wash the clock glass into the beaker.
3. Stir it with a glass rod to dissolve it.
4. Pour it through a funnel into a 1 litre volumetric flask.
5. Wash the glass rod, the beaker and the funnel with distilled water and add the washings to the flask.
6. Add more water, drop by drop with a dropper, until the bottom of the meniscus is resting on the mark.
7. Stopper the flask and invert the flask a few times to mix the solution.

Note: If you want to make up 250 cm^3 of solution, use ¼ of 10.6 g of sodium carbonate.

Figure 5.1   Preparing a standard solution of Na_2CO_3.

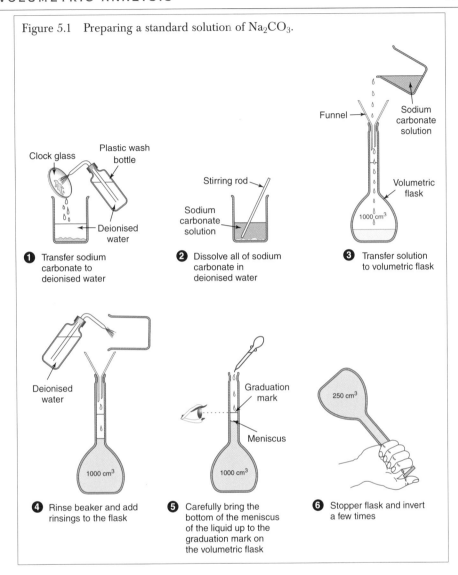

① Transfer sodium carbonate to deionised water

② Dissolve all of sodium carbonate in deionised water

③ Transfer solution to volumetric flask

④ Rinse beaker and add rinsings to the flask

⑤ Carefully bring the bottom of the meniscus of the liquid up to the graduation mark on the volumetric flask

⑥ Stopper flask and invert a few times

The procedure for titrations

See Figure 5.2.

1. Use a clean conical flask or one that has been washed out with distilled (or deionised) water. (Some water may be present in the flask as that will not change the number of moles of reactants that are added to the flask.)
2. Wash the burette with distilled (or deionised) water and then with some of the solution that it will contain. Hold it vertically in a stand. Use a small funnel to fill it with the solution. Remove the funnel and open the tap to fill the jet. Close the tap when the bottom of the meniscus is at the zero mark.

Figure 5.2   Titration procedure.

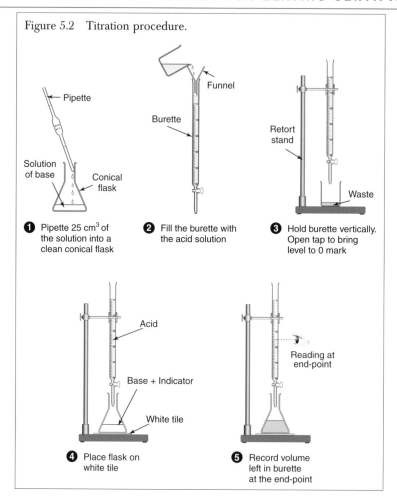

① Pipette 25 cm³ of the solution into a clean conical flask

② Fill the burette with the acid solution

③ Hold burette vertically. Open tap to bring level to 0 mark

④ Place flask on white tile

⑤ Record volume left in burette at the end-point

3. Wash the pipette with distilled (or deionised) water and with some of the solution that it will contain. Using a pipette-filler, fill the pipette with the solution to the mark. Empty the pipette into the flask, touching the tip against the inside of the flask.
4. Use a wash bottle to wash the liquid from the side of the flask to the bottom.
5. Add a few drops of suitable indicator. Place the flask over a white tile to see clearly the colour change at the end-point.
6. Open the tap of the burette and let the liquid mix with the liquid at the bottom. Swirl the flask to mix the liquids and use a wash-bottle to wash the liquids from the sides of the flask to the bottom. Close the tap when the indicator has made a permanent colour change. Record the volume of liquid still in the burette and calculate the volume that was used.
7. After the first rough titration, wash out the flask, and repeat the titration so that one drop brings about the end-point. Do it three times and get the average of the volumes that agree to within 0.1 cm³.

8. Use the formula:

$$\frac{V_1 M_1}{n_1} = \frac{V_2 M_2}{n_2}$$

to find M_1, where V stands for the volumes, M stands for the molarity, and n stands for the number of molecules in the balanced equation.

Mandatory experiment 6a: Standardisation of a hydrochloric acid (HCl) solution using a standard solution of sodium carbonate.

Standard solution: sodium carbonate Na_2CO_3

Indicator: methyl orange

End-point (when the burette contains the acid solution): yellow to pink

Example

25.0 cm^3 of a 0.05 M solution of sodium carbonate was titrated against a hydrochloric acid solution and the mean volume of hydrochloric acid used was 22.7 cm^3.
    The titration reaction is $Na_2CO_3 + 2HCl \rightarrow 2NaCl + H_2O + CO_2$.
    Calculate the concentration of the hydrochloric acid solution in mol l^{-1}.

Answer

Let 1 represent the HCl solution.

$$\frac{V_1 \times M_1}{n_1} = \frac{V_2 \times M_2}{n_2}$$

$$\frac{22.7 \times M_1}{2} = \frac{25 \times 0.05}{1}$$

$$\Rightarrow M_1 = \frac{25 \times 0.05 \times 2}{22.7}$$

$$= 0.11 \text{ M}$$

Example

25.0 cm^3 of a NaOH solution was titrated against a solution of 0.1 M HCl. After two accurate titrations the mean titre was 22.5 cm^3 of the HCl solution.
    The titration reaction is $HCl + NaOH \rightarrow NaCl + H_2O$.
    Calculate the concentration of the NaOH solution.

Answer

Let 1 represent the NaOH solution.

$$\frac{V_1 \times M_1}{n_1} = \frac{V_2 \times M_2}{n_2}$$

$$\frac{25 \times M_1}{1} = \frac{22.5 \times 0.1}{1}$$

$$\Rightarrow M_1 = \frac{22.5}{25}$$

$$M_1 = 0.9 \text{ M}$$

Mandatory experiment 6b: A hydrochloric acid/sodium hydroxide titration, and the use of this titration in making the salt sodium chloride.

Ordinary Level only

Indicator: methyl orange (or any indicator)

End-point: (when the burette contains the acid): yellow to pink.

Procedure

1. Pipette 25.0 cm^3 of the NaOH solution into a clean conical flask.
2. Add a few drops of indicator.
3. Add the HCl from the burette and measure the volume to achieve the end-point.
4. Repeat 3 times and calculate the average volume.
5. Mix the average volume with 25.0 cm^3 of the NaOH solution in a beaker.
6. Heat the solution to evaporate the water leaving sodium chloride.

HIGHER LEVEL

Mandatory experiment 7: Determination of the concentration of ethanoic acid in vinegar.

Standard solution: NaOH (or any other strong base. Sodium carbonate is unsuitable as it is a weak base and there are no indicators suitable for the titration of a weak acid, ethanoic acic, and a weak base).

Indicator: phenolphthalein.

End-point (when the burette contains the acid solution): pink to colourless.

Note: The vinegar is usually diluted (usually to 1/5th of its strength) in order to have a significantly large volume, and thus to reduce the margin of error when measuring the volume in the burette.

Example

50 cm^3 of vinegar was pipetted into a 250 cm^3 volumetric flask and distilled water was added to the mark and the flask was inverted a few times. The diluted vinegar was placed in a burette and titrated against 25 cm^3 of 0.1 M NaOH and the average titre was 16.0 cm^3.

The titration reaction is $CH_3COOH + NaOH \rightarrow CH_3COONa + H_2O$.

Calculate the concentration of the original vinegar:
(a) in terms of molarity
(b) in terms of % w/v.

Answer
(a)
Step 1. Let 1 represent the CH_3COOH solution.

$$\frac{V_1 \times M_1}{n_1} = \frac{V_2 \times M_2}{n_2}$$

$$\frac{16 \times M_1}{1} = \frac{25 \times 0.1}{1}$$

$$\Rightarrow M_1 = \frac{25 \times 0.1}{16}$$

$$\Rightarrow M_1 = 0.15625 \text{ M}$$

Step 2. The vinegar dilution factor was 50:250, i.e., 1:5 $\Rightarrow$ the molarity of the original vinegar is 5×0.15625, i.e., 0.78 M.

(b) The M_r of CH_3COOH is:

$2(12) + 4(1) + 2(16)$, i.e., $24 + 4 + 32$, i.e., 60

$\Rightarrow 0.78$ moles $= 0.78 \times 60$ g $= 46.8$ g.

Thus 1000 cm^3 of vinegar has 46.8 g of CH_3COOH

$\Rightarrow 100$ cm^3 of vinegar has 4.68 g.

Hence, the % w/v is 4.68%.

Mandatory experiment 8: Determination of the amount of water of crystallisation in hydrated sodium carbonate.

Standard solution: HCl (or any other strong acid)

Indicator: methyl orange

End-point (when the burette contains the acid solution): yellow to pink.

1. Weigh a definite amount of the sodium carbonate crystals, add them to distilled water in a beaker, stir to dissolve and bring the volume to 250 cm^3 in a volumetric flask.
2. By titrating against a standard solution of HCl, calculate the concentration of the Na_2CO_3 in the flask.
3. Calculate the number of moles of Na_2CO_3 that were in the flask, and hence in the crystals.
4. Calculate the mass of the Na_2CO_3 in the crystals.
5. Subtract from the mass of the crystals to find the mass of the water of crystallisation.
6. Express the mass of the water of crystallisation as a % of the hydrated crystals.
   Alternatively, calculate the number of moles of water of crystallisation, and express it as a ratio of the number of moles of Na_2CO_3 that were also in the crystals. Hence, in $Na_2CO_3x(H_2O)$ find the value of x.

Note: The molecular mass of the hydrated sodium carbonate crystals could be calculated by linking the number of moles that were present with the mass of crystals.

Example

7.77 g of sodium carbonate crystals was dissolved in water and made up to 500 cm^3 in a volumetric flask. The solution was titrated in 25 cm^3 samples against 0.075 M H_2SO_4 and the average titre was 20.0 cm^3.

The equation for the titration is:

$$Na_2CO_3 + H_2SO_4 \rightarrow Na_2SO_4 + H_2O + CO_2$$

(a) Calculate the concentration of the sodium carbonate solution in mol/l.
(b) Calculate the mass of Na_2CO_3 in the crystals.
(c) Calculate the water of crystallisation as a % mass.
(d) Calculate x in the formula of crystalline sodium carbonate, $Na_2CO_3 . x\ H_2O$.

Answer

(a) Let 1 represent the Na_2CO_3.

$$\frac{V_1 \times M_1}{n_1} = \frac{V_2 \times M_2}{n_2}$$

$$25 \times M_1 = 20 \times 0.075$$

$$\Rightarrow M_1 = \frac{20 \times 0.075}{25}$$

$$= 0.06\ M.$$

(b) The volume of the solution was 500 cm^3, hence the number of moles was 0.03 moles.

$$M_r \text{ of } Na_2CO_3 = 2(23) + 12 + 3(16), \text{ i.e., } 46 + 12 + 48, \text{ i.e., } 106.$$

Hence, 0.03 moles $= 0.03 \times 106$ g

$$= 3.18\ g.$$

(c) Mass of water in the crystals $= 7.77 - 3.18$

$$= 4.59\ g$$

$$\% \text{ mass} = \frac{4.59 \times 100}{7.77}$$

$$= 59.1\%$$

(d) M_r of $H_2O = 2(1) + 16$, i.e., 18

The number of moles of water in the crystals $= \dfrac{4.59}{18}$

$$= 0.255 \text{ moles.}$$

The number of moles of Na_2CO_3 in the crystals $= 0.03$ (see (b)).

Hence, 0.03 moles $Na_2CO_3 \equiv 0.255$ moles H_2O

$$\Rightarrow 1 \text{ mole } Na_2CO_3 = \frac{0.255}{0.03}$$

$$= 8.5$$

Hence x = 8.5

5.3   REDOX TITRATIONS

Primary standard for redox titrations: ammonium iron(II) sulfate

- It is obtainable in 100% purity, it is stable as it does not react with the gases of the air, and it has good solubility in water.
- However, when it is dissolved in water, **sulfuric acid must be added** to prevent it reacting with the water and oxygen present. Otherwise the solution becomes brown, as Fe^{2+} is oxidised to Fe^{3+}.
- Solutions should be made up with **distilled water** as tap water normally contains chlorine or chlorine compounds that are oxidising agents.

To prepare 250 cm^3 of a standard solution (0.1 M) of ammonium iron(II) sulfate.
(The formula of ammonium iron(II) sulfate is $(NH_4)_2SO_4.FeSO_4.6H_2O$ and its M_r is 392.)

Procedure

1. Weigh out on a clean clock glass (or 'boat') 9.8 g of the crystals.
2. Using a fine brush, transfer them to a beaker containing about 100 cm^3 of distilled water and about 20 cm^3 of dilute H_2SO_4.
3. With a glass rod, stir it to dissolve and pour it through a funnel into a clean 250 cm^3 volumetric flask. Wash the clock glass, beaker, rod and funnel, and add the washings to the flask. Add distilled water, drop by drop, to bring the bottom of the meniscus to the mark.
4. Stopper the flask and invert it 20 times to mix the solution.

Mandatory experiment 9: To determine the concentration of a potassium manganate (VII), KMnO₄, solution by titration with ammonium iron(II) sulfate (see Figure 5.3).

The balanced equation is provided:

$$MnO_4^- + 5Fe^{2+} + 8H^+ \rightarrow Mn^{2+} + 5Fe^{3+} + 4H_2O$$

Note: The MnO_4^- is purple and the Mn^{2+} is colourless, so **no indicator** is required. The **end-point is a permanent pale pink colour**.

Because of its strong dark colour, the **top of the meniscus** of the KMnO₄ solution in the burette is read.

The H^+ ions are provided by H_2SO_4, and not by HCl, which would be oxidised, or by HNO_3, which is an oxidising agent.

In the absence of sufficient H^+ ions, the MnO_4^- is reduced only as far as MnO_2, a brown solid. This indicates that more H_2SO_4 should be added, or the titration repeated with extra amount of H_2SO_4.

Procedure

1. Prepare the pipette and burette by washing them with distilled (or deionised) water and then with the solutions that they are to contain. Wash the conical flask with distilled (or deionised) water.
2. Pipette 20 cm^3 (or 25 cm^3) of the standard solution of ammonium iron(II) sulfate solution into the flask. Use a measuring cylinder to add about 20 cm^3 of dilute H_2SO_4.

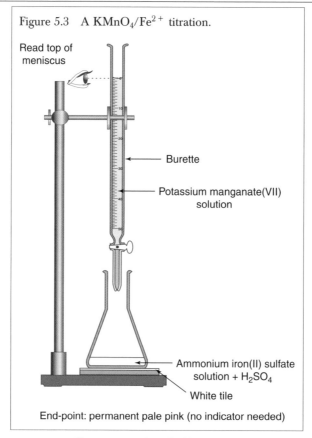

Figure 5.3   A $KMnO_4/Fe^{2+}$ titration.

Read top of meniscus

Burette

Potassium manganate(VII) solution

Ammonium iron(II) sulfate solution + H_2SO_4

White tile

End-point: permanent pale pink (no indicator needed)

3. Hold the burette vertically in a stand and fill it with the $KMnO_4$ solution. Open the tap to fill the jet and to bring the level to the 0 mark. Allow the solution into the flask until there is a permanent pale pink colour.
4. Read the burette and calculate the volume that was used.
5. Repeat the titration until the end-point is reached with one drop. Get the average from three titres that agree to within 0.1 cm^3.

Example
To calculate the molarity of the $KMnO_4$ solution.
25 cm^3 of a 0.1 M solution of a ammonium iron(II) sulfate was placed in a flask and an excess of dilute H_2SO_4 was added. It was titrated against a $KMnO_4$ solution and the average titre was 21.2 cm^3. Calculate the concentration of the solution.

Answer

$$\frac{V_1 \times M_1}{n_1} = \frac{V_2 \times M_2}{n_2}$$

Use the balanced equation provided above, and let solution 1 represent the unknown solution, i.e., the manganate solution.

$$\frac{21.2 \times M}{1} = \frac{25 \times 0.1}{5}$$

$$\Rightarrow M = \frac{25 \times 0.1}{5 \times 21.2}$$

$$= 0.024 \text{ M.}$$

Mandatory experiment 10: Determination of the amount of iron in an iron tablet (see Figure 5.4).

Procedure

1. Weigh the iron tablet(s) in a clean clock glass and brush it into a beaker containing about 100 cm³ of dilute H_2SO_4. (The H_2SO_4 prevents the oxidation of the Fe^{2+} to Fe^{3+} by dissolved oxygen from the air.) Use a glass rod to break it up to dissolve it. (Alternatively, crush the tablets with a pestle and mortar.)
2. Through a funnel pour it into a 250 cm³ volumetric flask. Wash the beaker, rod and funnel with distilled water and add the washings to the flask. Add water drop by drop until the bottom of the meniscus rests on the mark.
3. Stopper the flask and invert it a few times to mix the solution.
4. Pipette 25 cm³ of the iron solution into a clean flask, touching the tip against the inside. Use a measuring cylinder to add about 20 cm³ of dilute H_2SO_4. (The H_2SO_4 is needed to provide the H^+ ions for the oxidation reaction.)
5. Hold a burette vertically in a stand. Fill the burette with a standard solution of $KMnO_4$, open the tap to fill the jet and to bring the level to the zero mark.
6. Place the flask on a white tile and let in the $KMnO_4$ until a pale permanent pink colour remains. Record the volume that was used. Wash the flask and repeat. Get the average of three readings that agree to within 0.1 cm³.

Calculations

1. Use the balanced equation provided to calculate the molarity of the iron solution.
2. Calculate the number of moles of the iron in 250 cm³ of the solution. This is the number of moles that were in the tablet.
3. Calculate the mass of that number of moles of the iron or of the iron salt.

Example

Three iron tablets, which together weighed 1.5 g, were dissolved in an excess of sulfuric acid and it was brought to 250 cm³ in a volumetric flask. 25 cm³ of this solution was pipetted into a flask that contained excess sulfuric acid and it was titrated against a 0.01M solution of $KMnO_4$. The average titration value was 8.2 cm³. Calculate (a) the concentration of the iron solution (b) the mass of iron(II) sulfate in the tablets (c) the percentage of iron(II) sulfate in the tablets.

The balanced equation is $MnO_4^- + 5Fe^{2+} + 8H^+ \rightarrow Mn^{2+} + 5Fe^{3+} + 4H_2O$.

Answer

(a) Calculate the concentration of the iron solution in the volumetric flask.

   Let 1 represent the iron solution:

Figure 5.4   Finding the amount of iron in iron tablets.

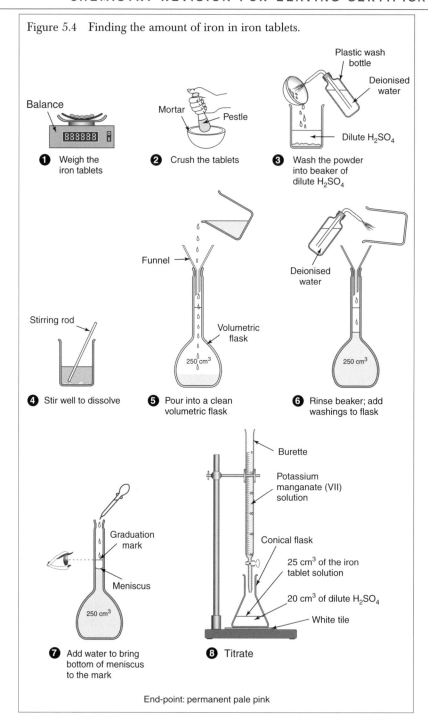

End-point: permanent pale pink

$$\frac{V_1 \times M_1}{n_1} = \frac{V_2 \times M_2}{n_2}$$

$$\frac{25 \times M}{5} = \frac{8.2 \times 0.01}{1}$$

$$\Rightarrow M = \frac{8.2 \times 0.01 \times 5}{25}$$

$$= 0.0164 \, \text{mol/L}.$$

(b) Calculate the number of moles of iron in the volumetric flask, i.e., in the tablets. Hence calculate the mass of iron.

There was $250 \, \text{cm}^3$ of the iron solution, hence the number of moles it contained was $0.0164/4$ moles, i.e., 0.0041 moles.

The iron was present as iron(II) sulfate, i.e., $FeSO_4$. Its M_r is $56 + 32 + 4(16)$, i.e., $56 + 32 + 64$, i.e., 152.

Thus, 0.0041 moles weighs 0.0041×152, i.e., $0.6232 \, \text{g}$.

(c) The % of iron sulfate in the tablets is:

$$\frac{0.623 \times 100}{1.5}$$

$$= 42.1\%.$$

Mandatory experiment 11: An iodine/thiosulfate titration (see Figure 5.5).

1. A solution of sodium thiosulfate can be standardised by titrating it against a standard solution of iodine. The iodine is formed by reacting excess potassium iodide with a definite volume of a standard solution of potassium manganate (the potassium iodide also keeps the iodine dissolved in the solution).

   The iodine is formed according to the equation:

   $$2MnO_4^- + 10I^- + 16H^+ \rightarrow 2Mn^{2+} + 5I_2 + 8H_2O$$

2. Iodine and thiosulfate react according to the equation:

   $$I_2 + 2S_2O_3^{2-} \rightarrow 2I^- + S_4O_6^{2-}$$

   Thus:

   $$2MnO_4^- \equiv 5I_2 \equiv 10 \, S_2O_3^{2-}$$

   $$\Rightarrow MnO_4^{2-} \equiv 5S_2O_3^{2-}.$$

The indicator

The iodine solution in the flask is red/brown. As the thiosulfate enters from the burette and reacts with the iodine the colour lightens and goes pale yellow. At that point a few drops of **starch indicator** is added to give a strong blue-black colour. The thiosulfate is added until the **end-point** is reached: the **blue-black colour disappears**.

Figure 5.5   An iodine/thiosulfate titration.

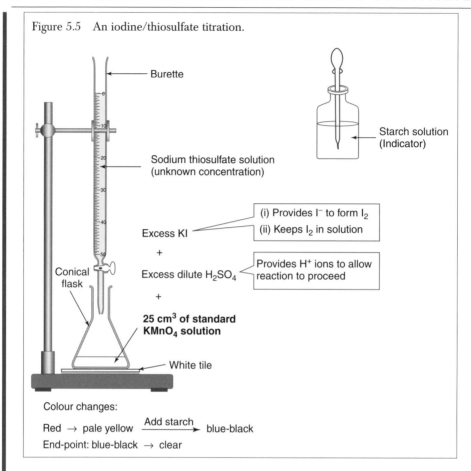

Burette

Starch solution
(Indicator)

Sodium thiosulfate solution
(unknown concentration)

Excess KI

(i) Provides I⁻ to form I_2
(ii) Keeps I_2 in solution

+

Excess dilute H_2SO_4

Provides H⁺ ions to allow
reaction to proceed

+

Conical
flask

**25 cm³ of standard
KMnO₄ solution**

White tile

Colour changes:

Red → pale yellow $\xrightarrow{\text{Add starch}}$ blue-black

End-point: blue-black → clear

Procedure

1. Wash the pipette and burette with water and with the liquids that they are to contain. Wash the conical flask with water. Hold the burette vertically in a stand.
   Fill it with the thiosulfate solution. Open the tap to fill the jet and bring the level to the 0 mark.
2. Pipette 25 cm³ of the standard KMnO₄ solution into the flask. Add about 10 cm³ of the KI solution and about 10 cm³ of dilute H_2SO_4. (The red-brown colour of iodine appears.)
3. Allow the thiosulfate solution into the flask until the colour goes very pale yellow. Add a few drops of starch solution. Continue adding the thiosulfate, drop by drop, until the blue-black colour clears. Read the volume in the burette and calculate the volume of thiosulfate that was used.
4. Wash out the flask and repeat the titration. Get the average of three readings that agree to within 0.1 cm³.

Example

25 cm^3 of a 0.02 M solution of KMnO4 was pipetted into a flask containing an excess of KI solution and dilute H_2SO_4. The thiosulfate solution was added from a burette and it required 23.5 cm^3 for the titration. Calculate the concentration of the thiosulfate solution.

Answer

Use the balanced equations provided and let 1 represent the thiosulfate solution.

$$5S_2O_3^{2-} \equiv MnO_4^-$$

$$\frac{V_1 \times M_1}{n_1} = \frac{V_2 \times M_2}{n_2}$$

$$\frac{23.5 \times M}{5} = \frac{25 \times 0.02}{1}$$

$$\Rightarrow M = \frac{25 \times 0.02 \times 5}{23.5}$$

$$\Rightarrow M = 0.106 \text{ mol/L}.$$

Mandatory experiment 12: Determination of percentage (w/v) of hypochlorite in bleach (see Figure 5.6).

- The hypochlorite ion ClO^- is a strong oxidising agent, which oxidises I^- ions to iodine molecules according to the equation provided:

$$ClO^- + 2I^- + 2H^+ \rightarrow Cl^- + I_2 + H_2O.$$

- The acid used is H_2SO_4 as the sulfate ion is stable under redox conditions. (HCl would be oxidised and HNO_3 is an oxidising agent.)
- The iodide ions must be **in excess** so that **all** of the hypochlorite ions can react to form iodine. Thus the number of iodine molecules that are formed is equal to the number of hypochlorite ions that were present.

To calculate the concentration of the iodine, the solution of iodine molecules can then be titrated against a **standard solution of sodium thiosulfate**. The balanced equation is provided: $I_2 + 2S_2O_3^{2-} \rightarrow 2I^- + S_4O_6^{2-}$.

Putting the two equations together links the ClO^- with the $S_2O_3^{2-}$:

$$ClO^- \equiv I_2 \equiv 2S_2O_3^{2-}$$

Bleach is very strong so it is usually **diluted** in order to increase the volumes in the titrations. (If a small volume of undiluted bleach is used, a greater % error is possible when measuring it.) A suitable dilution factor could be 1:10. Use a pipette to add 25 cm^3 to a 250 cm^3 volumetric flask and add distilled water, drop by drop, until the bottom of the meniscus rests on the mark. Stopper the flask and invert it 20 times to mix the solution.

Solutions **cannot be made with tap water** as it contains dissolved chlorine, an oxidising agent.

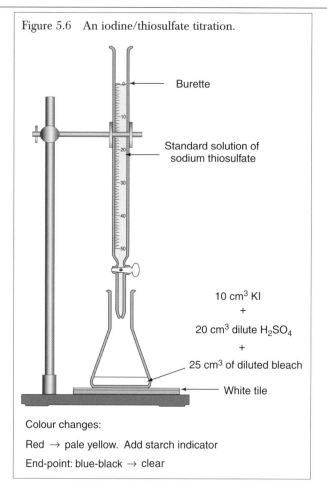

Figure 5.6   An iodine/thiosulfate titration.

Burette

Standard solution of
sodium thiosulfate

10 cm^3 KI
+
20 cm^3 dilute H$_2$SO$_4$
+
25 cm^3 of diluted bleach

White tile

Colour changes:

Red → pale yellow. Add starch indicator

End-point: blue-black → clear

Procedure

1. Pipette 25 cm^3 of the diluted bleach into a clean flask and use a measuring cylinder to add about 20 cm^3 of dilute H$_2$SO$_4$ and about 10 cm^3 of a potassium iodide solution. (An exact volume is not required so long as it provides an excess of the iodide.) The red/brown colour of iodine molecules appears.
2. Titrate it against a standard solution of sodium thiosulfate until the colour goes pale yellow. Add a few drops of starch solution as an indicator. Continue adding the thiosulfate solution, drop by drop, until the blue colour clears.
3. Record the volume added. Wash out the flask and repeat. Get the average of three titres that agree to within 0.1 cm^3.

   Use the combined balanced equation to calculate the concentration of the hypochlorite.

   Multiply by the dilution factor to find the concentration in the undiluted bleach.

Example

A 25.0 cm^3 of bleach was diluted to 250 cm^3. A 25 cm^3 portion was added to an excess of acidified potassium iodide solution and titrated against a standard 0.21 M sodium thiosulfate solution. The average titration figure was 20.7 cm^3.

1. Calculate the concentration of the bleach in moles per litre.
2. Express this concentration in terms of % w/v.

The equations for the reactions are:

$$ClO^- + 2I^- + 2H^+ \rightarrow Cl^- + I_2 + H_2O$$

$$2S_2O_3^{2-} + I_2 \rightarrow S_4O_6^{2-} + 2I^-$$

Answer

1. $ClO^- = I_2 = 2S_2O_3^{2-}$

Let 1 stand for the ClO^- solution.

$$\frac{V_1 \times M_1}{n_1} = \frac{V_2 \times M_2}{n_2}$$

$$\frac{25 \times M}{1} = \frac{20.7 \times 0.21}{2}$$

$$\Rightarrow M = \frac{20.7 \times 0.21}{2 \times 25}$$

$$= 0.087 \text{ moles/litre.}$$

Thus, the concentration in the undiluted bleach is 10×0.087 moles/litre, i.e., 0.87 moles/L.

2. The M_r of the bleach, NaClO, is $23 + 35.5 + 16$, i.e., 74.5.

Thus:

0.87 moles per litre $= 0.87 \times 74.5$ g, i.e., 64.82 g/litre.

To express this in % w/v we need to calculate the weight in 100 cm^3.

Thus:

1000 cm^3 contains 64.82 g

$\Rightarrow$ 100 cm^3 contains 6.482 g.

Thus the % w/v is 6.482 %, or 6.5%.

TEST YOURSELF

1. (a) State two differences between acids and bases.
   (b) According to the Arrhenius theory, define:
      (i) acid
      (ii) base.

    (c) What is meant by 'neutralisation'?

    (d) What is a salt?

*2. (a) According to the Bronsted–Lowry theory, define:

        (i) acid

        (ii) base.

    (b) What is a conjugate acid-base pair?

    (c) Identify the conjugate pairs in these reactions:

        (i) $CH_3COOH + H_2O \rightleftharpoons CH_3COO^- + H_3O^+$

        (ii) $NH_3 + H_2O \rightleftharpoons NH_4^+ + OH^-$.

3. $250 \ cm^3$ of a solution contained 4 g of sodium hydroxide (NaOH).

    (a) Calculate the concentration of the solution in:

        (i) $g \ L^{-1}$

        (ii) $mol \ L^{-1}$.

  *(b) Calculate the concentration in % (w/v).

  *(c) (i) If all of the solution was mixed with $750 \ cm^3$ of water what was the dilution factor?

        (ii) What is the concentration of the diluted solution in $mol \ l^{-1}$?

4. How many moles of solute are in:

    (a) $100 \ cm^3$ of a 1M solution?

    (b) $250 \ cm^3$ of a 0.1 M solution?

5. (a) What is a standard solution?

    (b) What are three properties that are essential in a primary standard?

    (c) Name a suitable primary standard in acid-base titrations.

    (d) Outline how to prepare $250 \ cm^3$ of a 0.1M solution of the primary standard named in (c).

6. (a) Name a suitable standard solution for the titration of an HCl solution.

    (b) Name a suitable indicator and state colour change at the end-point.

    (c) Outline how to prepare the burette with the HCl solution to begin the titration.

    (d) Outline how to put $25 \ cm^3$ of the standard solution into the conical flask.

    (e) Describe how to carry out the titration as accurately as possible.

7. (a) Name a suitable standard solution for the estimation of the concentration of ethanoic acid (CH_3COOH) in vinegar.

    (b) Name a suitable indicator and describe the colour change at the end-point.

    (c) Explain why a standard solution of sodium carbonate is not suitable for this titration.

    (d) Outline how you would dilute $50 \ cm^3$ of vinegar to $500 \ cm^3$.

    (e) The diluted vinegar was titrated against $25 \ cm^3$ of 0.1 M NaOH solution and the average titre was $22 \ cm^3$. Calculate the concentration of ethanoic acid in the vinegar in:

        (i) $mol \ L^{-1}$

        (ii) % w/v.

8. (a) State two reasons why ammonium iron(II) sulfate is used as a primary standard for redox titrations.

    (b) If the M_r of ammonium iron(II) sulfate is 392, outline how to prepare 250 cm^3 of a stable 0.1 M solution.

    (c) Why is an indicator not required for titrations with potassium manganate(IV)? What is the end-point?

    (d) If a brown solid appeared during a titration with potassium manganate(IV) what is it and what does that indicate?

9. In a titration to measure the amount of iron in iron tablets:
    (a) What standard solution is the iron solution titrated against?
    (b) Why is the iron dissolved in a solution of sulfuric acid?
    (c) Why is sulfuric acid added to the conical flask containing the iron solution?

10. (a) In iodine/thiosulfate titrations why cannot a standard solution of iodine be prepared by dissolving iodine?
    (b) How is a standard solution of iodine obtained?
    (c) What is the indicator, when is it added and what is the end-point?
    (d) What is the oxidising agent in bleach?
    (e) Why is the bleach usually diluted before measuring its concentration?

Chapter 6 – Fuels. Heats of reaction

6.1 FUELS

What are fuels?

Fuels are substances that provide energy (heat) when they are burned.

The most commonly used fuels are **hydrocarbons**, though **ethanol** is also used in countries that have cheap supplies of it from the fermentation of sugar. **Hydrogen** is another important fuel, which has the potential to become more widely used, as it does not cause air pollution.

Sources of hydrocarbons

The world's main sources are coal, natural gas and petroleum oil.

Oil refining

The main processes that take place in an oil refinery are fractionation and reforming.

Fractionation

The crude oil is heated to evaporate it and the gases are fed in to the bottom of the fractionating tower (see Figure 6.1). This consists of a series of bubble plates at different heights and at different temperatures. As the vapours move upwards they cool, and at their boiling point temperature they condense on the plates to form liquids. These liquids are removed from the tower as the fractions of the oil.

The fraction with the largest molecules has the highest boiling point and it is removed from the bottom of the tower. Going up the tower, the molecules get smaller and their boiling points become lower. One fraction comes out of the top of the tower as a gas – refinery gas.

The main fractions and their uses are:

- **Refinery gas**, C_1 to C_4 gases. The gases are separated. The methane and ethane of the refinery gas are burned in the oil refinery to provide heat. The propane and butane are liquefied under pressure to form liquid petroleum gas (LPG). This fuel is used for heating and in transport. It is different to natural gas, which is mainly methane. As these gases are odourless, mercaptans (compounds of sulfur) are added so that a gas leak can be easily detected by smell.
- **Light gasoline**, used as petrol.
- **Naphtha** is reformed and most of it is used as petrol and some of it provides the raw materials for making plastics, medicines etc.
- **Kerosene** (paraffin), used in planes and for home heating.
- **Gas oil** (diesel), used in transport and for home heating.
- **Residue**, used as fuel oil in power stations and as tar on roads.

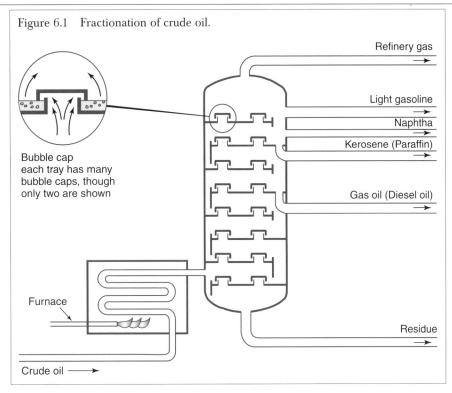

Figure 6.1   Fractionation of crude oil.

Bubble cap
each tray has many
bubble caps, though
only two are shown

Furnace

Crude oil ⟶

Refinery gas

Light gasoline

Naphtha

Kerosene (Paraffin)

Gas oil (Diesel oil)

Residue

Petrol

Petrol is a mixture of small hydrocarbon molecules. Their **octane rating is a measure of the tendency to cause knocking** in a car engine (see Figure 6.2).

Petrol with an octane rating of 100 is best for car engines. It burns smoothly without 'knocking'. **2,2,4-trimethylpentane** has an octane rating of **100**. **Heptane** has an octane rating of **0**, as it auto-ignites too easily, causing 'knocking'. Poor running of the engine also results in the emission of unburned components, causing air pollution.

HIGHER LEVEL

Molecules with the **highest octane** rating are:

*   smaller
*   more branched
*   in rings (cyclic), including aromatics.

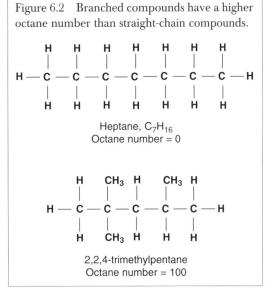

Figure 6.2   Branched compounds have a higher octane number than straight-chain compounds.

Heptane, C_7H_{16}
Octane number = 0

2,2,4-trimethylpentane
Octane number = 100

Anti-knock agents are added to petrol to raise its octane rating. These include **lead** (in the form of tetraethyl lead) and **oxygenates**. Unfortunately, lead causes health problems and also poisons the catalytic converters in the car exhausts which reduce air pollution.

HIGHER LEVEL

Oxygenates are oxygen containing organic substances, such as methanol, ethanol, and **methyl tert-butyl ether** (**MTBE**), which are added to petrol to increase its octane rating.

The octane rating is also improved by three **reforming processes**:

- **isomerisation**, whereby straight chain molecules break and reform as branched chains
- **dehydrocyclisation**, whereby chains become rings, including cycloalkanes and aromatics, by the removal of H atoms
- **catalytic cracking**, whereby using heat and catalysts, large hydrocarbon molecules are broken into smaller alkanes and one or more alkenes. The alkenes provide the raw materials for further industries, including making plastics. For example, $C_{10}H_{22} \rightarrow C_8H_{18}$ (octane) $+ C_2H_4$ (ethene).

Hydrogen as a fuel

At present, very few cars operate using hydrogen, but the development of hydrogen as a fuel is being encouraged for two reasons:

- when it is burned it forms only water, a **non-pollutant** $(H_2 + \frac{1}{2}O_2 = H_2O)$, and no CO_2, a major greenhouse gas.
- to **conserve hydrocarbons** for use in synthesis of plastics, pharmaceuticals, etc.

Hydrogen gas is at present used in the following industries:

- Manufacture of ammonia fertilisers $(3H_2 + N_2 \rightarrow 2NH_3)$
- Hydrogenation of vegetable oils to form margarine spreads. Vegetable oils, unlike animal fats, are unsaturated.

Hydrogen gas can be formed industrially by two methods:

- electrolysis of water, where a cheap supply of hydroelectricity is available
- steam reforming of natural gas: $H_2O + CH_4 \rightarrow 3H_2 + CO$. (This process is used to supply hydrogen in the manufacture of ammonia in Ireland.)

Ethyne as a fuel

Ethyne gas (C_2H_2) is burned with oxygen in the **oxyacetylene flame**, producing a high temperature for welding or cutting steel. (Ethyne is also known as acetylene.)

6.2 HEATS OF REACTION

What are exothermic and endothermic reactions?

In terms of heat change, there are two kinds of chemical reactions:

- **Exothermic** reactions release heat. They make their surroundings get warmer.
- **Endothermic** reactions absorb heat. Their surroundings get cooler.

For example, if you hold a thermometer in a test tube of water and add a spoonful of sodium hydroxide or anhydrous copper sulphate, the temperature rises. However, if you repeat using ammonium chloride, the temperature drops.

Burning a fuel is an exothermic reaction. A burning candle held under a test tube of water causes a temperature rise.

Another example of a heat change occurs when there is a **change of state**.

Heat is absorbed when a solid melts or when a liquid evaporates. Both changes cause their surroundings to cool down.

The opposite changes of state are exothermic: condensing a gas to liquid and the freezing of a liquid to a solid release heat.

What is the heat of a reaction?

The heat of a reaction is the heat change when substances react in molar quantities according to a balanced equation.

The combustion of methane is an exothermic reaction. When one mole is burned the amount of heat released is 890 kJ. This information is given in the following equation:

$$CH_4 + 2O_2 \rightarrow CO_2 + 2H_2O \quad \Delta H = -890 \text{ kJ mol}^{-1}$$

The minus sign indicates that heat is lost, i.e., that it is an exothermic reaction. An endothermic reaction has a plus sign.

The amount of heat, 890 kJ, is only released when **one mole** of the CH_4 reacts.

Mandatory experiment 13: Determination of the heat of reaction of hydrochloric acid with sodium hydroxide (see Figure 6.3).

The reaction is:

$$HCl + NaOH \rightarrow NaCl + H_2O$$

Procedure

1. With measuring cylinders, measure out 50 cm^3 of 1M HCl and 1M NaOH into separate polystyrene cups.
2. Measure their temperature, T_1, with a thermometer sensitive to 0.1°C.
3. Add one solution to the other and stir with the thermometer. Record the highest temperature, T_2.

Calculations

1. Calculate the amount of heat released by the reaction:
   Assuming the density of the HCl and NaOH solutions are the same as water, i.e., 1 g/cm^3, then the mass of the mixture is 100 g, or 0.1 kg.

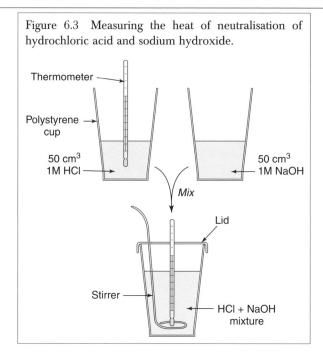

Figure 6.3 Measuring the heat of neutralisation of hydrochloric acid and sodium hydroxide.

Given that the specific heat capacity of the NaCl solution is 4060 J/kg/K, then the quantity of heat that was released by the reaction is $4060 \times 0.1 \times (T_2 - T_1)$.

(The equation to calculate the amount of heat that heats up a solution is often given as follows: Heat = $c \times m \times T$, where c = the specific heat capacity of the solution, m = the mass in kg of the solution, and T = the temperature rise (in °C or K).)

2. Calculate the heat of the reaction, i.e., the amount of heat that would be released if **one mole** of HCl reacted (or if one mole of water was formed).

The number of moles present in 50 cm^3 of 1M HCl = 50/1000, i.e., 0.05 mole.

Thus, 0.05 mole releases $4060 \times 0.1 \times (T_2 - T_1)$ joules

therefore one mole releases $\dfrac{4060 \times 0.1 \times (T_2 - T_1)}{0.05}$ joules

Measuring the heat of combustion, or the calorific value of a food, or the kilogram calorific value of a fuel

The heat of combustion of a fuel, and the calorific value of a food, can be measured in a bomb calorimeter (see Figure 6.4). The **heat of combustion** is the heat change when **one mole** of a substance is **completely burned** in an excess of oxygen.

For example, the reaction for the combustion of methane, CH_4 is as follows:

$$CH_4 + 2O_2 \rightarrow CO_2 + 2H_2O$$

A bomb calorimeter consists of a thick-walled vessel that contains a heating element. The fuel is weighed and placed inside and the lid is screwed down.

Oxygen is forced inside under pressure. (If an excess of oxygen is not present, then the fuel is not completely oxidised and some CO is produced, instead of CO_2.)

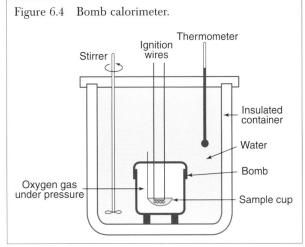

Figure 6.4   Bomb calorimeter.

The bomb is placed inside a container of water and its temperature is recorded. The wire is heated with an electric current to ignite the fuel. The water in the container is stirred and the highest temperature is recorded. The rise in the temperature is used to calculate the amount of heat released from the fuel, or food. This is then calculated as the heat of combustion, i.e., the amount of heat that would be released by burning one mole of the fuel.

Comparing energy values of foods and fuels

Non-chemists, such as engineers, fuel merchants, dieticians, lay people, etc. can use the heat values in fuels and in foods in amounts other than moles, in order to make comparisons.

- **Calorific value of a food**. This is the heat, in kJ or calories, that is released when **100 g** of the food is burned. (1 calorie = 4.2 joules) This value allows a balanced diet to be calculated for people of different ages or with different levels of activity.
- **Kilogram calorific value** of a fuel is the amount of heat that is released when 1 kg of the fuel is burned. This value allows the cost of different fuels to be compared, or the size of a boiler that is needed to supply heat to a building or industrial process to be calculated.

HIGHER LEVEL

Heat of formation

The heat of formation is the heat change when one mole of a substance is formed from its element in their standard states. (The heat of formation of an element is assumed to be zero.)

From the values of the heat of formation, the heat of a reaction can be calculated as follows:

Heat of a reaction = heats of formation of the products – the heats of formation of the reactants.

Example

The heats of formation of H_2O, H_2S and SO_2 are -286 kJ mol^{-1}, -21 kJ mol^{-1} and -297 kJ mol^{-1} respectively. Calculate the heat of reaction for this reaction:

$$2H_2S + SO_2 \rightarrow 3S + 2H_2O$$

Answer

Heat of reaction: heats of formation of products – heats of formation of reactants

$$\Delta H = 3(0) + 2(-286) - 2(-21) - (-297)$$

$$= -572 + 42 + 297$$

$$= -572 + 339$$

$$= -233 \text{ kJ mol}^{-1}$$

The **heat of formation of a substance can also be calculated** from its heat of reaction and knowing the heats of formation of the products.

Example

The heat of combustion of methane (CH_4) is -879 kJ mol^{-1}. The heats of formation of CO_2 and of H_2O are -393 kJ mol^{-1} and -286 kJ mol^{-1}. Calculate the heat of formation of methane.

Answer

The balanced equation for the reaction is:

$$CH_4 + 2O_2 \rightarrow CO_2 + 2H_2O \quad \Delta H = -879$$

$\Delta H =$ heats of formation of products – heats of formation of reactants:

$$-879 = -393 + 2(-286) - \Delta H_f(CH_4) - 2(0)$$

$$-879 = -393 - 572 - \Delta H_f(CH_4)$$

$$\Delta H_f(CH_4) = -393 - 572 + 879$$

$$\Delta H_f(CH_4) = -965 + 879$$

$$= -86 \text{ kJ mol}^{-1}$$

Hess's law

The heat change for a reaction is equal to the sum of the heat changes for intermediate reactions.

The above example could also be solved using Hess's law. The reaction that is required is:

$$C + 2H_2 \rightarrow CH_4 \quad \Delta H \text{ unknown}$$

The reactions that are given are as follows:

(i) $CH_4 + 2O_2 \rightarrow CO_2 + 2H_2O$ $\Delta H = -879$
(ii) $C + O_2 \rightarrow CO_2$ $\Delta H = -393$
(iii) $H_2 + \frac{1}{2}O_2 \rightarrow H_2O$ $\Delta H = -286$.

To get the required equation, we can use the above equations as they are, or reverse them, or multiply them. There are two rules to follow:

- If we reverse an equation, we reverse the sign of the ΔH.
- If we multiply an equation, we multiply the value of the ΔH.

The reaction that we must build up in intermediate steps is:

$C + 2H_2 \rightarrow CH_4$

Thus, we need an equation with C on the left; another equation with $2H_2$ on the left, and another equation with CH_4 on the right. Then we add them together:

$C + \cancel{O_2} \rightarrow C\cancel{O_2}$ $\Delta H = -393$ (equation ii)

$2H_2 + \cancel{O_2} \rightarrow 2\cancel{H_2}O$ $\Delta H = -572$ (doubling equation iii)

$\underline{C\cancel{O_2} + 2\cancel{H_2}O \rightarrow CH_4 + 2\cancel{O_2}}$ $\Delta H = 879$ (reversing equation i)

$C + 2H_2 \rightarrow CH_4$ $\Delta H = 879 - 965$

$$= -86 \text{ kJ/mol}$$

Law of conservation of energy

In a chemical reaction energy cannot be created or destroyed, but it can be changed from one form to another.

Bond energy

The bond energy is the energy required to break one mole of covalent bonds and completely separate the atoms.

In a reaction, **energy is absorbed to break bonds** in the reactants and **energy is released when new bonds are formed** in the products. The heat of the reaction is the difference between the energy needed to break the bonds and the energy released when the new bonds are formed (see Figure 6.5).

Figure 6.5   Structural formulas of reactants and products.

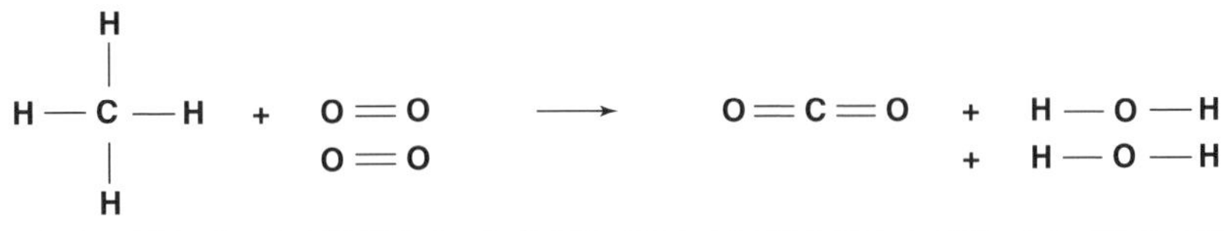

For instance, the reaction between methane and oxygen:

$$CH_4 + 2O_2 \rightarrow CO_2 + 2H_2O$$

In the methane molecule there are four C–H bonds that break, and in the oxygen molecule there is one O=O bond. Thus the energy that must be used to separate the atoms is the bond energy of the C–H bond multiplied by four, plus the bond energy of the O=O bond multiplied by two (there are two O_2 molecules in the reaction).

When the atoms react to form CO_2 and H_2O the energy that is released is the bond energy of the C=O bond multiplied by two, plus the bond energy of the O–H bond multiplied by four.

The difference between the energy input to break the bonds in the reactants and the energy released by forming the new bonds in the products is the heat of the reaction.

TEST YOURSELF

1. (a) Define 'fuel'.
   (b) What are three sources of hydrocarbons?
   (c) (i) What is one advantage of using hydrogen as a fuel?
       (ii) Outline two ways of producing hydrogen on an industrial scale.
   (d) What is the main use of ethyne as a fuel?
2. Outline what happens in a fractionation tower in an oil refinery.
3. Name six products of a fractionation tower and state the main use for each fraction.
4. (a) What do the initials LPG stand for?
   (b) Compare natural gas and LPG.
   (c) Name the substance that is added to these gases to give them an odour.
5. (a) What does the octane number of petrol measure?
   (b) Name a substance with an octane number of:
       (i) 100
       (ii) 0.
   (c) What are the problems associated with using lead to increase the octane number?
   (d) Outline three processes that are carried out in an oil refinery to increase the octane rating of petrol.
*6. (a) Outline three structural features of alkane molecules that give them a high octane rating.
   (b) (i) What are oxygenates?
       (ii) Name two oxygenates.
       (iii) What is the function of adding oxygenates to petrol?
7. (a) (i) What are exothermic reactions?
       (ii) Give two examples of exothermic reactions.
       (iii) Describe a change of state that is exothermic.
   (b) (i) What happens to the temperature in an endothermic reaction?
       (ii) Outline a change of state that is endothermic.
       (iii) What happens to the temperature when the change of state is taking place?

8. (a) Define 'heat of reaction'.
   (b) The heat of reaction for the combustion of methane (CH_4) releases 890 kJ. Write an equation for the heat of reaction.

9. (a) Outline the procedure to measure the heat of reaction for the reaction between HCl and NaOH.
   (b) When 50 cm^3 of 1M HCl was added to 50 cm^3 of 1M NaOH in a plastic container, the temperature rose from 17°C to 21°C. The density of the solution was 1 g/cm^3 and its specific heat capacity was 4200 $J/kg^{-1}\,°C^{-1}$. Calculate the heat of reaction.
   (c) Why is the heat of reaction for ethanoic acid and NaOH less than for the reaction for HCl and NaOH?

10. (a) Define 'heat of combustion'.
    (b) Describe a bomb calorimeter and outline how it is used to measure the heat of combustion of a fuel.
    (c) Define 'kilogram calorific value'. State one use for such values.
    (d) Define 'calorific value of a food'. State one use for such values.

*11. (a) Define 'heat of formation'.
     (b) Outline how the values of heat of formation may be used to calculate the heat of a reaction.
     (c) Given that the heats of formation of water, carbon dioxide and ethyne are -286, -394 and 227 $kJ\,mol^{-1}$ respectively, calculate the heat of combustion of ethyne.
     (d) Define 'bond energy'. List the bonds broken and the bonds formed in the combustion of ethyne.

*12. (a) State Hess's law.
     (b) Use Hess's law to calculate the heat of formation of methane, given that its heat of combustion is -879 $kJ\,mol^{-1}$, and the heats of formation of carbon dioxide and water are -393 and -286 $kJ\,mol^{-1}$ respectively.

Chapter 7 – Rates of reaction

7.1 MEASURING THE RATE OF A REACTION

The rate of a chemical reaction is a measure of **how fast** the reaction is taking place. It can be measured as the change in the amount of one of the reactants, or one of the products, per second (or other unit of time).

The amount of a substance can be measured in concentration (moles per litre/mol L^{-1}), or mass, or volume (for gases). Thus, the usual definition of **the rate of a reaction is the change in the concentration of a reactant or product per unit of time**.

Mandatory experiment 14: Monitoring the rate of production of oxygen from hydrogen peroxide, using manganese dioxide as a catalyst (see Figure 7.1).

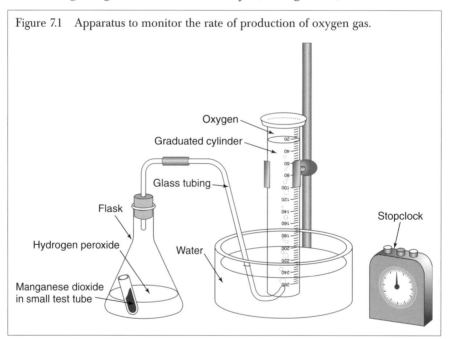

Figure 7.1   Apparatus to monitor the rate of production of oxygen gas.

Procedure

Mix the manganese dioxide with the hydrogen peroxide and measure the volume of oxygen in the graduated cylinder every 10 seconds. Graph the volume against time.

The rate of the reaction is measured by the **slope** of the graph (see Figure 7.2):

- The slope was most steep at the beginning as the rate of the reaction was fastest.
- The slope became less steep as the reaction slowed down.
- It levelled off when the reaction had stopped.

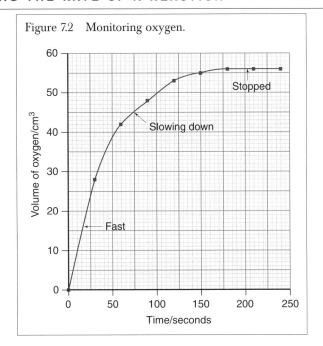

Figure 7.2   Monitoring oxygen.

HIGHER LEVEL

The average and instantaneous rates

See Figure 7.3.

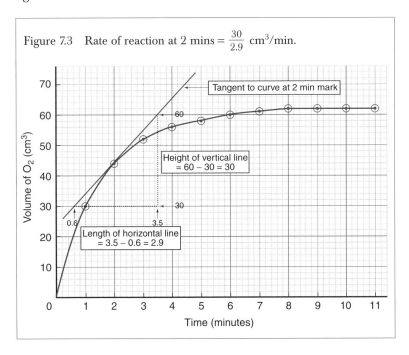

Figure 7.3   Rate of reaction at 2 mins $= \dfrac{30}{2.9}$ cm^3/min.

- The **average rate** of the reaction can be calculated by dividing the **overall change** in the amount of the reactant by the **overall time** for the reaction.
- The **instantaneous rate** at any particular time is measured as the **slope of the tangent** at the point in the graph that corresponds with that time. The slope can be measured by dividing the vertical by the horizontal components.

The factors that affect the rate of a reaction

The rate of a reaction may be affected by the following factors:

- the nature of the reactants
- the concentration of the reactants
- the temperature
- the size of the particles of solid
- the presence of a catalyst.

Nature of the reactants

Ionic substances that have dissolved in water are able to collide and react without further dissociation. Thus, the reaction between ionic substances can be completed almost **instantaneously**.

Covalent molecules must collide with sufficient energy – the **activation energy**, to break some covalent bonds. In a liquid or gas the speed of the molecules varies, and only a small percentage have a very fast speed. Thus, many of the molecules do not react after colliding because they do not have the activation energy. Thus more time (and energy) is needed for all of the molecules to react to complete the reaction.

Concentration of the reactants

Molecules and ions only react when they collide. Thus, the rate of a reaction depends on the number of collisions per second. **Increasing the concentration** of the molecules **increases the frequency of collisions** and thus increases the rate of the reaction.

Temperature

Increasing the temperature of a liquid or gas increases the rate of a reaction for two reasons:

- The speed of the molecules increases and thus they **collide more frequently**.
- The number of molecules that have the **activation energy** to react is significantly increased, and **so more of the collisions are effective**.

The second effect has the greater influence, and therefore an increase of just 10°C can often double the rate of a reaction.

Particle size

If the reactant is a **solid**, it reacts faster when it is ground up as a **powder**. This is because the small particles of the powder have **more surface area** and more molecules are exposed to the liquid or gas around them.

Dust explosions in mines and flour silos are cases of explosively fast reactions!

Catalysts

A catalyst alters the rate of a chemical reaction and is not used up by the reaction.

Most catalysts **speed up** reactions, and they are used in industry to save money by reducing temperatures that are needed for a fast rate of reaction, or in reducing the size of reaction vessels that are needed to satisfy the demand for the product.

Substances that stop the action of catalysts are called **catalyst poisons**. The industrial raw materials must be checked to ensure that none are present before they enter the reaction vessel.

Catalytic converters (see Figure 7.4) are present in car exhausts to reduce the amount of air pollutants, such as CO, which is injurious to humans, and NO which contributes to acid rain. The catalysts include **platinum, palladium and rhodium**. They form a finely divided surface over which the exhaust gases pass. They catal-

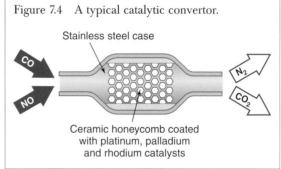

Figure 7.4   A typical catalytic convertor.

Stainless steel case

Ceramic honeycomb coated with platinum, palladium and rhodium catalysts

yse the reaction of CO and NO into CO_2 and N_2. $(2CO + 2NO = 2CO_2 + N_2)$. Lead is a poison to the catalysts; hence one reason why leaded petrol has been phased out.

Enzymes are catalysts that living organisms produce in the form of proteins. For example, the digestive enzymes in humans break down large food molecules, and the digestive enzymes produced by bacteria are included in biological washing powders.

An **autocatalyst** is the product of a reaction that speeds up the reaction. For example, in the titration between MnO_4^- and Fe^{2+} (page 79), the Mn^{2+} ions formed are catalysts. $MnO_4^- + 5Fe^4 + 8H^+ \rightarrow Mn^{2+} + 5Fe^{3+} + 4H_2O$.

HIGHER LEVEL

Theories of catalyst action

Surface adsorption

A **heterogeneous** catalyst is one that exists in a **different state** to the reactants. This typically means a solid catalyst in a liquid or gaseous reaction, for example, in a catalytic converter: $2CO + 2NO - (Pt) \rightarrow 2CO_2 + N_2$.

The reactant molecules are **adsorbed** on to the surface of the catalyst, by weak bonds, and thus increasing their concentration. Therefore the reaction rate increases. For this reason the surface area is increased by finely dividing the catalyst.

Intermediate formation

A **homogeneous catalyst** is in the **same state** as the reactants, for example, dissolved cobalt(II) salts catalyse the reaction between a solution of potassium sodium tartrate and hydrogen peroxide. The reaction generates heat and produces CO_2 gas which bubbles up. As this happens the pink colour of the catalyst changes during the reaction to green, but the colour changes back to pink again at the end of the reaction. The green colour is due to an intermediate compound. It is explained as follows:

uncatalysed reaction – A reacts slowly with B to produce AB:

A + B (slow) → AB

catalysed reaction – the catalyst C reacts **quickly** with A to produce an **intermediate compound** AC, and this reacts **quickly** with B to produce AB and to release C unchanged.

A + C (fast) → AC

AC + B (fast) → AB + C

The effect of a catalyst on activation energy

The activation energy is the minimum energy that colliding particles need to react. The catalysed reaction has a lower activation energy. More of the molecules can react by this pathway, thus increasing the rate of the reaction (see Figure 7.5).

The influence of temperature on activation energy

The energy of the molecules in a liquid or gas varies – a few have very little energy, a few have very large amount of energy, and most are in between. The proportion that has enough energy for the activation energy is low.

Raising the temperature raises the average energy of all molecules but it can significantly increase the number that has the activation energy. Typically, an increase of 10°C doubles the number that has the activation energy, and thus doubles the number that can react when they collide. This explains why a small temperature rise results in such a large increase in the rate of reaction (see Figure 7.6).

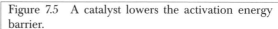
Figure 7.5   A catalyst lowers the activation energy barrier.

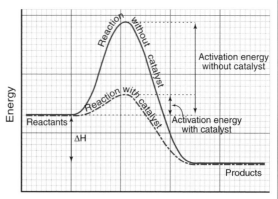
Note: ΔH is the same for the catalysed and uncatalysed reaction. The above reaction is exothermic.

Figure 7.6   A rise in 10°C can double the number of molecules with the activation energy.

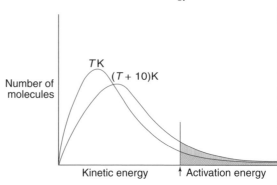

Mandatory experiments 15: Studying the effects on the reaction rate of (i) concentration and (ii) temperature using sodium thiosulphate solution and hydrochloric acid.

The reaction is the reaction of sodium thiosulfate and hydrochloric acid to produce a suspension of sulfur (and SO_2 gas, an irritant to some people).

$$2HCl + Na_2S_2O_3 \rightarrow 2NaCl + S + SO_2 + H_2O$$

The effect of concentration on the rate of reaction

See Figures 7.7 and 7.8.

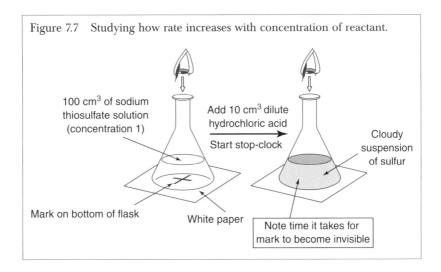

Figure 7.7 Studying how rate increases with concentration of reactant.

Procedure

1. Use a graduated cylinder to place 100 cm³ of a solution of sodium thiosulfate into a conical flask and position the flask on paper that has an X mark.
2. Quickly add 10 cm³ of dilute HCl, swirl to mix, and start a stop-clock.
3. Record how long it takes before the X becomes invisible under the cloud of sulfur that forms in the reaction. Calculate the rate of the reaction as 1/time.
4. Dilute the thiosulfate solution with distilled water to 80%, 60%, 40%, 20% and repeat.
5. Make a graph of the rate versus the concentration.

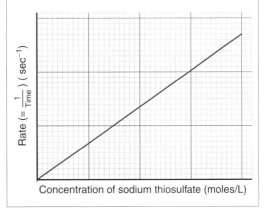

Figure 7.8 The straight line through the origin shows that rate is directly proportional to concentration.

Result

A straight line, going through the origin shows that they are directly proportional.

The effect of temperature on the rate of reaction

See Figure 7.9.

Procedure

1. Use a graduated cylinder to place 100 cm^3 of a solution of sodium thiosulfate into a conical flask and position the flask on paper with an X mark.
2. Measure the temperature with a thermometer.
3. Quickly add 10 cm^3 of dilute HCl, swirl to mix, and start a stop-clock.
4. Record how long it takes before the X becomes invisible under the cloud of sulfur that forms. Calculate the rate as 1/time.
5. Repeat but heat the solutions to 30°C, 40°C, 50°C, 60°C, and 70°C on a hot plate.
6. Make a graph of rate of reaction versus the temperature.

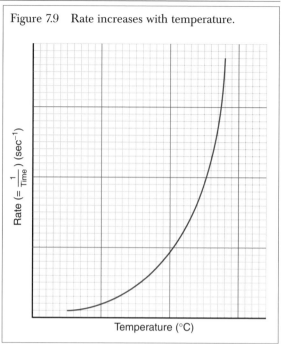

Figure 7.9   Rate increases with temperature.

Result

Increasing the temperature causes an increase in the rate, but not in direct proportion.

TEST YOURSELF

1. (a) What is meant by 'rate of reaction'?
   (b) In the reaction between zinc and hydrochloric acid the rate of the reaction slowed over time. Suggest two reasons why the rate decreased.
   (c) In what form should the zinc be added to the acid in order to have a fast rate of reaction?
   (d) Suggest a method of slowing down the rate of a reaction.
2. (a) With the aid of a labelled diagram, describe how to show the change in the rate of reaction over time of the catalysed reaction of hydrogen peroxide.
   (b) Sketch the graph you would expect.
*3. (a) Use Figure 7.10 to calculate the average rate of the reaction.
   (b) Calculate the rate at 30 seconds.
4. Outline simple experiments to show that the rate of a reaction is affected by:
   (a) temperature
   (b) particle size
   (c) concentration of the reactants.

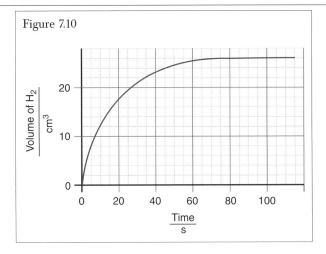

Figure 7.10

5. Explain the following:
   (a) the reaction between ionic substances is faster than one with covalent substances
   (b) increasing the temperature speeds up a chemical reaction
   (c) an increase in the concentration of the reactants increases the rate of the reaction.
6. (a) What is a catalyst?
   (b) Name a catalyst in a car's catalytic converter, and outline the reaction that is catalysed and the benefits to the environment.
   (c) What is a catalyst poison?
   (d) What are biological catalysts?
*7. (a) Distinguish between a homogeneous catalyst and a heterogeneous catalyst.
   (b) Outline how a heterogeneous catalyst works.
   (c) Outline how a homogeneous catalyst works. Outline an experiment to support the theory.
   (d) With the aid of a labelled energy profile diagram of an exothermic reaction, explain the effect of a catalyst.

Chapter 8 – Hydrocarbons. Chloroalkanes

8.1 HYDROCARBONS

What are hydrocarbons?

Hydrocarbons are compounds of hydrogen and carbon only. In everyday life they are important as fuels, solvents and the raw materials for plastics.

Sources of hydrocarbons: coal, petroleum oil, and natural gas are **fossil sources** that will one day be exhausted. Some hydrocarbons, for example, methane, can be made by **anaerobic decomposition** of plant and animals remains by bacteria. This can happen in landfills, slurry pits and in special digesters, where the gas is produced as a fuel. The escape of methane into the atmosphere should be reduced, as it is a major **greenhouse gas**, more damaging than CO_2.

The structure of hydrocarbon molecules

There are two kinds of hydrocarbons:

* **aliphatic** hydrocarbons have molecules in chains or rings of carbon atoms
* **aromatic** hydrocarbons have a **benzene ring** of 6 carbon atoms, where the bonds are intermediate between single and double.

Benzene ring

Aliphatic hydrocarbons

There are three series of aliphatic hydrocarbons, (alkanes, alkenes, alkynes), depending on whether there are single bonds, or a double bond or a triple bond between some of the carbons in the chain. This difference results in significantly different chemical properties between the three groups. Thus each group forms a homologous series of compounds that share characteristic chemical properties.

A **homologous series** is a group of compounds with similar chemical reactions due to having the same functional group. They have a gradual variation in physical properties, and they differ from each other by CH_2.

Alkanes

Alkanes have **single bonds only** between the carbon atoms; they are therefore **saturated compounds**. Their general formula is C_nH_{2n+2}. The first five members of this series are:

* methane CH_4
* ethane C_2H_6
* propane C_3H_8
* butane C_4H_{10}
* pentane C_5H_{12}.

From butane onwards there are different ways to arrange the carbon atoms in the chain, forming molecules that are either branched or unbranched. This gives rise to isomers.

Isomers are substances that have the same molecular formula but different structural formulas.

To name the isomer, find the longest chain and name it as the parent molecule, and then name the branches (side groups) with the number of the carbon atom that has the branch attached. Number the parent chain from the end that gives you the lowest number for the carbon that has the first branch.

See Figure 8.1 for the structural formulas of the first five alkanes and their isomers.

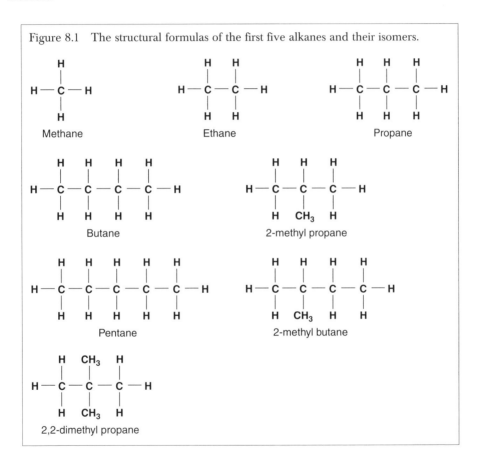

Figure 8.1   The structural formulas of the first five alkanes and their isomers.

Other alkanes (not including their isomers) include the following (see Figure 8.2 for their structural formulas):

- hexane C_6H_{14}
- heptane C_7H_{16}
- octane C_8H_{18}
- 2,2,4-trimethylpentane (iso-octane).

Figure 8.2   The structural formulas of more alkanes.

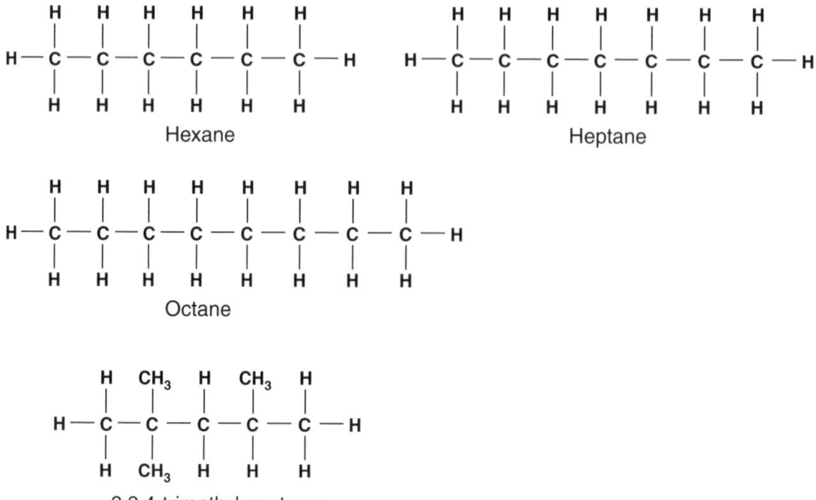

Hexane

Heptane

Octane

2,2,4-trimethyl pentane

Cyclohexane C_6H_{12} has a ring structure, but unlike an aromatic benzene ring C_6H_6, the carbon atoms are joined by single bonds (see Figure 8.3).

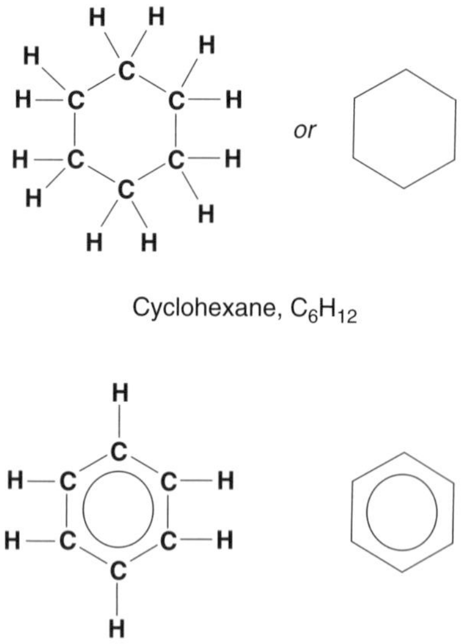

Alkenes

Alkenes are a homologous series, of general formula C_nH_{2n}, where there is a **double bond between two of the carbon atoms**; thus they are **unsaturated**. From butene onwards there are isomers, not only in branching, but also in the location of the double bond. The carbon after which the double bond is found is numbered, again numbering from the end that gives the lower number.

The first four members of the series are:

- C_2H_4 ethene
- C_3H_6 propene
- C_4H_8 but-1-ene
- but-2-ene.

See Figure 8.4 for their structural formulas.

Alkynes

The alkynes are another homologous series. They are characterised by the presence of a **triple bond between two carbon atoms**; thus they are

Figure 8.3   Cyclohexane and benzene.

Cyclohexane, C_6H_{12}

Benzene, C_6H_6

Figure 8.4   The structural formulas of the first four alkenes.

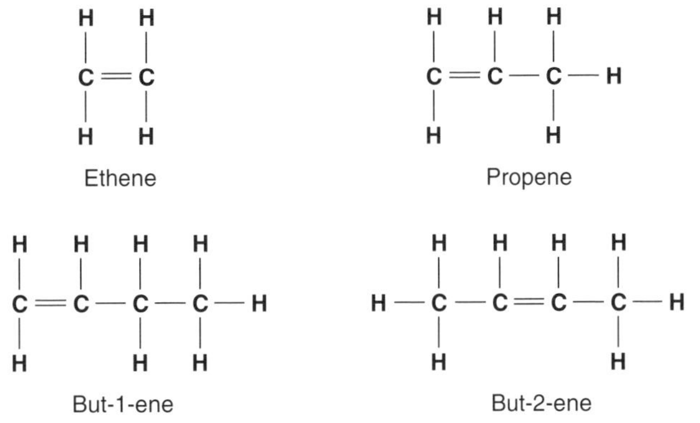

Ethene

Propene

But-1-ene

But-2-ene

unsaturated. The general formula is C_nH_{2n-2}. Only ethyne, C_2H_2, is on the Leaving Cert course.

H–C≡C–H

The physical properties of hydrocarbons

The molecules are non-polar and thus the intermolecular forces are van der Waals forces. The size of the force increases as the M_r increases.

Hydrocarbons are:

- soluble in cyclohexane
- insoluble in water
- gases when the M_r is small (C_1 to C_4). As the M_r increases they become liquids with a low boiling point (C_5 to C_{17}), or solids with a low melting point.

The reactions of the alkanes

Combustion

Alkanes are fuels of major importance (for example, petrol, diesel, etc.), used in transport, heating and for making electricity. Natural gas contains methane.

$CH_4 + 2O_2 \rightarrow CO_2 + 2H_2O$

$C_8H_{18} + 12\frac{1}{2}O_2 \rightarrow 8CO_2 + 9H_2O$

Substitution

Because alkanes contain only **saturated bonds**, they react by **replacing** H atoms with different atoms.

For example, by reacting with **chlorine** they form chloroalkanes, for example, chloromethane and chloroethane.

$CH_4 + Cl_2 \rightarrow CH_3Cl + HCl$

$C_2H_6 + Cl_2 \rightarrow C_2H_5Cl + HCl.$

By reacting with **bromine** they form bromoalkanes, for example, bromoethane and dibromoethane.

$$C_2H_6 + Br_2 \rightarrow C_2H_5Br + HBr$$

$$C_2H_5Br + Br_2 \rightarrow C_2H_4Br_2 + HBr$$

HIGHER LEVEL

Mechanism of substitution by free radicals

The reaction between **methane** and **chlorine** takes place in **sunlight**, where the UV light provides sufficient energy to break the bond in the chlorine molecule to form two separate chlorine atoms (radicals), each with seven outer electrons, and thus reactive. The presence of the unpaired electron that they have available for bonding is shown as a dot: Cl*.
  A radical is a reactive atom with an unpaired electron.
  The reaction takes place in steps as follows:
1. **Initiation**. This step forms radicals:

$$Cl_2 + UV \text{ light} \rightarrow Cl* + Cl*$$

2. **Propagation**. This step changes one radical into another. The Cl* attacks the CH_4 molecule to take away and bond with a H atom, forming HCl and a radical CH_3*:

$$CH_4 + Cl* \rightarrow HCl + CH_3*$$

The CH_3* radical can react in two ways. It might take another propagation step, where it attacks a Cl_2 molecule to take away and bond with a Cl atom to form CH_3Cl and a Cl* radical ($CH_3* + Cl_2 \rightarrow CH_3Cl + Cl*$), or a termination step might occur.
3. A **termination** step is where the CH_3* bonds with a Cl* radical to form:

$$CH_3Cl \ (CH_3* + Cl* \rightarrow CH_3Cl)$$

A similar reaction scheme can be produced, starting with ethane, forming chloroethane, etc.
  The **evidence** for this reaction is as follows:

- A short exposure to UV light causes a large amount of product to be formed. This is because the formation of just one radical leads to a **chain reaction** where one reaction leads to another in the propagation steps.
- Trace quantities of ethane (and of butane, in the reaction beginning with ethane) are found among the products. This happens when CH_3* joins with CH_3* to form C_2H_6.
- Other substances, for example, tetraethyl lead can speed up the reaction. This is because these substances also produce free radicals, which can increase the number of radicals formed from the methane (or ethane).

Reactions of the alkenes

Alkenes have a double bond between two carbon atoms. One of these bonds can be broken to allow each carbon atom to make another bond to a different atom.

This kind of reaction is also possible with the alkynes, as they have a triple bond. Thus, a molecule with a double or a triple bond is **unsaturated** and it is capable of **addition** reactions.

An addition reaction happens when an unsaturated compound adds on another atom to each of the carbon atoms in the double or triple bond.

1. Reaction with hydrogen forms alkanes:

$$C_2H_4 + H_2 \rightarrow C_2H_6$$

2. Reaction with chlorine forms dichloroalkanes:

$$C_2H_4 + Cl_2 \rightarrow C_2H_4Cl_2$$
(1,2-dichloroethane)

3. Reaction with bromine forms dibromoalkanes:

$$C_2H_4 + Br_2 \rightarrow C_2H_4Br_2$$
(1,2-dibromoethane)

4. Reaction with water forms alcohols:

$$C_2H_4 + H_2O \rightarrow C_2H_5OH$$
(ethanol)

5. Reaction with hydrogen chloride forms chloroalkanes:

$$C_2H_4 + HCl \rightarrow C_2H_5Cl$$
(chloroethane)

See Figure 8.5 for the structural formulas for the above reactions.

6. **Polymerisation**. Alkene molecules can react with one another to form long chains of polymers, which are used as plastics. Thus alkenes, often produced by the cracking of long chain alkanes in the petrochemical industry to make more petrol, are the raw materials for the manufacture of plastics.

Figure 8.5   The structural formulas of reactions.

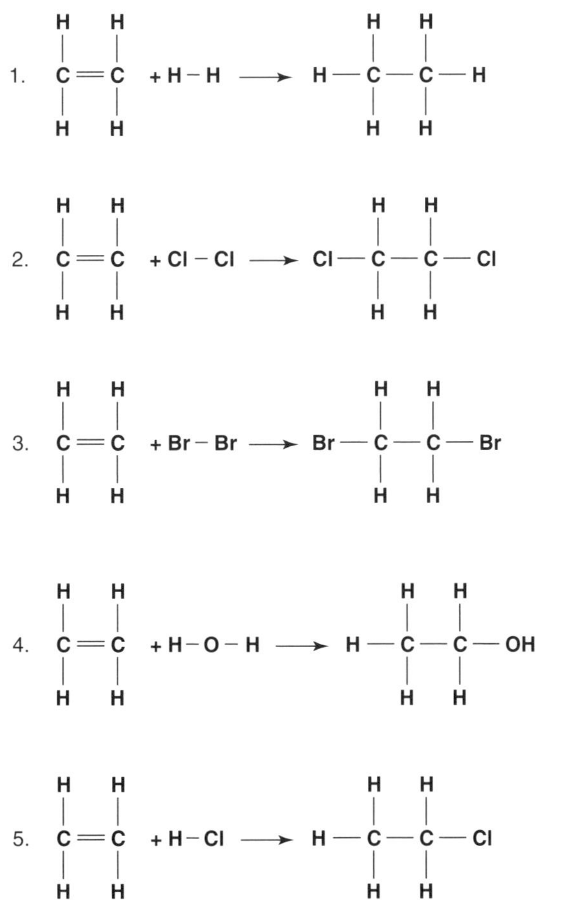

- n × ethene → poly(ethene), usually called polythene, used to make bags.
- n × propene → poly(propene), usually called polypropylene, used to make ropes.

HIGHER LEVEL

The mechanism of ionic addition of ethene and bromine

1. As the bromine molecule approaches the area of the ethene molecule with the double bond it becomes **polarised**, and eventually the bond breaks forming a Br^+ ion close to the double bond, and a Br^- ion.
2. The Br^+ ion is attracted to the double bond and attacks it. One of the bonds breaks and the pair of electrons forms a new bond to the Br. This leaves the other C atom with a + charge (a carbonium ion).
3. The Br^- ion is attracted to the C^+ atom and uses a pair of electrons to form a bond.

Thus, a Br has been added on to each of the C atoms of the double bond. See Figure 8.6.

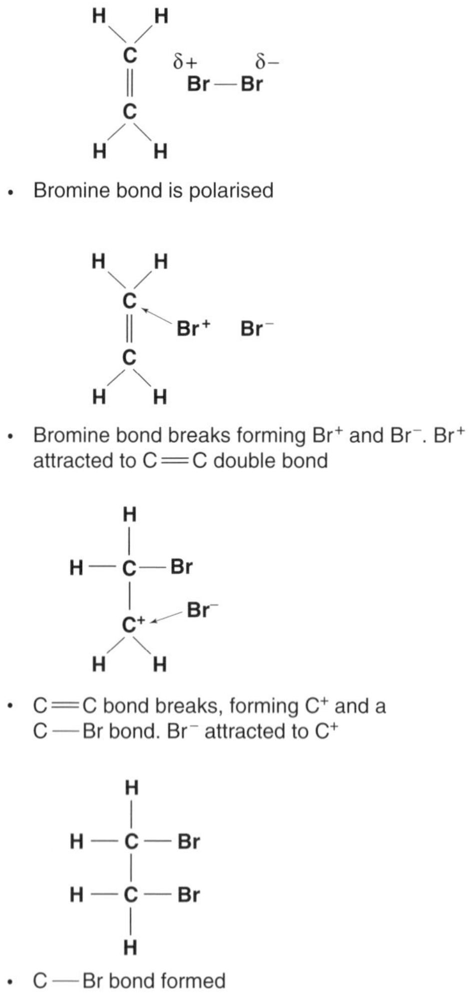

Evidence for the mechanism of ionic addition

See Figure 8.7.

If water containing NaCl is present in the reaction between bromene and ethene, the products include 2-bromoethanol, 1-bromo-2-chloroethane as well as 1,2-dibromoethane. These extra products could form by the reaction of the Cl^- ion or the OH^- ion with the C^+ on the ethene after the Br^+ had bonded to the other C atom of the double bond.

Figure 8.6 Ionic additions of ethene and bromine.

- Bromine bond is polarised

- Bromine bond breaks forming Br^+ and Br^-. Br^+ attracted to C=C double bond

- C=C bond breaks, forming C^+ and a C—Br bond. Br^- attracted to C^+

- C—Br bond formed

Figure 8.7 The mechanism of ionic addition.

1-bromo-2-chloroethane

2-bromoethanol

Similar mechanisms occur when **HCl** forms H^+ and Cl^- ions, and when **Cl$_2$** forms Cl^+ and Cl^- ions, when the molecules are polarised by the double bond of ethene.

Mandatory experiment 16: Laboratory preparation of ethene and its properties

See Figure 8.8.

Ethene can be prepared by the dehydration of ethanol, using hot Al_2O_3 as a catalyst.

$$C_2H_5OH \xrightarrow{(Al_2O_3)} C_2H_4 + H_2O$$

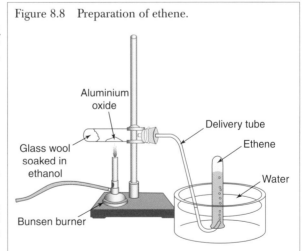

Figure 8.8 Preparation of ethene.

The properties of ethene

- It burns in air with slightly smoky flame.
- In tests for unsaturation, it decolourises acidified $KMnO_4$ and bromine water.

Mandatory experiment 17: Laboratory preparation of ethyne and its properties

See Figure 8.9.

Ethyne is prepared by the reaction of calcium carbide and water.

$$CaC_2 + 2H_2O \rightarrow C_2H_2 + Ca(OH)_2$$

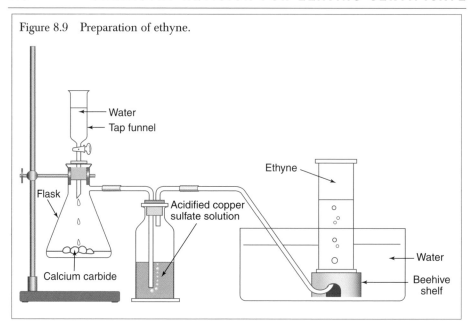

Figure 8.9   Preparation of ethyne.

Observations: the calcium carbide fizzes and changes from brown and grey to white. The copper sulfate solution changes from blue to brown and black.

Because of impurities in the calcium carbide, such as Ca_3P_2 and CaS, the reaction also produces PH_3 (phosphine) and H_2S (hydrogen sulphide), poisonous gases. They are removed by passing the gases through acidified copper sulphate.

The properties of ethyne

- It burns in air with a very smoky flame. It burns better and produces a very hot flame when mixed with oxygen gas, in the oxyacetylene flame, which is used in welding and cutting.
- In tests for unsaturation, it decolourises acidified KMnO4 and bromine water.

Aromatic hydrocarbons

Aromatic compounds contain a benzene ring. Benzene, C_6H_6, has bonds between the carbon atoms that are intermediate in length between a single and a double bond. The molecule is **planar**.

HIGHER LEVEL

Part of the bond is a **sigma (σ) bond** between adjacent carbon atoms and the other part consists of a ring of six **delocalised electrons** that circle above and below the plane of the six carbon atoms, forming a **pi (π) bond**.

This ring is very difficult to break, thus the structure is very stable and the molecule is much less reactive than a molecule with double bonds such as ethene. Unlike ethene, benzene does not undergo addition reactions.

Other aromatic compounds include C_7H_8 methylbenzene (also called toluene), which is a common industrial solvent, and ethylbenzene C_8H_{10}. Methylbenzene is insoluble in water but it is soluble in cyclohexane (see Figure 8.10).

Figure 8.10   Some examples of aromatic hydrocarbons.

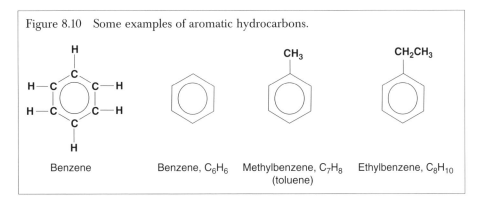

Benzene   Benzene, C_6H_6 Methylbenzene, C_7H_8 Ethylbenzene, C_8H_{10}
(toluene)

Useful aromatic compounds

Many biological substance, for example, steroids, cholesterol, some hormones, etc. are aromatic. Some have been found to be carcinogenic, for example, benzene.

Aromatic compounds are used in industry, in the following examples:

- pharmaceuticals for example, aspirin
- herbicides
- detergents
- dyes.

Some acid-base **indicators** are also aromatic, for example, phenolphthalein and methyl orange.

HIGHER LEVEL

8.2   CHLOROALKANES

Chloroalkanes have a molecular structure where one or more atoms of H of an alkane molecule have been replaced with Cl atoms. There is a large number of chloroalkanes, depending on the number of C atoms in the chain and on the number of Cl atoms; for instance, chloromethane, trichloromethane, 1,1-dichloroethane, 1,2-dichloroethane, 1,2,2,3-tetrachlorobutane etc. (see Figure 8.11).

The physical properties of chloroalkanes

The bond between the C and Cl is polar and because of the lack of symmetry, the molecules have a **polar end**. Thus, there are weak dipole-dipole attraction between the molecules. This means that they are **liquids with low boiling points**.

Due to their weak polarity they are **insoluble in water** but they are soluble in other non-polar liquids, for example, cyclohexane. Thus, they are useful as **solvents**, for example, in the dry cleaning industry, with a wide range of solubility.

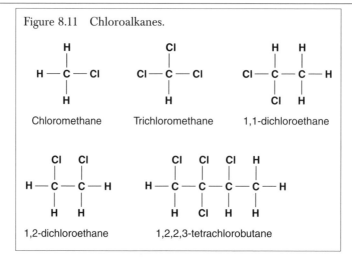

Figure 8.11   Chloroalkanes.

A useful property of the **fully halogenated alkanes** is that they are **non-flammable**, and so they are used as flame retardants in upholstery, or as fire extinguishers.

TEST YOURSELF

1. (a) What are hydrocarbons?
   (b) Distinguish between aliphatic and aromatic hydrocarbons.
   (c) Define:
      (i) saturated
      (ii) unsaturated.
2. (a) What are alkanes?
   (b) What are isomers?
   (c) Draw the structural formulas of:
      (i) pentane
      (ii) 2-methylbutane
      (iii) 2,2-dimethylpropane.
   (d) Are the three substances in part (c) isomers? Explain your answer.
   (e) Explain why a mixture of the three substances in part (c) can be separated by distillation.
3. (a) What is the functional group of the alkenes?
   (b) Draw the structural formulas of
      (i) but-1-ene
      (ii) but-2-ene.
4. (a) What is the functional group of the alkynes?
   (b) Draw the structural formula of ethyne.
5. (a) Compare the solubility of hydrocarbons in:
      (i) water
      (ii) cyclohexane.

(b) Explain why the smaller members of the hydrocarbons are gases at room temperature and the larger members are liquids or solids.

6. (a) Write a balanced equation for the combustion of heptane.
   (b) What is meant by a substitution reaction?
   (c) Using structural formulas, write a balanced equation for the reaction of ethane and chlorine.
   (d) Using structural formulas, write a balanced equation for the conversion of ethane to bromoethane.

*7. (a) What is a radical?
   (b) Describe the mechanism for the reaction of methane and chlorine to form chloromethane.
   (c) Outline one piece of evidence for the reaction mechanism you have described.

8. (a) What is meant by an addition reaction?
   (b) (i) Which series of hydrocarbons are capable of addition reactions?
       (ii) Name a homologous series that does not undergo addition reactions.
   (c) Write balanced equations for the reactions of ethene with:
       (i) hydrogen
       (ii) chlorine
       (iii) bromine
       (iv) hydrogen chloride
       (v) water.
   (d) Draw the structural formula of:
       (i) propene
       (ii) two units of poly(propene).

*9. (a) Outline the mechanism of the addition of HCl or Br_2 or Cl_2 to ethene.
   (b) Explain how the addition of bromine to ethene in the presence of sodium chloride can form 1-bromo-2-chloroethane.

10. (a) With the aid of a labelled diagram describe the laboratory preparation of ethene.
    (b) Describe a test to show that ethene is unsaturated.

11. (a) With the aid of a labelled diagram describe how to prepare a sample of pure ethyne in the laboratory.
    (b) Describe a test to show that ethyne is unsaturated.
    (c) Outline one industrial use for ethyne.

12. (a) Define 'aromatic hydrocarbons'.
    (b) Draw the structural formula of:
        (i) benzene
        (ii) methylbenzene
        (iii) ethylbenzene.
    (c) What is one industrial use for methylbenzene?
    (d) List three kinds of industrial products that contain aromatic compounds.
    (e) Compare the solubility of methylbenzene in:
        (i) water
        (ii) cyclohexane.

*(f) Describe the kinds of bonds between the carbon atoms in the molecule of benzene.

*12. (a) What are chloroalkanes?

(b) State one use for chloroalkanes.

(c) Draw the structural formulas of:
   (i) 1,1-dichloroethane
   (ii) 1,2-dichloropropane
   (iii) 2,2,3-trichlorobutane.

(d) Do you expect chloroalkanes to be solid, liquid or gas at room temperature? Explain your answer.

(e) Outline the solubility of chloroalkanes in:
   (i) water
   (ii) cyclohexane.

Chapter 9 – Alcohols. Aldehydes and ketones. Carboxylic acids. Esters. Organic synthesis

9.1 ALCOHOLS

AlcOHols are a homologous series of chemicals that have an OH group attached to a carbon atom. Thus, the **OH** (hydroxyl) group is their **functional group**.

The first four members are:

- methanol CH_3OH
- ethanol C_2H_5OH
- propanol C_3H_7OH
- butanol C_4H_9OH.

Depending on the number of carbon atoms that the carbon with the OH is attached to, there are primary and secondary alcohols:

- **primary alcohols**. The carbon with the OH is joined to **one** other carbon atom (or none in the case of methanol).
- **secondary alcohols**. The carbon with the OH is joined to **two** other carbon atoms. (Note that propan-2-ol and butan-2-ol are secondary alcohols.)

See Figure 9.1.

Figure 9.1   Alcohols.

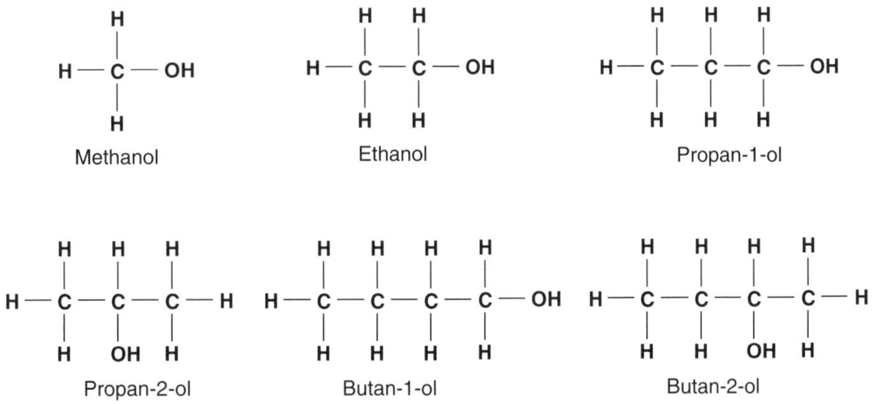

The physical properties of the alcohols

The H atom bonded to the O can form a **hydrogen bond** to other alcohol molecules and to water. The non-polar part of the molecule ensures that alcohols mix with non-polar solvents. Consequently alcohols are:

- liquids with relatively high boiling points (only lower than carboxylic acids of similar M_r)
- soluble in water and in non-polar solvents such as cyclohexane.

The solubility in water decreases as the size of the molecule increases, due to the larger non-polar end. Hence, methanol is soluble in water but butan-1-ol is not.

Uses for alcohols

Ethanol is commonly made by **fermentation** of sugar by yeast to make **beers** and **wine**. These liquids are distilled to increase the concentration of ethanol, to make whiskey and brandy.

Alcohols are flammable and they can be added to **motor fuels** in countries that can produce them cheaply by fermentation.

Ethanol is a **solvent**, which is sold cheaply as methylated spirits. Methylated spirits is about 90% ethanol and it is sold without the excise duty that is normally taxed on alcoholic drinks. To prevent its use in drinks, **methanol**, a poison, is added and a blue dye is also added to identify it. The methanol is thus a **denaturing agent**.

The reactions of alcohols

1. **Dehydration** (or elimination). Water can be removed from ethanol to form ethene by passing the ethanol vapour over hot Al_2O_3. See Figure 9.2.

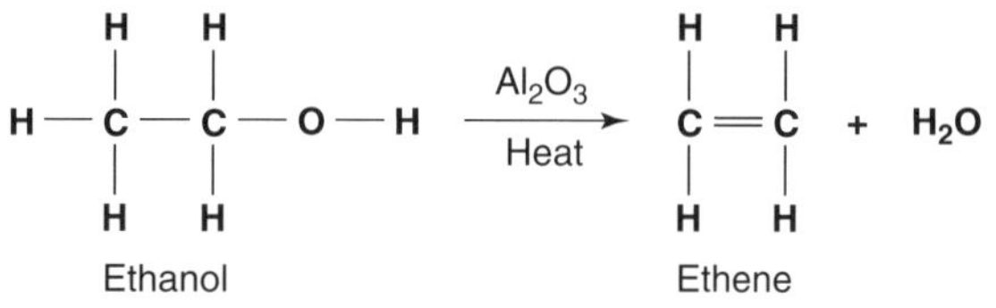

2. **Oxidation**. The removal of 2H atoms, converts a primary alcohol to an aldehyde (**al**cohol **dehydro**genated), and a secondary alcohol to a ketone.

Figure 9.2   The structural formula for dehydration of ethanol.

The normal oxidising agents are hot acidified $KMnO_4$ or $Na_2Cr_2O_7$. These oxidising agents, if they are in excess, can continue to oxidise and convert the aldehyde to an acid (but they cannot oxidise a ketone).

Ethanol to ethanal (see Figure 9.3):

$$C_2H_5OH \rightarrow CH_3CHO \text{ (or } C_2H_4O)$$

and

$$Cr_2O_7^{2-} \rightarrow Cr^{3+}$$

Figure 9.3   The structural formula for oxidation of ethanol.

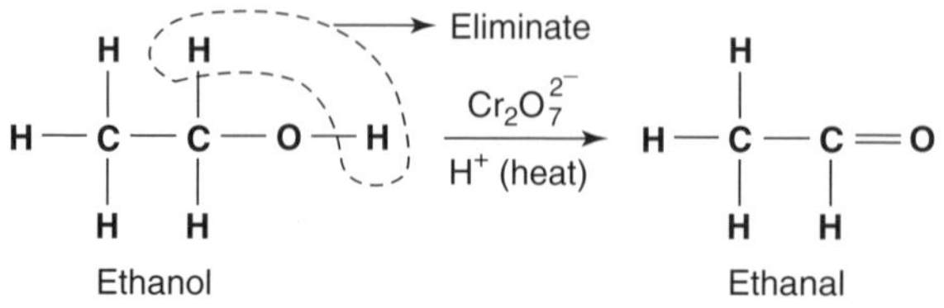

Ethanal to ethanoic acid (see Figure 9.4):

$$CH_3CHO \text{ (or } C_2H_4O) \rightarrow CH_3COOH$$

and

$$Cr_2O_7^{2-} \rightarrow Cr^{3+}$$

Figure 9.4   The structural formula for oxidation of ethanal.

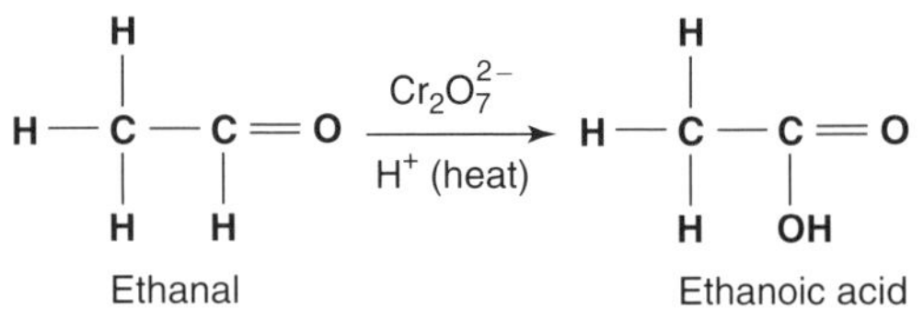

HIGHER LEVEL

3. **Esterification**. An alcohol reacts with an acid to form an ester and water.
   For example, methanol and ethanoic acid → methylethanoate + water. This reaction is usually catalysed with H_2SO_4 (see Figure 9.5).

Figure 9.5   The structural formula for esterification of methanol.

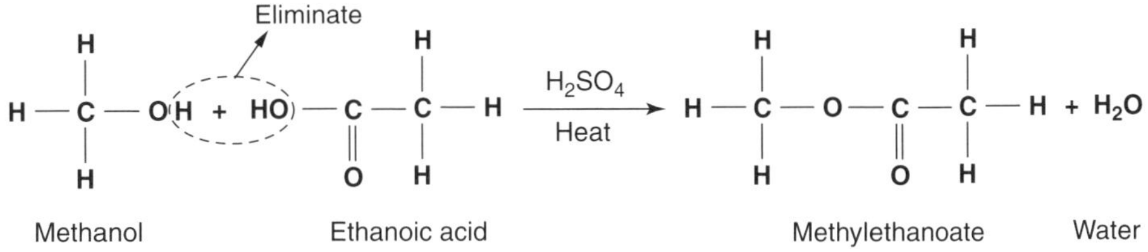

4. **Reaction with sodium**. A piece of sodium floats on the alcohol and reacts slowly with it, forming hydrogen gas and an ionic product from the alcohol.
   In this reaction alcohols act like acids by breaking the O–H bond to release H^+ ions and form a negative ion. The sodium quickly removes the H^+ ions by changing them to H atoms.

$$C_2H_5OH + Na \rightarrow C_2H_5ONa + \tfrac{1}{2}H_2$$

9.2   ALDEHYDES AND KETONES

Aldehydes and ketones have a **carbonyl group: C=O**. This is a **polar bond** and thus the molecules form **dipoles**, which attract each other, though not as strongly as

a H-bond. They dissolve easily in water because the negatively charged O atom is attracted by H-bonds to the H atoms of water. The rest of the molecule is non-polar.
   They have the following properties:

- liquids of fairly low boiling point (higher BP than hydrocarbons but lower than alcohols of similar M_r)
- soluble in water (when the molecule is small) and also very soluble in non-polar solvents, such as cyclohexane.

Aldehydes: the functional group is **RCHO**. The first four members of the series are as follows:

- methanal HCHO
- ethanal CH_3CHO
- propanal C_2H_5CHO
- butanal C_3H_7CHO.

See Figure 9.6

Note: Benzaldehyde is present in almonds.

Figure 9.6   The structural formula of aldehydes.

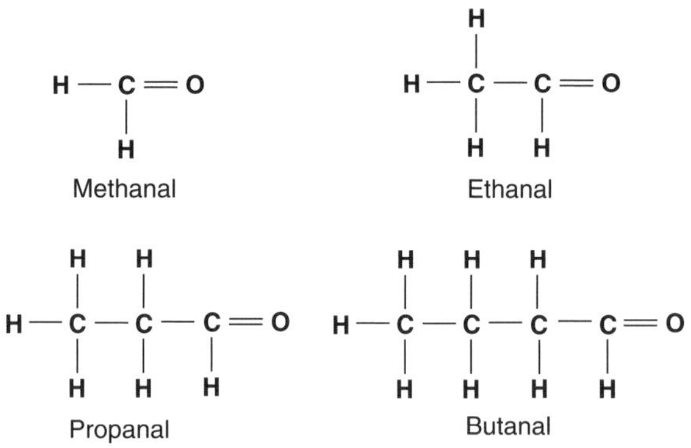

Methanal

Ethanal

Propanal

Butanal

HIGHER LEVEL

Ketones: the functional group is **RCOR**. The first two members are as follows:

- propanone CH_3COCH_3
- butanone $CH_3COC_2H_5$ (or $C_2H_5COCH_3$).

See Figure 9.7.

Figure 9.7   The structural formula for propanone and butanone.

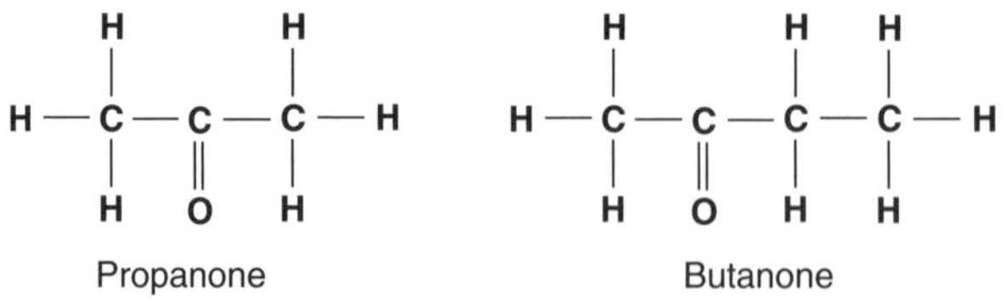

Propanone

Butanone

The reactions of the aldehydes and ketones

Aldehydes are formed by the oxidation of primary alcohols. Thus, aldehydes can be reduced to the corresponding primary alcohol. Likewise, ketones can be reduced to a secondary alcohol.

Reduction. By mixing their vapours with hydrogen gas and passing them over hot nickel catalyst, aldehydes and ketones are reduced to their corresponding alcohols.

Ethanal is reduced to ethanol; propanone is reduced to propan-2-ol $(CH_3CHO + H_2 \xrightarrow[\text{Heat}]{\text{Ni}} C_2H_5OH.)$. See Figure 9.8.

Figure 9.8   The structural formula for reduction of ethanal and propanone.

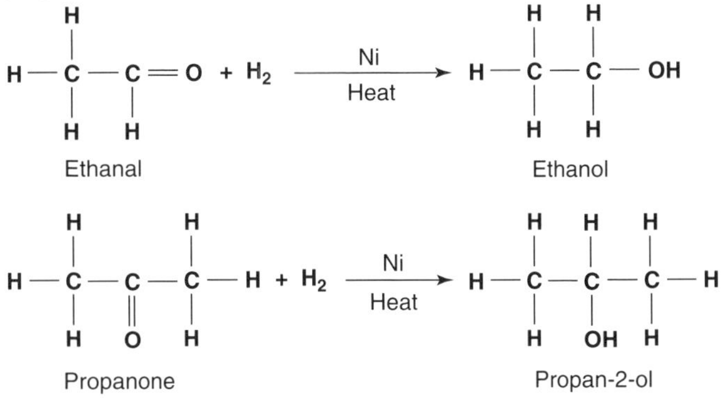

Oxidation. **This distinguishes aldehydes from ketones**, because aldehydes can be easily oxidised to carboxylic acids, but ketones cannot.

Aldehydes are oxidised by acidified potassium permanganate and by Fehlings solution. (See Figure 9.9).

Figure 9.9   The structural formula for oxidation of ethanal.

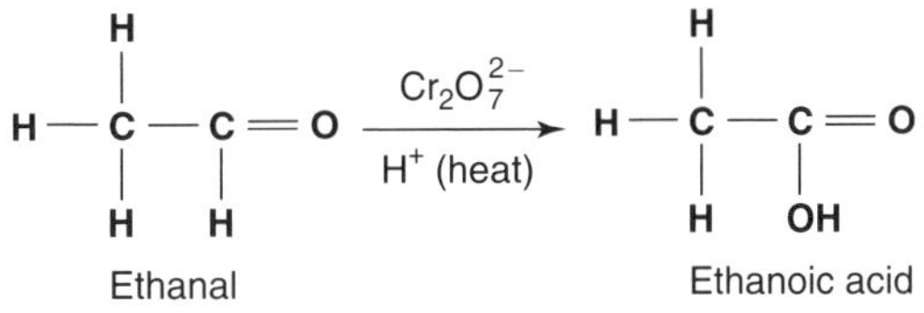

Mandatory experiment 18a: Preparation of ethanal (see Figure 9.10).

To prevent the oxidation of the ethanal to ethanoic acid there are two features of the preparation:

*   The oxidising agent is kept to a minimum and diluted in an excess of the alcohol.
*   The apparatus allows for immediate distillation of the aldehyde.

Figure 9.10   The laboratory preparation of ethanal.

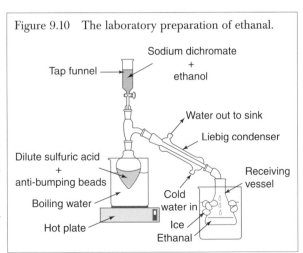

The receiving vessel is surrounded by icy water because ethanal has a low boiling point, i.e., it is a volatile liquid.

Procedure

1. Mix the sodium dichromate with the alcohol and place it in the dropping funnel.
2. Place water in the flask and slowly add concentrated H_2SO_4 to it, carefully swirling it and cooling it in icy water.
3. Add anti-bumping beads for smooth boiling.
4. Heat it in a water bath to avoid overheating. Heat the flask to boiling and then remove the heat.
5. Add the mixture from the tap funnel drop by drop at a rate that keeps the reaction boiling.
6. Observe that the orange dichromate changes to green Cr^{3+}.

HIGHER LEVEL

Percentage yield

Using the balanced equation that is given, you can calculate the maximum amount of ethanal that could have been made if all of the ethanol was converted to ethanal. The actual amount that was made can be expressed as a percentage of the maximum possible.

Example

8.94 g of sodium dichromate ($Na_2Cr_2O_7.2H_2O$, $M_r = 298$) and 6.9 cm^3 of ethanol (density $= 0.8$ g cm^{-3}) were used to make ethanal. The yield of ethanal was 1.62 g. Calculate the percentage yield. The equation for the reaction is:

$$3C_2H_5OH + Cr_2O_7^{2-} + 8H^+ \rightarrow 3CH_3CHO + 2Cr^{3+} + 7H_2O$$

Answer

1. Calculate the number of moles of both reactants.
   (a) Moles of $Cr_2O_7^{2-} = 8.94/298 = 0.03$ mole.
   (b) Mass of $C_2H_5OH = 6.9 \times 0.8 = 5.52$ g.
   M_r of $C_2H_5OH = 2(12) + 6(1) + 16$, i.e. $24 + 6 + 16, = 46$.
   Moles of $C_2H_5OH = 5.52/46 = 0.12$ mole.

2. Find out which reactant is in excess and which is limiting.
   According to the equation, one mole of $Cr_2O_7^{2-}$ requires three moles of C_2H_5OH. Therefore 0.03 mole requires 0.09 mole of C_2H_5OH, but 0.12 mole are present. Thus, the ethanol is in excess and only 0.09 mole of it can react.

3. Calculate the maximum theoretical yield.
   According to the equation 0.09 mole of ethanol can produce 0.09 mole of ethanal. M_r of $CH_3CHO = 2(12) + 4(1) + 1(16)$, i.e., $24 + 4 + 16, = 44$.
   Thus, 0.9 mole of ethanal $= 0.09 \times 44 = 3.96$ g.

4. Calculate the percentage yield.

$$\% \text{ yield} = \frac{\text{actual yield} \times 100}{\text{max. theoretical yield}}$$

$$= \frac{1.62 \times 100}{3.96}$$

$$= 40.9\%$$

Mandatory experiment 18b: Properties of ethanal

In all of the following reactions the ethanal is a reducing agent, and is oxidised to ethanoic acid.

If the same tests are performed with a **ketone**, a **negative** result is found in every case.

1. When it is heated, it decolourises an acidified solution of $KMnO_4$ from purple to clear.

CH_3CHO (Ethanal) $\rightarrow CH_3COOH$ (ethanoic acid); MnO_4^- (purple) $\rightarrow Mn^{2+}$ (clear)

2. When it is heated, it changes Fehling's solution from blue to red.

CH_3CHO (ethanal) $\rightarrow CH_3COOH$ (ethanoic acid); Cu^{2+} (blue) $\rightarrow Cu^+$ (red)

3. When it is heated, it changes ammoniacal silver nitrate to a silver mirror.

CH_3CHO (ethanal) $\rightarrow CH_3COOH$ (ethanoic acid); $Ag^+ \rightarrow Ag$.

9.3   CARBOXYLIC ACIDS

The **functional group** of the carboxylic acids (see Figure 9.11) is **RCOOH**. This contains **two polar bonds**: C=O, and the O–H. Thus, the molecules form **two hydrogen bonds** between each other, as well as with molecules of water. The rest of the molecules are non-polar.

The properties of carboxylic acids include:

- liquids of high boiling points
- soluble in water and in non-polar solvents, such as cyclohexane.

Figure 9.11   Carboxylic acid group.

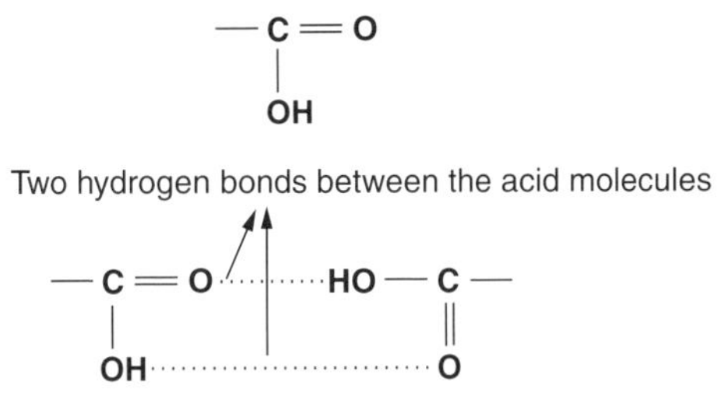

$$-C = O$$
$$|$$
$$OH$$

Two hydrogen bonds between the acid molecules

$$-C = O \cdots\cdots HO - C -$$
$$| \qquad\qquad\qquad\quad ||$$
$$OH \cdots\cdots\cdots\cdots\cdots\cdots O$$

The first four members of the series are:

- HCOOH methanoic acid
- CH_3COOH ethanoic acid
- C_2H_5COOH propanoic acid
- C_3H_7COOH butanoic acid.

See Figure 9.12.

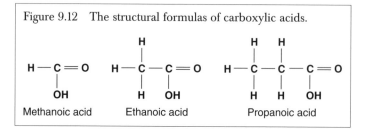

Figure 9.12   The structural formulas of carboxylic acids.

Methanoic acid   Ethanoic acid   Propanoic acid

Presence of carboxylic acids in nature

Methanoic acid is in **nettle stings** and in ant bites. **Ethanoic acid** is formed naturally in wines by the oxidation of ethanol to make **vinegar**. Ethanoic acid is used to convert wood and cotton to cellulose acetate (rayon). **Propanoic acid** and **benzoic acid** (and their salts) are **food preservatives**.

HIGHER LEVEL

Why are carboxylic acids acidic?

Carboxylic acids are acidic in water, i.e., the O–H bond breaks and they donate H^+ ions to water. This forms a negative ion that stabilises itself by spreading the negative charge over its two oxygen atoms.

Carboxylic acids are weak acids as the negative ion acts as a base and accepts H^+ ions to return to the undissociated state. But by delocalising the charge the negative ion is made less reactive as a base, thus forming an acidic solution of H^+ ions.

Alcohols are not acidic in water as the negative charge that forms when its O–H bond breaks remains on the one O atom, and it immediately reacts with the H^+ ion to return to its undissociated state (see Figure 9.13).

Figure 9.13   Acids are acidic in water because the negative charge is delocalised.

Mandatory experiment 19: Preparation and properties of ethanoic acid (see Figure 9.14).

Note: The **oxidising agent is in excess** to ensure that the ethanal that is produced as an intermediate in the reaction is also oxidised to ethanoic acid, and thus all of the ethanol is oxidised to ethanoic acid. This increases the percentage yield.

Figure 9.14   Apparatus for refluxing and distilling.

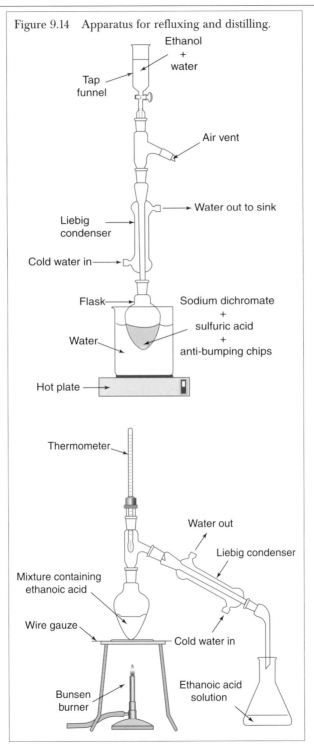

The mixture is **refluxed** to return the intermediate product, ethanal, to the flask for its complete oxidation. The ethanal condenses in the Liebig condenser.

The orange colour of dichromate changes to the green colour of chromium ions.

The mixture in the dropping funnel is added drop wise to the flask as the reaction is exothermic and it could boil up too vigorously and shatter the apparatus.

The air vent allows the gases formed to escape; otherwise the apparatus could come apart or shatter.

Procedure

1. Place water in the flask and slowly add concentrated H_2SO_4 to it, carefully swirling it and cooling it in icy water. Add the sodium dichromate and some anti-bumping beads.
2. Set up the apparatus for reflux, including an air-vent between the condenser and the dropping funnel. Place the alcohol in the dropping funnel.
3. Connect the condenser to the cold-water tap and to the sink.
4. Allow the alcohol to drop slowly through the condenser into the flask.
5. Heat the flask gently in a beaker of boiling water for about 20 minutes.
6. Adjust the condenser for distillation to remove the ethanoic acid. Remove the water bath and heat the flask with the Bunsen burner. (This is because the boiling point of ethanoic acid (118°C) is higher than 100°C).

Impurities that are removed with the ethanoic acid include water, ethanol, ethanal, and ethylethanoate.

The reactions of the carboxylic acids

Carboxylic acids have the usual **acidic reactions** (though slower than in strong acids). Ethanoic acid has the following properties:

- it changes blue litmus red
- it reacts with magnesium to form salt and hydrogen gas (the name of the salt that is formed is magnesium ethanoate)

$$2CH_3COOH + Mg \rightarrow (CH_3COO)_2\,Mg + H_2$$

- it reacts with sodium hydroxide to form salt and water (the name of the salt is sodium ethanoate)

$$CH_3COOH + NaOH \rightarrow CH_3COONa + H_2O$$

- it reacts with sodium carbonate to form salt, water and carbon dioxide gas

$$2CH_3COOH + Na_2CO_3 \rightarrow 2CH_3COONa + H_2O + CO_2.$$

HIGHER LEVEL

9.4   ESTERS

An ester is formed in the reaction of an acid and an alcohol:

Acid + alcohol $\rightleftharpoons$ ester + water.

The catalyst is concentrated H_2SO_4.

In this reaction the OH group of the acid and the H of the OH group of the alcohol are removed to form water, and the two remaining parts combine to form an ester. The name of the ester has the alcohol part ending in 'yl' and the acid part ending in 'oate'. For instance, methanol and ethanoic acid react to form methyl ethanoate. Ethanol and methanoic acid react to form ethyl methanoate. Other esters with up to four carbon atoms include methyl methanoate, methyl propanoate and ethyl ethanoate (see Figure 9.15).

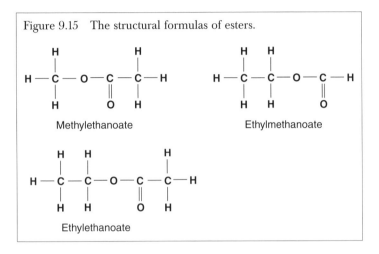

Figure 9.15   The structural formulas of esters.

The physical properties of esters

Esters have a **polar C=O group** and so they form weak **dipole–dipole attractions** with each other. The O atom is also attracted to the H atoms of water molecules by **hydrogen bonds**. The rest of the molecule is non-polar. Accordingly esters of low M_r have the following properties:

- liquids with low boiling points
- soluble in water (when the molecule is small) and in non-polar solvents such as cyclohexane.

Esters, such as ethyl ethanoate, are used as **solvents** in glues, etc.

Another characteristic is that many esters have a **fruity smell**, and in nature they give fruits and wines their aromas.

Fats

The most common esters in nature are **fats**. Fats are formed from an alcohol with three OH groups, propane-1,2,3,-triol, which is usually called glycerol, and three long chain acids, usually called fatty acids (see Figure 9.16).

Figure 9.16   The structure of fat, with three molecules of stearic acid joined to glycerol.

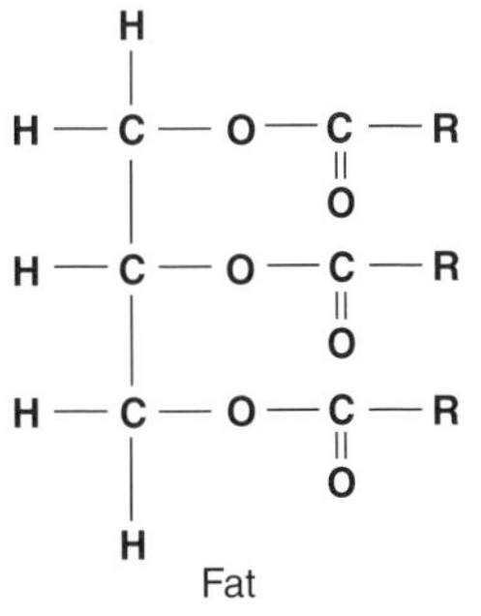

The reactions of esters

Esters have just one reaction of importance – their **hydrolysis**. A hydrolysis reaction is one where water reacts with a large molecule to split it in two, and one end acquires a H and the other an OH from the water.

Esters are formed by removing a H from an alcohol and an OH from an acid to form H_2O; thus the hydrolysis of an ester splits it to reform the alcohol and acid.

Acid + alcohol $\rightleftharpoons$ ester + H_2O

The forward reaction is a condensation reaction; the reverse reaction is a hydrolysis reaction.

Saponification: base hydrolysis of an ester

When fat (an ester of glycerol and fatty acids) is hydrolysed using a solution of a base, the products are glycerol (an alcohol), and the salts of the fatty acids. These salts are soaps.

Fat + NaOH → glycerol + sodium salts of the fatty acids

HIGHER LEVEL

See Figure 9.17.

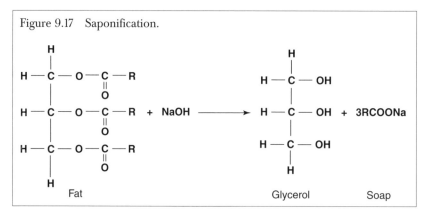

Figure 9.17   Saponification.

Fat   Glycerol   Soap

The soap works because its ionic end mixes with water and its long non-polar end mixes with grease and dirt molecules, thus bringing them into the water.

Mandatory experiment 20: Preparation of soap (see Figure 9.18).

Procedure

1. Place the fat in a flask and dissolve it in ethanol. Add the sodium hydroxide and some anti-bumping pieces.
2. Connect the flask to a condenser that is set up for refluxing.
3. Heat the flask in a water bath and boil it for about 20 minutes to complete the reaction.

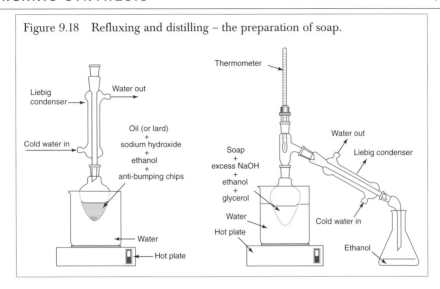

Figure 9.18   Refluxing and distilling – the preparation of soap.

4. Change the condenser for distillation and heat it to remove the ethanol. (The ethanol can be reused and it would contaminate the soap.)
5. Add the contents of the flask to a beaker of brine. This causes the soap to precipitate, as it is insoluble.
6. Filter to remove the soap and wash it with brine to remove any sodium hydroxide.

Molecular Shapes: tetrahedral or planar?

The organic molecules that have only single bonds are tetrahedral in shape. Molecules with a double bond are planar (see Table 9.1).

Table 9.1   Tetrahedral and planar compounds

Tetrahedral	Planar
Alkanes	Alkenes
Chloroalkanes	Aldehydes
Alcohols	Ketones
	Carboxylic acids
	Esters
	Aromatics

9.5   ORGANIC SYNTHESIS

The petrochemical industry provides the raw materials for the industrial synthesis of many products. The conversion of the raw materials to the finished products involves bond breaking and bond formation. In general, bond breaking requires energy, while bond forming releases energy.

The manufacture of PVC from ethene

PVC is a polymer, made by joining together large numbers of chloroethene molecules. Its technical name is poly(chloroethene). See Figure 9.19.

Ethene is available as a by-product from the cracking of large alkanes to make smaller molecules for the petrol market.

Chloroethene cannot be prepared from ethene by substitution. The route involves the following:

$$Ethene + Cl_2 \rightarrow CH_2Cl - CH_2Cl \rightarrow CH_2CHCl + HCl$$

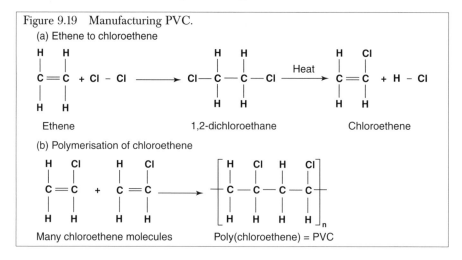

Figure 9.19   Manufacturing PVC.
(a) Ethene to chloroethene
    Ethene   1,2-dichloroethane   Chloroethene
(b) Polymerisation of chloroethene
    Many chloroethene molecules   Poly(chloroethene) = PVC

Synthesis routes in organic chemistry

Figure 9.20 shows the synthesis of alkenes, alkanes, alkynes, alcohols, aldehydes, acids, esters and chloroalkanes.

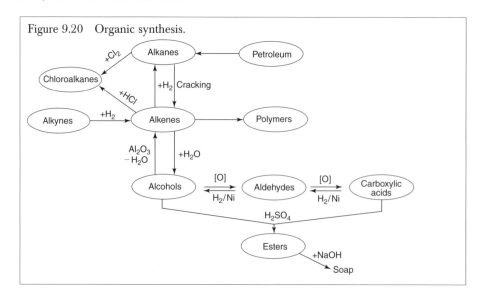

Figure 9.20   Organic synthesis.

TEST YOURSELF

1. (a) What is the functional group of alcohols?
   (b) Describe how the functional group affects the boiling point and the solubility of alcohols.
   (c) Compare and explain the solubility in water of ethanol and butan-1-ol.
2. (a) Distinguish between the structure of a primary and a secondary alcohol.
   (b) Draw the molecular structure of:
     (i) propan-1-ol
     (ii) butan-2-ol.
   (c) State two industrial uses for alcohols.
   (d) Explain why methanol can be used as a 'denaturing' agent.
3. (a) With the aid of a labelled diagram describe how ethanol can be converted to ethene.
   (b) What kind of reaction converts ethanol to ethene?
4. (a) What are the products of the reaction of ethanol and sodium?
   (b) Explain why this reaction can be termed 'acidic'.
5. (a) Name a suitable oxidising agent to oxidise ethanol. Outline the conditions necessary for the reaction and state the colour change for the oxidising agent.
   (b) Ethanol can be oxidised to two products. Name these products and draw their structural formulas.
6. (a) Aldehydes have a carbonyl group. Draw the structure of the carbonyl group. Describe how this group affects the boiling point and the solubility of aldehydes.
   (b) Draw the structural formulas of:
     (i) methanal
     (ii) propanal
     (iii) butanal.
7. Aldehydes can be oxidised by:
     (i) potassium manganate(VII)
     (ii) Fehling's solution
     (iii) ammoniacal silver oxide.
   (a) Name the product of the oxidation of ethanal and draw its structural formula.
   (b) Draw an equation to show the reaction of each of the oxidising agents and state the difference that is observed.
8. (a) With the aid of a labelled diagram outline how to prepare a sample of ethanal in the laboratory.
   (b) State two observations as the liquid in the dropping funnel reacts with the contents of the heated flask.
   (c) Outline two precautions that should be taken to ensure the maximum yield of ethanal.
   (d) Why is the receiving vessel surrounded by icy water?
*8. (a) Draw the structural formulas of:
     (i) propanone
     (ii) butanone.

(b) Outline the conditions for the reduction of aldehydes and ketones. State the products of the reduction of:
   (i) propanone
   (ii) propanal.
(c) What is observed when propanone is heated with acidified potassium manganate(VII)?
(d) Describe and explain the solubility of propanone in:
   (i) water
   (ii) cyclohexane.

9. (a) What is the functional group of carboxylic acids?
  (b) Explain why carboxylic acids have higher boiling points than other organic compounds of similar molecular mass.
  (c) Name three carboxylic acids and state a use for each one in nature or in industry.
  (d) Draw the structural formulas of:
    (i) propanoic acid
    (ii) butanoic acid.
  (e) Show with equations the reaction of ethanoic acid with:
    (i) magnesium
    (ii) sodium hydroxide
    (iii) sodium carbonate.

10. (a) With the aid of a labelled diagram outline how to prepare and collect ethanoic acid in the laboratory.
  (b) State two precautions to ensure the maximum yield of ethanoic acid.
  (c) Name two other products that are collected with the ethanoic acid. Suggest how to get a purer sample of the acid.

*11. Explain why the carboxylic acid molecule acts as an acid in water.

*12. (a) Draw the structural formulas of:
    (i) methyl methanoate
    (ii) methyl ethanoate
    (iii) methyl propanoate.
  (b) What are two physical properties of esters?
  (c) What characteristic do they impart of fruits and wines?
  (d) Outline how to prepare a small amount of methyl ethanoate in the laboratory.
  (e) What are the products of the acid catalysed hydrolysis of ethyl methanoate?

13. (a) What are the raw materials for the manufacture of soap?
  (b) Apart from soap, name another product of the reaction.
  (c) With the aid of a labelled diagram outline the laboratory preparation of soap.

*14. (a) Draw the structural formula of:
    (i) fat
    (ii) glycerol
    (iii) soap.
  (b) Explain how soap is able to bring grease into solution with water.

15. (a) Draw the structural formulas of:
    (i) ethene
    (ii) chloroethene.
   (b) What is the common name (abbreviation) for poly(chloroethene)?
   (c) Draw the compound formed when ethene reacts with chlorine. This compound can be converted to chloroethene. Name the other product of this conversion.

Chapter 10 – Extraction of natural products. Recrystallisation and determination of melting point. Instrumentation in analysis

10.1 EXTRACTION OF NATURAL PRODUCTS

Natural products that are used today include:

- **colourings**, for example, carotenes, marigold yellow, etc.
- **perfumes**, for example, lavender oil, rose oil, etc.
- **flavourings**, for example, vanilla, almond oil, etc.
- **medicines**, for example, morphine, codeine, etc.

Natural products may be removed by steam distillation or by solvent extraction.

Steam distillation

When a mixture of water and an **immiscible liquid** is heated it boils at a temperature that is lower than the boiling points of either liquid.

Plants contain oily liquids that have relatively high boiling points and which are also unstable at high temperatures. By passing steam into a natural material, the water mixes with the volatile oils and heats them, and they boil off and are removed together. When the mixture is cooled they both condense, with the oils separating from the water. (Because the oils are removed as an essence they are called essential oils.)

The **advantage** of this method is that the oily material is **distilled at a lower temperature** to avoid breaking down the oils.

Mandatory experiment 21: Extraction of clove oil from cloves by steam distillation (see Figure 10.1).

Procedure

1. Boil water in a flask that has a tube running upwards from the water to the outside as a safety outlet. It allows steam to escape if there is a blockage in the apparatus.
2. Pass the steam through a trap to remove condensed water and into a flask containing the cloves. Surround the connecting tubes with cotton wool to insulate them to keep the steam above 100°C.
3. Connect the flask to condenser and collect the distillate. It has a milky colour and smells of cloves.
4. Add the distillate to a separating funnel and remove the bottom aqueous layer.

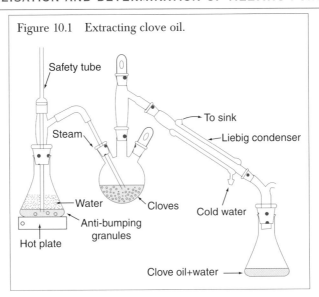

Figure 10.1   Extracting clove oil.

Solvent extraction

Procedure

1. When two solid substances are mixed together with a **solvent that dissolves only one of the components**, the insoluble substance can be removed by filtration and, by evaporating the solvent, the other substance is obtained.
2. In a **liquid–liquid extraction**, for example, when one or more substances are mixed in water, another solvent may be found that is immiscible with water and dissolves one of the substances and not the other. For instance, cyclohexane dissolves oils but not salts. By shaking it with an aqueous mixture of oils and salts, the oils leave the water and dissolve in the cyclohexane. Allowing the mixture to settle in a separating funnel, the aqueous layer is first removed by opening the tap. The cyclohexane solution can then be removed and its solute recovered by evaporating the solvent.

10.2   RECRYSTALLISATION AND DETERMINATION OF MELTING POINT

 Mandatory experiment 22: Recrystallisation of benzoic acid and determination of its melting point.

Separation of the benzoic acid from the impurity

- A solvent (water) is selected that dissolves the benzoic acid but in which the impurity is insoluble.
- A hot solvent is used in order to dissolve the maximum amount of benzoic acid in the minimum quantity of solvent. This reduces the amount of benzoic acid that will still be dissolved when the solvent is cooled.
- The insoluble impurity is removed by filtration.

- The filter paper and the funnel should be preheated to prevent crystallisation in the paper by standing it in a flask of boiling solvent, or by pouring some hot solvent through it.
- For faster filtration, the filter paper can be folded in a fluted manner to make more surface area, or else use a Buchner funnel and flask, and a suction pump.
- The filtrate, which contains the benzoic acid, is allowed to cool slowly, allowing the benzoic acid to crystallise out, or it may need to be heated to evaporate the solvent.

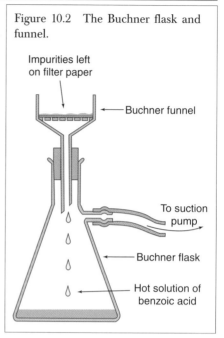

Figure 10.2   The Buchner flask and funnel.

Procedure
See Figure 10.2.

1. Place the mixture in a beaker, add boiling water to it and keep it boiling on a hot-plate. Stir it until all of the benzoic acid has just dissolved. (Use minimum volume of water.)
2. Flute a filter paper and place it in a funnel or use a Buchner funnel and flask. Stand the funnel in a flask of boiling water to heat it, or pour a small amount of boiling water through it and discard it. Quickly add the dissolved acid and collect the filtrate. If crystals form in the filter paper, add a small amount of boiling water to dissolve them.
3. Heat the filtrate until crystals begin to form and then allow it to cool slowly.
4. Filter to remove the crystals and wash them with ice-cold water. Dry them in an oven at 80°C.

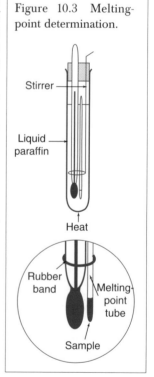

Figure 10.3   Melting-point determination.

Measurement of the melting point

Measuring the melting point is useful:

- to identify a substance – the melting point of a substance is a characteristic property.
- to confirm if it is pure – the melting point of a pure substance is sharp; if the substance is impure it melts over a range of temperatures.

Procedure
See Figures 10.3 and 10.4.

1. Grind the dry crystals in a mortar.
2. Fill a melting point tube with the powder by tapping it downwards.

Method A. Attach the melting point tube to a thermometer and hold it in a tube of liquid paraffin. Heat it gently in a Bunsen burner and record the temperature when it melts, or the temperature range over which it completes its melting.

Method B. Place the tube inside an aluminium block that contains a thermometer. Heat the block and record the temperature when it melts, or the temperature range over which it completes its melting.

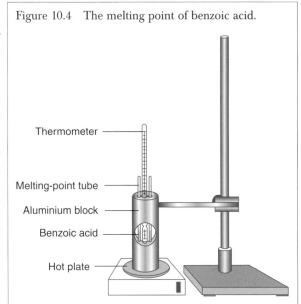

Figure 10.4   The melting point of benzoic acid.

Thermometer

Melting-point tube

Aluminium block

Benzoic acid

Hot plate

10.3   INSTRUMENTATION IN ANALYSIS

Chromatography

Chromotography is a widely used method of **separating small amounts of substances for analysis**, i.e., to identify them. It is based on the different solubilities of the components of a mixture for a stationary phase and for a mobile phase.

- The mixture is positioned on a **stationary phase**, such as paper or silica. The components have different affinities for this phase and some are more strongly adsorbed to it than others.
- A **mobile phase** is introduced and it carries the mixture forward. The components that were least strongly adsorbed to the stationary phase are carried faster and move further along in a fixed amount of time, thus separating from each other.

Thin-layer chromatography (TLC)

TLC is used to identify the components of a mixture (see Figure 10.5), for example, the individual pigments in a sample of paint.

- The **stationary phase is a thin layer of silica** (or other material) that has been prepared on a glass (or plastic or aluminium) plate.
- The **mobile phase is a solvent** in which the components of the mixture dissolve.

The solvent is placed in a tank to about 1 cm depth for about 1 hour to saturate the air with the solvent vapour.

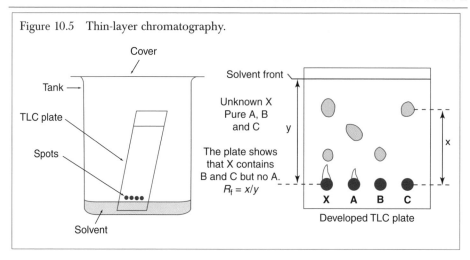

Figure 10.5 Thin-layer chromatography.

The mixture is obtained in as concentrated a form as possible by dissolving it in a small amount of solvent. A line is drawn about 3 cm from one end of the plate and a spot of the mixture is applied. The plate is placed in the tank. The tank is covered and left to stand for a few minutes until the solvent arrives at the other end of the plate. The plate is removed and allowed to dry.

Result

The components of the mixture have moved different distances. The ratio of the distance that each component has moved relative to the distance the solvent moved is its **R_f value**. By repeating with pure samples of the possible components and measuring their R_f values, the identity of the components can be found by matching the R_f values.

Paper chromatography

This is similar to thin-layer chromatography, whereby the stationary phase is a strip of chromatography paper.

Mandatory experiment 23: Separation of a mixture of indicators using paper chromatography or thin-layer chromatography or column chromatography (see Figure 10.6).

Procedure

1. Add solvent (a mixture of water, ethanol and ammonia) to cover the base of the tank to a depth of about 1 cm. Place the cover on top and allow it to stand for about 1 hour to saturate the air with the vapour.
2. Make a pencil line about 3 cm from the bottom of the chromatography paper or thin layer plate. Use a capillary tube to place a small spot of each indicator and the mixture at separate positions on the pencil mark. Make the spot concentrated by drying it and re-applying.

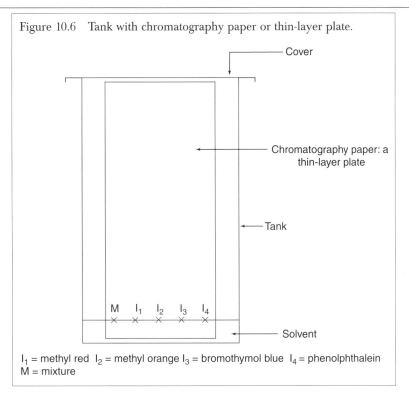

Figure 10.6   Tank with chromatography paper or thin-layer plate.

Cover

Chromatography paper: a thin-layer plate

Tank

M I_1 I_2 I_3 I_4

Solvent

I_1 = methyl red I_2 = methyl orange I_3 = bromothymol blue I_4 = phenolphthalein
M = mixture

3. Stand the chromatography paper in the tank until the solvent has almost reached the top.
4. Remove the paper and let it dry.
5. Observe the separation of the components of the mixture. (The phenolphthalein is coloured pink by holding the paper in a stream of ammonia vapour.) Identify the components by matching the distance they travelled with the distance travelled by the pure indicators. Alternatively, measure the R_f of each component and of each indicator.

Gas chromatography (GC)

- The **stationary phase is a liquid** that is supported on a porous solid bed inside a long coiled column. The column is heated inside an oven.
- The **mobile phase is an inert gas** (for example, nitrogen or argon).
- The components must be **volatile**, i.e., they must evaporate when heated without decomposing.

The mixture is injected into the bottom of the column where it is heated to **evaporate** it, and an inert gas – the 'carrier' gas – carries it forward through the column. The different solubilities of the components for the liquid stationary phase causes them to move at different speeds. The arrival of the components at the end of the column is detected (see Figure 10.7).

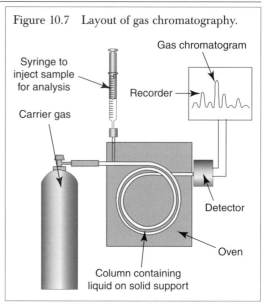

Figure 10.7   Layout of gas chromatography.

The gas chromatograph is usually connected to a **mass spectrometer (MS)** to measure the molecular mass of the separated components so that they can be **identified**.

GC–MS is used to identify drugs in athletes, the composition of pollutants, etc.

High-performance liquid chromatography (HPLC)

- **The stationary phase** is a finely divided solid held inside a column.
- **The mobile phase** is a **solvent** that is **pumped under pressure** through the column.

As the components leave the column they are detected, and usually passed to a mass spectrometer to identify them. The process is commonly used with **non-volatile substances**, particularly in the food industry, where it identifies growth promoters in meat, vitamins, and food additives (see Figure 10.8).

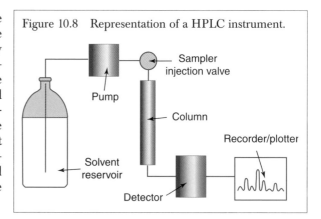

Figure 10.8   Representation of a HPLC instrument.

HIGHER LEVEL

Infra-red (IR) spectrometry

Within a molecule the bonds between the atoms can absorb infra-red radiation, and different bonds absorb different wavelengths (or frequencies). When the **spectrum of infra-red radiation** is passed through a sample the combination of all of the bonds in a molecule results in a **characteristic absorbance pattern**.

An IR spectrum shows the relative absorbance of each wavelength of IR (see Figure 10.9).

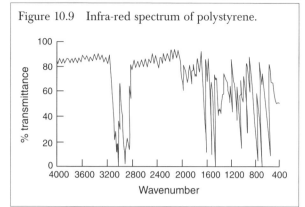

Figure 10.9   Infra-red spectrum of polystyrene.

- It forms a unique **fingerprint** that can **identify a substance** when its spectrum is compared with a database of known substances.
- It also indicates the **nature of the bonds** that are present, which helps to identify it if it is a new substance.

Ultra-violet (UV) spectrometry

Atoms also absorb UV radiation and molecules have a characteristic absorption spectrum that may be used **to identify them**. This is done by measuring the relative absorption of each wavelength (see Figure 10.10).

UV spectroscopy is also used in **quantitative analysis**, by measuring the amount of a particular wavelength of UV light that is absorbed. By comparing with the amount absorbed by known concentrations, the unknown concentration can be calculated.

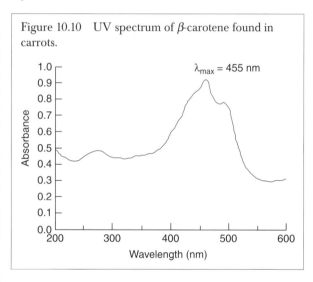

Figure 10.10   UV spectrum of β-carotene found in carrots.

TEST YOURSELF

1. (a) Name two useful natural organic compounds or groups of compounds.
   (b) What advantage have natural products over synthetic products?
   (c) What is an advantage of steam distillation over extraction methods that use high temperatures?
   (d) How is the product extracted by steam distillation separated from the steam?

2. (a) Name solvents for:
      (i) salts
      (ii) non-polar substances.
   (b) In the process of separating benzoic acid from impurities, explain why the minimum amount of hot water is used to dissolve the benzoic acid.
   (c) Outline how the benzoic acid can be quickly separated from the insoluble impurities.
   (d) How is the benzoic acid removed from the solution?
   (e) What are two reasons for measuring the melting point of a substance?
3. Chromatography uses a stationary phase and a mobile phase.
   (a) What is the purpose of chromatography?
   (b) In thin-layer chromatography, name the stationary phase and a mobile phase.
   (c) Why is the solvent placed in the chromatography tank 1 hour before using it?
   (d) What is the 'R_f' value? What is the purpose of measuring it?
   (e) Name the stationary phase and the mobile phase in gas chromatography.
   (f) What do the letters GC–MS stand for?
   (g) What kinds of substances are not suitable for separation in gas chromatography?
   (h) What are the stationary phase and the mobile phase in HPLC?
*4. (a) For what purpose are IR and UV spectroscopy both used?
   (b) What additional information is available from an IR absorbance spectrum?
   (c) For which additional purpose is UV spectroscopy used?

Chapter 11 – Equilibrium. pH

11.1 EQUILIBRIUM

What is a reversible reaction?

A reversible reaction is one that **goes in both directions**. The products of the forward reaction are the reactants for the reverse reaction. For example:

$$N_2 + 3H_2 \rightleftharpoons 2NH_3$$

Dynamic equilibrium

If you begin just with the reactants of the forward reaction, as time passes the concentration of the reactants falls and the concentration of the products rises. Consequently the rate of the forward reaction falls, while the rate of the reverse reaction rises. Eventually a time is reached when there is **equilibrium**, i.e., **the rate of the forward reaction equals the rate of the reverse reaction**. Both reactions continue, but there is no change in the concentrations of any of the reactants.

The equilibrium constant

If a reversible reaction is represented as follows:

$$A + B \rightleftharpoons C + D$$

then when equilibrium is reached, if the concentrations of the reactants are measured and put in the following relationship

$$\frac{[C] \times [D]}{[A] \times [B]}$$

a value is found for that reaction. This value is called the **equilibrium constant, K_c,** and its value is always true, no matter what the original conditions are, provided the temperature is not changed. If the reaction is repeated with different concentrations of the substances involved, but at the same temperature, the same value is found.

Only a change in temperature changes the value of the K_c.

Note:

- When more than one molecule is present in the balanced equation, the concentration of that substance is raised to the power of the number of molecules in the equation.
  For instance, for the reaction $N_2 + 3H_2 \rightleftharpoons 2NH_3$

$$K_c = \frac{[NH_3]^2}{[N_2] \times [H_2]^3}$$

- If there is the **same number of molecules** in the forward and reverse reactions, then the volume of the container may be ignored, and the number of moles is used instead of the concentration. In other cases, the concentration must be calculated as the number of **moles per litre**.
- If the reaction is represented in an equation with different ratios, then the K_c changes accordingly.

How to calculate the K_c

Ethanoic acid and ethanol react to form ethylethanoate and water as follows:

$$CH_3COOH + C_2H_5OH \rightleftharpoons CH_3COOC_2H_5 + H_2O$$

Calculate the K_c for the above reaction, at 298K, if one mole of CH_3COOH and one mole of C_2H_5OH are mixed in a 1-litre vessel and allowed to come to equilibrium, and the equilibrium mixture contained 0.33 mole of CH_3COOH.

What to do

1. Calculate how many moles of the reactants had reacted to reach the equilibrium stage, and hence how many moles of the products were present.
2. Make a table to show the number of moles of each substance at the initial stage, and at equilibrium.
3. Write the expression for the K_c, put in the values at equilibrium, and calculate.

Answer

1. The information given states that one mole of CH_3COOH was present at the start and 0.33 mole was present at equilibrium. Hence 0.67 mole of it reacted. From the equation, this means that 0.67 mole of C_2H_5OH also reacted. It also means that 0.67 mole of both products are now present at equilibrium.

2.

	CH_3COOH	C_2H_5OH	$CH_3COOC_2H_5$	H_2O
Initial concentration	1	1	0	0
At equilibrium	0.33	0.33	0.67	0.67

3.

$$K_c = \frac{[CH_3COOC_2H_5] \times [H_2O]}{[CH_3COOH] \times [C_2H_5OH]}$$

$$= \frac{0.67 \times 0.67}{0.33 \times 0.33}$$

= 4. (There are no units in this reaction as the number of molecules in the forward and reverse reactions were equal.)

HIGHER LEVEL

Using the K_c in calculations, calculate the equilibrium concentrations at 298K if two moles of CH_3COOH and three moles of C_2H_5OH are mixed together. The K_c at 298K is 4.

What to do

1. Let x stand for the number of moles of one reactant that has reacted to reach equilibrium. Use x to calculate the number of moles of each substance present at equilibrium.
2. Use the K_c expression and the value of K_c that is given.
3. Solve for x, and hence the concentrations of the other substances at equilibrium.

Answer

1. Let x = moles of CH_3COOH that reacted to reach equilibrium. Hence, by looking at the equation, x moles of C_2H_5OH also reacted, and x moles of each product was formed.

Concentration	CH_3COOH	C_2H_5OH	$CH_3COOC_2H_5$	H_2O
Initially	2	3	0	0
At equilibrium	2 − x	3 − x	x	x

2. $K_c = \dfrac{[CH_3COOC_2H_5] \times [H_2O]}{[CH_3COOH] \times [C_2H_5OH]}$

$4 = \dfrac{(x) \times (x)}{(2-x) \times (3-x)}$

$4 = \dfrac{x^2}{6 - 5x + x^2}$

$4(6 - 5x + x^2) = x^2$

$24 - 20x + 4x^2 = x^2$

$3x^2 - 20x + 24 = 0$

$x = \dfrac{20 \pm \sqrt{20^2 - 4(3)(24)}}{2(3)}$

$= \dfrac{20 \pm \sqrt{400 - 288}}{6}$

$= \dfrac{20 \pm \sqrt{112}}{6}$

$= \dfrac{20 \pm 10.6}{6}$

= 1.6 or 5.1 (5.1 does not make sense, as only two moles of CH_3COOH was present initially).

3. Hence, the concentrations at equilibrium are as follows:
- $CH_3COOH = 2.0 - 1.6$, i.e., 0.4
- $C_2H_5OH = 3.0 - 1.6$, i.e., 1.4
- $CH_3COOC_2H_5 = 1.6$
- $H_2O = 1.6$.

Chatelier's principle

When a system at equilibrium is subjected to a stress, the system alters to oppose the stress.
Stress to a system can arise from a change in concentration, or temperature, or pressure (the latter, for reactions involving gases only).

Changing concentrations

For example, if a reversible reaction is represented by the following equation:

$$A + B \rightleftharpoons C + D$$

then **if the amount of either A or B is increased, the system alters to remove it** and more of C and D will be produced. The equilibrium mixture will have more of C and D, but the K_c will still be the same.
If more of either C or D is added the system alters to remove it and more of A and B will be produced.

Changing temperature

$$A + B \rightleftharpoons C + D \quad \Delta H = -$$

In the above example the forward reaction is exothermic, and therefore the reverse reaction is endothermic.
Thus, **if the temperature is lowered** the system alters to increase the temperature and thus the **exothermic reaction is increased**. The equilibrium mixture is changed to increase the products of the forward reaction.
Increasing the temperature results in the endothermic reaction increasing and thus the reverse reaction increases.

Changing the pressure

This applies only to reactions involving gases, and also only when there is a different number of molecules in the forward and reverse reactions.

$$A_{(g)} + 2B_{(g)} \rightleftharpoons 4C_{(g)}$$

In the above equation the forward reaction involves three gas molecules reacting to form four gas molecules.
Thus, **if the pressure is reduced the system alters to increase the number of molecules** and so the forward reaction is increased and the equilibrium mixture will have more of the product.
If the pressure is increased the system alters to reduce the number of molecules and so the reverse reaction is increased.

For example, in the manufacture of ammonia by the Haber process, the reaction is:

$$N_2 + 3H_2 \rightleftharpoons 2NH_3 \qquad \Delta H = -92 \text{ kJ mol}^{-1}$$

When the **pressure is increased**, the forward reaction increases, as this changes four molecules to two molecules to reduce the pressure. This increases the yield of ammonia. A **low temperature** also increases the amount of ammonia in the equilibrium mixture, but it slows down the reaction so for a fast reaction a temperature of 400°C is used.

In the industrial manufacture of ammonia, the process takes place at high pressure (over 200 atmospheres) to increase the yield of ammonia in the equilibrium mixture.

Another example is in the manufacture of sulfuric acid, when SO_2 reacts with O_2 to form SO_3.

$$SO_2 + \tfrac{1}{2}O_2 \rightleftharpoons SO_3 \qquad \Delta H = -98 \text{ kJ mol}^{-1}$$

This operation is also done at slightly **increased pressure** to increase the amount of SO_3 in the equilibrium mixture. Further increase in pressure adds to cost without significant increased yield. The yield in the equilibrium mixture is also increased by low temperature, but this slows down the reaction, so it operates at 450°C for a fast reaction.

Adding a catalyst

This has **no effect on the equilibrium mixture**, apart from bringing the system to equilibrium **faster**.

Mandatory experiments 24: To demonstrate the effects of both temperature changes and concentration changes on an equilibrium mixture.

Example

$$\underset{\text{Blue}}{CoCl_4^{2-}} + 6H_2O \rightleftharpoons \underset{\text{Red}}{Co(H_2O)_6^{2+}} + 4Cl^- \quad \Delta H = -$$

(i) Dissolve some cobalt chloride in water in a test tube.

By adding some **more Cl^-**, in the form of concentrated HCl, the **red colour changes to blue**, as the system removes the Cl^- by increasing the reverse reaction.

By adding **more H_2O** to the **blue solution the colour changes to red**, as the system removes the H_2O by increasing the forward reaction.

(ii) By **heating the red solution** in a beaker of very hot water the colour **changes to blue**. The reverse reaction is endothermic and it is increased when the temperature is increased.

When the **blue solution is cooled** in a beaker of ice the colour **changes to red**. The forward reaction is exothermic and it is increased when the temperature is reduced.

Example

$$\underset{\text{Orange}}{Cr_2O_7^{2-}} + H_2O \rightleftharpoons \underset{\text{Yellow}}{2CrO_4^{2-}} + 2H^+$$

Dissolve some sodium dichromate (orange) in water in a test tube.

By **adding an alkali** (for example, NaOH) the **orange colour changes to yellow**. This is because the OH^- ions remove the H^+ ions ($H^+ + OH^- \rightarrow H_2O$), so the system makes more H^+ ions by increasing the forward reaction.

By **adding an acid** (for example, HCl) the **yellow solution changes to orange**, as the system removes the added H^+ ions by increasing the reverse reaction.

Example

$$Fe^{3+} + CNS^- \rightleftharpoons Fe(CNS)^{2+}$$
Yellow   Red

Mix together solutions of iron(III) chloride and potassium thiocyanate. A blood-red colour is produced.

Add some concentrated HCl (or other source of Cl^- ions) and the **red colour changes to yellow**. This is because the Fe^{3+} and the Cl^- ions form a complex ion and so the reverse reaction increases to produce more Fe^{3+} ions.

Add some thiocyanate solution to the yellow solution and the **colour changes to red**. The equilibrium has shifted to the right to remove the CNS^- ions.

11.2   pH

What does the pH scale measure?

The pH scale **measures the acidity or alkalinity of a solution**. The scale extends from 0 to 14. pH 7 is neutral. Below 7 a solution is acidic and the lower the pH the more acidic it is. pH 0 is the most acidic. pH 8 is a weakly alkaline solution and it becomes more alkaline as the pH increases.

The pH scale is limited to **dilute solutions** of acids and alkalis. It does not include the acidity of very concentrated strong acids or strong alkalis.

0   1   2   3   4   5   6   7   8   9   10   11   12   13   14
   strong acids   weak acids   neutral   weak alkalis   strong alkalis

Measuring pH

Add a few drops of universal indicator solution (or a piece of universal indicator paper) and match the colour with the colour chart. Alternatively, a pH meter gives a direct reading.

Calculating pH

pH is defined as:

$$pH = -\log_{10}[H^+]$$

The pH of an alkaline solution: $14 - pOH$

where $pOH = -\log_{10}[OH^-]$

Examples

1. Calculate the pH of a 0.2M HCl solution.

$[H^+] = 0.2$

$$pH = -\log[H^+]$$

$$= -\log(0.2)$$

$$= -(-0.6989)$$

$$= 0.7$$

2. Calculate the pH of 0.4M H_2SO_4 solution.

$[H^+] = 2 \times 0.4$, i.e., 0.8.

$$pH = -\log[H^+]$$

$$= -\log(0.8)$$

$$= -(-0.0969)$$

$$= 0.1$$

3. Calculate the pH of a 0.3M NaOH solution.

$[OH^-] = 0.3$

$$pOH = -\log[OH^-]$$

$$= -\log(0.3)$$

$$= -(-0.5228)$$

$$= 0.5$$

$$pH = 14 - pOH$$

$$= 14 - 0.5$$

$$= 13.5$$

4. Calculate the pH of a solution that has 20 g of NaOH in 500 cm^3 of solution.

M_r of NaOH $= 23 + 16 + 1$, i.e., 40.

$$\text{Moles of NaOH} = \frac{20}{40}$$

$$= 0.5 \text{ mole.}$$

There are 0.5 mole in 500 cm^3 of this solution.
Therefore, 1 litre has 1.0 mole, i.e., the solution is 1M NaOH.

$$[OH^-] = 1$$

$$pOH = -\log(1)$$

$$= -(0)$$

$$pH = 14 - pOH$$

$$= 14 - 0$$

$$= 14.$$

HIGHER LEVEL

The self-ionisation of water

Water molecules dissociate according to the equation:

$$H_2O \rightleftharpoons H^+ + OH^-$$

($\Delta H = +$, which indicates that the forward reaction is endothermic)
As this is a reversible reaction it reaches equilibrium and there is a K_c expression:

$$K_c = \frac{[H^+] \times [OH^-]}{[H_2O]}$$

Thus:

$$K_c \times [H_2O] = [H^+] \times [OH^-]$$

Because only a very small number of molecules are dissociated at any one time, the $[H_2O]$ at equilibrium is the normal concentration of water molecules. Therefore, the $K_c \times [H_2O]$ is also a constant, represented as K_w, and it is called the **ionic product of water**.
Thus:

$$K_w = [H^+] \times [OH^-]$$

At 25°C the value of the K_w is 1×10^{-14}.

Example

Calculate the pH of pure water at 25°C:

$$[H^+] \times [OH^-] = 10^{-14}$$

Because the H^+ ions only came from the dissociation of water molecules, the $[H^+]$ equals $[OH^-]$, or $[H^+]^2 = 10^{-14}$.

Thus:

$$[H^+] = 10^{-7}$$

$$pH = -\log[H^+]$$

$$= -\log(10^{-7})$$

$$= -(-7)$$

$$= 7$$

Note: The value of K_w changes with a change of temperature (the **K_w increases as the temperature increases**, because the dissociation of water is endothermic). Therefore at temperatures other than 25°C (298K) the pH of pure water is not 7, even though the water is still neutral as it still has an equal concentration of H^+ and OH^- ions.

Calculating the pH of solutions of a weak acid or a weak base

A weak acid, such as CH_3COOH, is only partly dissociated at any one time. This is because its dissociation is reversible, and it establishes equilibrium.

$$CH_3COOH \rightleftharpoons CH_3COO^- + H^+$$

Thus:

$$K_c = \frac{[CH_3COO^-] \times [H^+]}{[CH_3COOH]}$$

or:

$$[CH_3COO^-] \times [H^+] = K_c \times [CH_3COOH]$$

Because each H^+ ion is matched by one CH_3COO^- ion, the equation can be written as:

$$[H^+]^2 = K_c \times [CH_3COOH]$$

or:

$$[H^+] = \sqrt{K_c \times [CH_3COOH]}$$

To simplify the calculation, and because only a small fraction of the acid molecules are dissociated at any one time, we assume that the concentration of the acid molecules at equilibrium is the same as the initial concentration.

Thus:

$[H^+] = \sqrt{K_c \times [CH_3COOH]}$ that was added to the water.

Therefore the pH $= -\log(\sqrt{K_c \times [CH_3COOH]})$.

The dissociation constant of an acid is called **the acid dissociation constant**, and is termed **K_a**. Likewise, for a base there is the **base dissociation constant, K_b**.

- The pH of a weak acid $= -\log(\sqrt{K_a \times \text{concentration of the acid}})$.
- The pOH of a weak base $= -\log(\sqrt{K_b \times \text{concentration of the base}})$.

Acid/base indicators

An acid/base indicator is either a **weak acid or a weak base**. It partly ionises, by donating or accepting a H^+, forming an **ion that has a different colour to the molecule**.

If the indicator is an acid, represented as HA, it dissociates as follows:

$$HA \text{ (colour 1)} \rightleftharpoons H^+ + A^- \text{ (colour 2)}$$

When it is placed in an acid solution, the equilibrium shifts to the left (to remove H^+ ions in accordance with Le Chatelier's principle), and colour 2 disappears and colour 1 predominates.

In an alkaline solution, the OH^- reacts with the H^+ to form H_2O, and so the equilibrium shifts to the right (to produce more H^+ in accordance with Le Chatelier's principle), and colour 1 disappears while colour 2 predominates.

If the indicator is a base, represented as B, it accepts H^+ in a reversible reaction as follows:

$$H^+ + B \text{ (colour 1)} \rightleftharpoons HB^+ \text{ (colour 2)}$$

In an acid solution, colour 2 predominates as the system shifts to the right to use up the H^+ ions, and in an alkaline solution colour 1 predominates.

Acid/base titration curves

An acid/base titration curve (see Figures 11.1–11.4) is typically found by adding alkali in measured amounts to an acid solution (or vice versa) and measuring the pH at every addition.

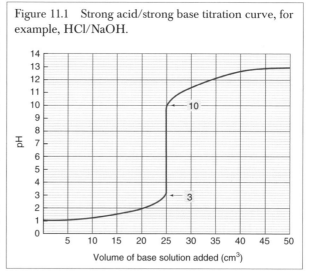

Figure 11.1   Strong acid/strong base titration curve, for example, HCl/NaOH.

Note:

1. The pH changes slowly at the very low and very high pHs, but changes quickly near to pH7. This is because the **pH scale is logarithmic** (it requires 10 times more OH^- ions to move from pH 0 to 1 as it does to move from 1 to 2, and so on). Therefore near pH7 one drop of a strong acid or strong base can change the pH value by a few points.

2. For every curve involving either a strong acid or a strong alkali there is a **vertical region around the point of neutralisation** – there is none for the titration of a weak acid and a weak base.

   (Not all salts are neutral. The salts of a weak acid are alkaline and the salts of a weak base are acidic. Thus the point of neutralisation is pH7 for titrations of strong acids and strong bases, but above or below 7 if either of the acid or base is weak.)

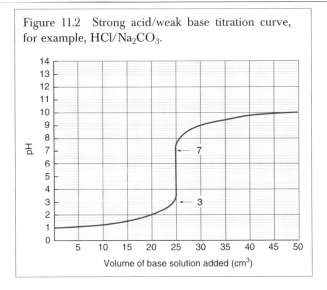

Figure 11.2   Strong acid/weak base titration curve, for example, HCl/Na_2CO_3.

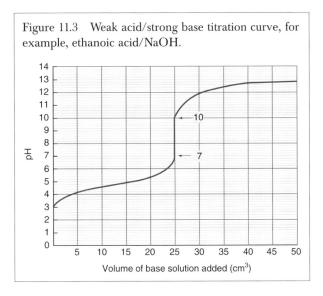

Figure 11.3   Weak acid/strong base titration curve, for example, ethanoic acid/NaOH.

3. Each indicator has **a range of pH during which it changes colour completely:**

- methyl orange: red 3.2–yellow 4.4
- litmus: red 5.0–blue 8.0
- bromothymol blue: yellow 8.0–blue 9.6
- phenolphthalein: colourless 8.2–red 10.0.

To indicate that neutralisation has occurred the indicator must change colour completely during the vertical section.

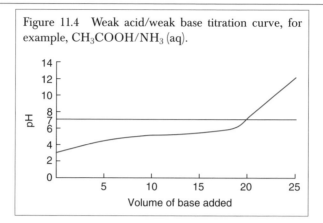

Figure 11.4   Weak acid/weak base titration curve, for example, CH_3COOH/NH_3 (aq).

4. To select a suitable indicator for a titration, find one that has **its pH colour range within the vertical section of the titration curve**. Therefore:

- strong acid/strong base: any of the above indicators
- strong acid/weak base (for example, HCl and Na_2CO_3): methyl orange
- weak acid/strong base (for example, vinegar and NaOH): phenolphthalein
- weak acid/weak base: no indicator suitable as there is no vertical region in the titration curve.

TEST YOURSELF

1. (a) Explain what is meant by 'dynamic equilibrium'?
   (b) Express the K_c for these reactions:
       (i) $HCOOH + C_2H_5OH \rightleftharpoons HCOOC_2H_5 + H_2O$
       (ii) $H_2 + I_2 \rightleftharpoons 2HI$
       (iii) $N_2 + 3H_2 \rightleftharpoons 2NH_3$.

2.

$$CH_4 + H_2O \rightleftharpoons CO_2 + 3H_2$$

The forward reaction is endothermic.

   (a) How will the concentration of hydrogen at equilibrium be affected by increasing the temperature?
   (b) When 32 g of methane and 54 g of water vapour were reacted in a 20-litre container there was 10 g of hydrogen at equilibrium. Calculate the K_c.

3.

$$2HI \rightleftharpoons H_2 + I_2$$

Two moles of hydrogen iodide were placed in a 2-litre vessel at 683 K. The K_c at that temperature is 0.0156. Find the number of moles of hydrogen iodide present at equilibrium.

4. (a) State Le Chatelier's principle.

   (b)

$$Cr_2O_7^{2-} + H_2O \rightleftharpoons 2CrO_4^{2-} + 2H^+$$

$$Fe^{3+} + CNS^- \rightleftharpoons Fe(CNS)^{2+}$$

   (i) Explain why adding sodium hydroxide solution to an orange solution containing dichromate ions changed the colour to yellow.

   (ii) When iron(III) chloride is added to potassium thiocyanate solution the colour changes to red. Explain why this is so and explain how the colour could be reversed.

5. Cobalt chloride was dissolved in some water and formed a red solution, according to the equation:

$$CoCl_4^{2-} \text{ (blue)} + 6H_2O \rightleftharpoons Co(H_2O)_6^{2+} \text{ (red)} + 4Cl^- \quad \Delta H = -$$

   (a) What could be added to the solution to change the colour to blue? Explain your answer.

   (b) Would you heat or cool the red solution to change the colour to blue? Explain your answer.

6. Sodium dichromate was dissolved in water to form an orange solution. The reaction between the dichromate ion and water is according to this equation:

$$Cr_2O_7^{2-} \text{ (orange)} + H_2O \rightleftharpoons 2CrO_4^{2-} \text{ (yellow)} + 2H^+$$

   (a) What could be added to the orange solution to change the colour to yellow? Explain your answer.

   (b) How could you change the yellow solution to orange? Explain your answer.

7. (a) Define pH and explain the significance of the pH values.

   (b) Calculate the pH of these solutions:
      (i) 0.4M HCl
      (ii) 0.5M H_2SO_4
      (iii) 2 g of NaOH in 250 cm^3

*8. (a) What is the 'ionic product of water'?

   (b) Use the ionic product of water to calculate the pH of water at 25°C.

   (c) The value of the ionic product of water is higher at 30°C than at 25°C. What effect has that on the pH of pure water at 30°C? Explain why the water is still neutral.

*9. (a) Write an expression for the K_a of CH_3COOH.

   (b) The K_a for CH_3COOH at room temperature is 1.8×10^{-5}.
      (i) What does the small value of the K_a indicate about ethanoic acid?
      (ii) Calculate the pH of a 0.1M solution.

   (c) Calculate the pH of a 0.2M solution of urea when its K_b is 1.5×10^{-14}.

*10. (a) Using HA to represent an indicator that is a weak acid, explain how the indicator changes colour from acid to alkaline solutions.

   (b) Name an indicator for these titrations:
      (i) HCl and NaOH
      (ii) HCl and ammonia solution
      (iii) ethanoic acid and NaOH.

   (c) Explain why no indicator is suitable for a titration of a weak acid/weak base.

Chapter 12 – Water hardness. Waste water analysis

12.1 WATER HARDNESS

What is hard water? Hard water is **difficult to lather with soap**. It contains dissolved salts of **calcium** and **magnesium**. The calcium and magnesium ions react with the soap ions (for example, stearate ions) to form an insoluble scum:

$$Ca^{2+} + \text{stearate ion} \rightarrow \text{calcium stearate (scum)}$$

It is only after all the dissolved calcium and magnesium ions have formed scum that the soap is free to lather.

Temporary hardness

This hardness is caused by **calcium hydrogencarbonate** or **magnesium hydrogencarbonate**.

The source of the hydrogencarbonates is the reaction between rain water and limestone. Limestone contains calcium carbonate and magnesium carbonate; rain contains CO_2 dissolved in the water. The reaction is as follows:

$$CaCO_3 + CO_2 + H_2O \rightarrow Ca(HCO_3)_2$$

Temporary hardness is **removed by boiling** the water, because the calcium and magnesium hydrogencarbonates **change to carbonates** which are insoluble. This removes the calcium and magnesium ions from the water, making it softer.

$$Ca(HCO_3)_2 \rightarrow CaCO_3 + H_2O + CO_2$$

The presence of carbonates in limescale in kettles is shown by the reaction with HCl – it releases CO_2 which turns limewater white.

Permanent hardness

This is caused by calcium or magnesium salts that are not affected by heat, for example, **calcium nitrate**, **calcium chloride**, **magnesium sulfate**, etc. These are present in the rocks through which the water supply passes.

Deionising water

Water can be **softened** by passing it through an **ion-exchange** resin that swaps Na^+ ions for Ca^{2+} and Mg^{2+} ions.

When the resin has lost all of its Na^+ ions, they can be replenished by passing a concentrated solution of NaCl through it. This releases the calcium and magnesium ions as the Na^+ ions are taken up by the resin.

Water can also be **deionised** (see Figure 12.1). There are natural (for example, zeolites) and artificial ion-exchange materials can swap H^+ ions for positive ions, and **OH⁻** ions for negative ions, thus **removing all ions** from the water and replacing them with ions that combine to form water:

$$H^+ + OH^- \rightarrow H_2O$$

They not only soften the water because they remove Ca^{2+} and Mg^{2+} ions, but they also purify the water to a great degree.

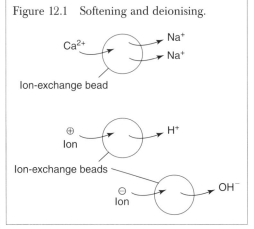

Figure 12.1 Softening and deionising.

HIGHER LEVEL

- **Deionised water** has no salts, but it could contain **impurities** of covalent substances, such as hydrocarbon oils etc.
- **Distilled water** is pure water, which was heated (boiled) to evaporate it, and the vapour cooled to condense it back to liquid. **All impurities are removed in the process.**

Mandatory experiment 25: Determination of total suspended solids (expressed as ppm) by filtration.

Procedure

1. Dry a filter paper in an oven at 100°C and weigh it on a balance sensitive to 0.01 g.
2. Fold the paper, hold it in a funnel, and pass 100 cm³ of water through it.
3. Dry the paper in an oven and weigh it.
4. Calculate the mass of solids in 100 cm³, and hence in 1 litre.
5. Express the answer in mg/L, i.e., ppm.

Determination of total dissolved solids

Procedure

1. Weigh a clean beaker.
2. Add 100 cm³ of filtered water and reweigh.
3. Heat the beaker in an oven at 100°C until all of the water has evaporated.
4. Weigh the beaker and the dissolved salts.
5. Calculate the mass of dissolved solids in 100 cm³, and hence in 1 litre.
6. Express the answer in mg/L, i.e., ppm.

Determination of pH

Procedure

Add a few drops of universal indicator and match the colour with the pH colour chart. Alternatively, use a pH meter. The pH meter uses an electrode that allows H^+ ions to pass through a membrane.

Mandatory experiment 26: Colorimetric experiment to estimate the amount of free chlorine in swimming-pool water (using a comparator or a colorimeter).

Procedure

Chlorine is present in swimming pools to kill bacteria by oxidising them. It is present in its free (active) state as HOCl (hypochlorous acid) and the hypochlorite ion OCl^-.

Comparator method

Procedure

1. Fill one tube with distilled water.
2. Fill the other tube with the swimming-pool water, add the sachet of DPD, stopper and mix.
3. Place both tubes in the comparator and view them in strong white light.
4. Rotate the colour disc and match the pink colour. Read the value of free chlorine.

Colorimeter method

See Figure 12.2.

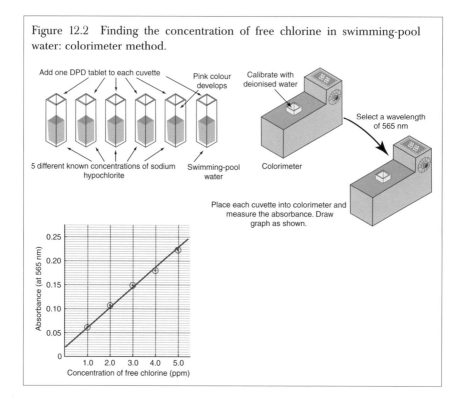

Figure 12.2   Finding the concentration of free chlorine in swimming-pool water: colorimeter method.

Procedure

1. Prepare a range of diluted hypochlorite solutions of known chlorine concentration.
2. Add a tablet of DPD to each.
3. Set the colorimeter to a fixed wavelength.
4. Fill a tube with each diluted solution, place it in the colorimeter and measure the transmittance of the light.
5. Repeat for the sample of swimming-pool water.
6. Make a graph of transmittance versus concentration of free chlorine. From the graph find the concentration that corresponds with the transmittance of the sample.

Note: Colorimetric analysis is based on the production of a coloured product of the substance being measured. An increased concentration of the substance results in a stronger colour and hence it lowers the transmittance of light. The transmittance is proportional to the strength of the colour and therefore to the concentration of the substance being measured.

By selecting a particular wavelength, other materials in the water that can also absorb light are eliminated.

HIGHER LEVEL

Mandatory experiment 27: Estimation of total hardness using ethylenediamine-tetraacetic acid (EDTA).

See Figure 12.3.

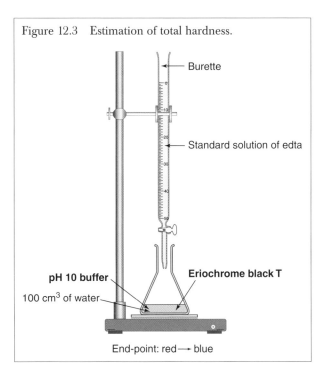

Figure 12.3   Estimation of total hardness.

The EDTA ion (ethylenediaminetetraacetic acid) combines with calcium and magnesium ions as follows:

$$EDTA + Ca^{2+} \rightarrow EDTACa$$

Procedure

1. Pipette 100 cm^3 of the water into a conical flask.
2. Add a small amount of pH10 buffer.
3. Add a pinch of eriochrome black indicator. The colour is wine-red.
4. Place the EDTA solution in a burette (washed and prepared in the usual way).
5. Add the EDTA into the flask until the colour changes to blue.
6. Repeat to get the average of three results that agree to within 0.1 cm^3.
7. Calculate the molarity of Ca^{2+} in the water, and express your answer in terms of mg/L (ppm) of CaCO$_3$.

Note: The EDTA solution is stored in plastic, as it reacts with glass and removes its metal ions.

Mandatory experiment 28: Estimation of dissolved oxygen by redox titration.

See Figure 12.4.

Procedure

1. Fill a clean bottle with the water sample.
2. Add 1 cm^3 of concentrated manganese sulphate and 1 cm^3 of concentrated alkaline potassium iodide.
   A **white precipitate** of manganese hydroxide forms which is quickly oxidised by the oxygen in the water to a **brown precipitate** of manganese oxide.
3. Add 2 cm^3 of concentrated H$_2$SO$_4$. Stopper the bottle and invert to mix.
   The brown precipitate disappears and the **yellow colour** of iodine appears.
4. Titrate 100 cm^3 of the iodine solution against standard solution of sodium thiosulfate, using starch as an indicator near the end-point.
5. Calculate the concentration of the O$_2$ in moles/litre. Express the answer in mg/L, i.e., ppm.

Equations

$$Mn^{2+} + 2OH^- \rightarrow Mn(OH)_2 \text{ (white)}$$

$$2Mn(OH)_2 + O_2 \rightarrow 2Mn_2O_3 \text{ (brown)}$$

$$Mn_2O_3 + 2I^- \rightarrow I_2 + 2Mn^{2+} + 3H_2O$$

Thus, O$_2$ ≡ 2I$_2$ (different formulas of the manganese oxide may be used, and hence different equations, but the ratio of O$_2$ to 2I$_2$ still results).

In the titration between I$_2$ and thiosulfate, the equation is as follows:

$$I_2 + 2S_2O_3^{2-} \rightarrow 2I^- + S_4O_6^{2-}$$

To calculate the concentration of O$_2$ in the titration sample:

$$O_2 \equiv 4S_2O_3^{2-}$$

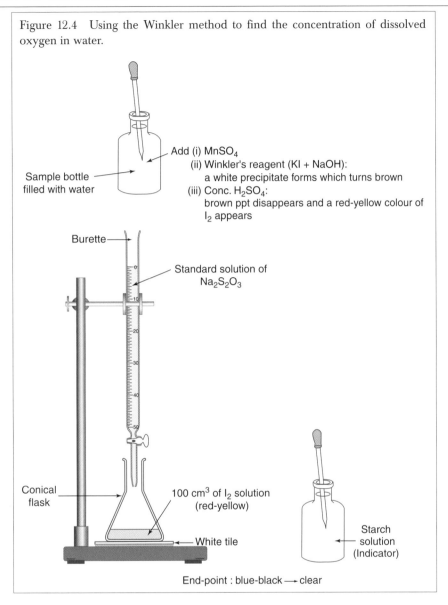

Figure 12.4   Using the Winkler method to find the concentration of dissolved oxygen in water.

Add (i) MnSO$_4$
    (ii) Winkler's reagent (KI + NaOH):
        a white precipitate forms which turns brown
    (iii) Conc. H$_2$SO$_4$:
        brown ppt disappears and a red-yellow colour of
        I$_2$ appears

Sample bottle filled with water

Burette

Standard solution of Na$_2$S$_2$O$_3$

Conical flask

100 cm^3 of I$_2$ solution (red-yellow)

White tile

Starch solution (Indicator)

End-point : blue-black ⟶ clear

Note:

- The **Winkler reagents are as concentrated as possible** in order not to displace any of the water sample, and to sink to the bottom, reacting with any oxygen present.
- The sample bottle is clean so as not to trap any air bubbles.
- Tap water contains chlorine, an oxidising agent, thus increasing the apparent amount of oxygen present in the water.

The treatment of drinking water

To make water suitable for consumption it undergoes a number of processes at a water treatment plant (see Figure 12.5).

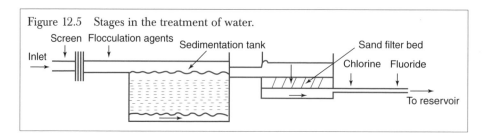

Figure 12.5   Stages in the treatment of water.

1. **Screens** remove any floating debris, if the source of water is a river or lake.
2. **Flocculation** agents are added. These cause small particles of clay, etc., to clump together forming larger particles, so that they sink faster. Common flocculation agents include **alum** and polyelectrolytes.
3. The water is passed to large **sedimentation** or settling tanks where the suspended sand and clay particles sink.
4. Final removal of solids is usually done by **filtration** through beds of fine sand.
5. **Chlorination** by chlorine gas or hypochlorite is done to kill pathogenic bacteria.
6. Compounds of **fluoride**, such as hexafluorosilicilic acid, are added to strengthen tooth enamel in order to help reduce tooth decay.
7. The **pH may need to be adjusted** to prevent corrosion inside metal pipes. Lime is used to raise the pH.

Note: Drinking water must look clean, be free of pathogens, and not exceed safe levels of chemicals. Nitrates from excessive use of fertilisers must be controlled, as they can be toxic to infants.

Water pollution

Sewage, and other biodegradable wastes, must be treated before it can be discharged to a river or lake, otherwise it causes pollution. Waste water can be released when it has a low **BOD** (biochemical oxygen demand), usually less than 20 ppm, and does not exceed **European Union limits** for toxic substances, for example, **heavy metals** such as cadmium, lead, etc., and nitrates, phosphates, etc.

Pollution from sewage arises from two effects:

- **Depletion in the oxygen levels**. When bacteria multiply and break down the waste material, they consume oxygen at the same time. This can result in a fish kill.
- **Eutrophication**, i.e., enrichment in the amount of algae. Plant nutrients, such as **nitrates and phosphates**, are released in the breakdown of the waste. In many aquatic habitats phosphate is the limiting factor, i.e., it is in short supply. As the phosphate level rises the growth of algae rises in proportion. When the algae die they are broken down by bacteria. This depletes the oxygen, causing a fish kill. Another problem is that some algae are toxic.

HIGHER LEVEL

Pollution also arises from the presence of **heavy metal** ions, such as Pb^{2+}, Hg^{2+}, and Cd^{2+}, which are toxic to humans and animals. (The ions of the light metals, such as the alkali metals and alkaline earth metals are important components of many animals and plants and are not toxic.) They mainly arise from particular industries, including mining, electronics, and leather tanning, etc., although domestic batteries are another source. Their discharge in waste water requires a licence from the EPA, which implements the EU standards in Ireland.

12.2   WASTE WATER ANALYSIS

Biochemical (or biological) oxygen demand (BOD)

BOD is a measure of how much oxygen will be taken out of the water in a river or lake as the waste material is broken down by bacteria. It is defined as **the depletion in the oxygen concentration as the waste is broken down over five days in darkness at 20°C**.

Darkness is needed to **prevent photosynthesis** by plants, which produces oxygen. The temperature must remain constant, as oxygen is less soluble in warm water and the rate of microbial action is faster in warm water. 20°C represents the highest average temperature of rivers and lakes in Ireland and the United Kingdom.

Note: Water often has an oxygen concentration of around 10 ppm. Thus, a waste with a BOD higher than this cannot be fully broken down in the BOD test. It must be diluted. The waste may also need to be oxygenated, by bubbling air through it, to increase its oxygen concentration in order to have a **complete breakdown within the five days**.

Example

A sample of waste was diluted by mixing 50 cm^3 of it with 200 cm^3 of well-oxygenated water. Its oxygen concentration was measured at 12.0 ppm. After five days in the dark at 20°C the oxygen concentration was 5 ppm. Calculate the BOD.

Answer

BOD of diluted waste was $12 - 5$, i.e., 7 ppm.
Dilution factor was 1:5 (, i.e., 50 cm^3 in 250 cm^3).
BOD of undiluted waste was 5×7, i.e., 35 ppm.

Analysis of heavy metals

The **atomic absorption spectrometer** (**AAS**) is used to measure the concentration of metals, such as lead, cadmium, mercury, etc.

Treatment of sewage

Sewage treatment can take place in three stages:

1. **Primary (physical) treatment**. Solids are screened from the waste water and more solids are removed by allowing the waste to settle in tanks.
2. **Secondary (biological) treatment**. The liquid is passed into tanks and air is introduced into it. Bacteria feed on the waste, breaking it down to simpler substances. After primary and secondary treatment, the BOD of most sewage has been reduced to safe levels and it can be discharged to a river or to the sea.
3. **Tertiary (chemical) treatment**. This treatment is mainly to **reduce the levels of nitrates and phosphates**, the plant nutrients that cause eutrophication in lakes and estuaries. As this treatment is expensive it is normally only considered where a problem of eutrophication has arisen in a lake or estuary, and not where discharge to the sea is allowed.

HIGHER LEVEL

By adding various substances and adjusting the pH, insoluble compounds of nitrogen and phosphorus are **precipitated** and removed in settling tanks.

TEST YOURSELF

1. (a) Define hard water. What causes hardness in water?
   (b) (i) Define temporary hardness.
       (ii) Name a substance that causes temporary hardness.
       (iii) Outline how that substance is formed in limestone areas of the country.
       (iv) Describe what happens when water with temporary hardness is boiled.
   (c) Name a substance that causes permanent hardness.
2. (a) Explain how an ion-exchange resin can soften hard water.
   (b) Explain how water is deionised.
   *(c) Compare deionised and distilled water.
3. 100 cm^3 of a water sample was found to contain 0.05 g of dissolved solids. Calculate the concentration of dissolved solids in ppm.
4. 50 cm^3 of water was titrated against 0.01M solution of EDTA and the mean titre was 16.4 cm^3.
   (a) Name the indicator used in the titration and state the colour change at the end-point.
   (b) What was added to the flask to ensure an accurate end-point?
   (c) Using H_2Y^{2-} to represent the EDTA anion and M^{2+} to represent the cation causing hardness the reaction is as follows:

   $$H_2Y^{2-} + M^{2+} \rightarrow MY^{2-} + 2H^+$$

   Calculate the total hardness of the water in terms of ppm of calcium carbonate.
   (d) Outline how to measure the temporary hardness of the water sample.

5. (a) To determine the oxygen concentration in a bottle of water to which two very concentrated solutions were added. Identify what is present in these solutions. State what you observe if there is oxygen present in the water.

   (b) State what you observe when concentrated sulfuric acid is next added to the bottle.

   (c) What standard solution is used to titrate against the water sample?

6. (a) Outline the main steps in the physical and chemical treatment of drinking water.

   (b) What use is made of the following substances in the treatment of drinking water:
       (i) aluminium sulfate
       (ii) chlorine
       (iii) lime
       (iv) hexafluorosilicic acid.

7. (a) Explain why the discharge of untreated sewage into rivers causes fish kills.

   (b) What is meant by 'eutrophication'? Outline the effect of eutrophication on human and fish life.

   *(c) Name two plant nutrients that can cause eutrophication.

   *(d) Identify three heavy metal ions that can cause water pollution and name two industrial sources.

8. Outline the main stages in the treatment of sewage.

*9. (a) Explain 'BOD' and its significance.

   (b) Outline how the BOD is measured.

   (c) Why is a sample of sewage usually diluted before carrying out a BOD test?

   (d) 25 cm^3 of a sample of sewage was diluted to 1 litre with well-oxygenated water and the oxygen concentration was found to be 12.8 ppm. A bottle was filled with the diluted sewage and stored for five days under standard conditions for a BOD test. Its dissolved oxygen was then found to be 8.2 ppm. Calculate the BOD of the sewage.

Chapter 13 – Option 1A: Industrial chemistry. Case studies. Option 1B: Atmospheric chemistry

13.1 OPTION 1A: INDUSTRIAL CHEMISTRY

Principles of industrial chemistry

There are several different areas of the chemical industry:

- pharmaceuticals and fine chemicals – medicines, etc.
- agrochemicals – fertilisers, insecticides, herbicides, etc.
- household products – cleaning products, toiletries, etc.
- bulk chemicals – nitric acid, ammonia, magnesium oxide.

Types of production operations

Batch process

The feedstock (raw materials) is added to a vessel, for example, a stainless steel reactor, stirred and heated at a controlled temperature until the reaction has gone to completion. The vessel is then emptied, cleaned and reused.

Advantages:

- The vessel can be easily used for other processes so many different processes can take place at different times in the one factory.
- Capital costs are low.

Disadvantages:

- It is labour-intensive.
- Contamination can occur.

Continuous process

The feedstock is continuously fed into the reactor and the products are displaced.

Advantages:

- It uses computer-controlled automation, so labour costs are low.
- There is little risk of contamination.

Disadvantages:

- The reactor is specialised for just one reaction.
- Capital costs are high.
- Unreacted reactants must be separated from the product and returned to the reactor.

Chemical, economic and social factors that affect the operation of a chemical plant are:

- the **feedstock**, its supply and preparation
- the methods of achieving a **fast rate** of reaction, for example, catalysts, temperature, pressure
- the ways of achieving a **high product yield**, i.e., eliminating side reactions, altering the equilibrium
- the use or disposal of **co-products** of the main reactions
- **waste reduction** and waste disposal (integrated waste licence from the EPA)
- **quality control** of the product
- the **safe operation** of plant and monitoring of hazards
- **costs** of: plant construction and maintenance (fixed costs); raw materials; energy (heat exchangers to reduce energy requirements); waste treatment (reuse, recycling); co-products (finding a market)
- **site location**, i.e., access to transport for feedstock and products and the workforce; space for operation and storage of feedstock and product
- the supply of suitably resistant **materials for plant construction** – specialists needed.

13.2   CASE STUDIES

Study any one of the following case studies:

- **ammonia manufacture**
- **nitric acid manufacture**
- **magnesium oxide manufacture**.

Ammonia manufacture

Ammonia, NH_3, is made from the following feedstock:

- methane (natural gas)
- steam
- air.

The process took place in the IFI plant in Cork Harbour, near a source of natural gas – Kinsale gas field – and water. There is a rail connection to Arklow, to where the ammonia was transported to make nitric acid and nitrogen fertilisers.

The process involves the following steps (see Figure 13.1):

1. **Removal of sulfur compounds** from the natural gas (added to give the gas an odour in case it leaks), which are catalyst poisons.

2. **Steam reforming to form hydrogen gas**: the methane reacts with steam at a high temperature and over a nickel catalyst:

HIGHER LEVEL

$$CH_4 + H_2O \rightarrow CO + 3H_2$$

The carbon monoxide also reacts with steam, which makes more hydrogen gas.

Figure 13.1   Ammonia manufacture.

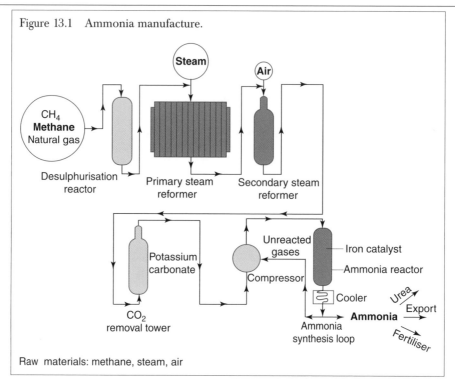

Raw materials: methane, steam, air

HIGHER LEVEL

$$CO + H_2O \rightarrow CO_2 + H_2$$

3. **Air is added**. The **oxygen** reacts with the left-over methane and with the left-over carbon monoxide (its removal is necessary as it is a catalyst poison). The nitrogen of the air will be part of the reaction with hydrogen to make the ammonia.

HIGHER LEVEL

$$CH_4 + 2O_2 \rightarrow 2H_2O + CO_2$$
$$CO + O_2 \rightarrow CO_2$$

4. **Removal of CO$_2$**: The carbon dioxide reacts with potassium carbonate to form potassium hydrogencarbonate. This reaction is reversed in another plant, and the carbon dioxide is a useful by-product, which is used to make urea, as well as carbonated drinks.

HIGHER LEVEL

$$CO_2 + H_2O + K_2CO_3 \rightleftharpoons 2KHCO_3$$

5. **Formation of ammonia by the Haber process**: the hydrogen and nitrogen gases are pressurised to **300 atmospheres** and the temperature is brought to about **400–500°C**. They are passed over an **iron catalyst**.

The reaction is reversible and it is exothermic:

$$N_2 + 3H_2 \rightleftharpoons 2NH_3$$

By Le Chatelier's principle, the equilibrium is richest in NH_3 at high pressure and at low temperatures. However, there are costs associated with increasing the pressure. Because low temperatures slow down the rate of reaction too much the operating temperature is a compromise between a fast rate of reaction (high temperature) and an equilibrium mixture richest in ammonia (low temperature).

6. **Removal of ammonia**: the gases are cooled rapidly and the ammonia liquefies. The unreacted gases are recycled back to the reactor.

Urea synthesis

Urea is a fertiliser with a very high percentage of nitrogen.

It is produced by reacting liquid ammonia with carbon dioxide, a product of the production of ammonia.

HIGHER LEVEL

$$2NH_3 + CO_2 \rightarrow CO(NH_2)_2 + H_2O$$

The solution of urea is evaporated and pellets of urea are produced by spraying it against a draft of rising hot air.

Nitric acid manufacture

The feedstock to make nitric acid consists of the following:

- ammonia
- air
- water.

The nitric acid produced by IFI is used to make **nitrate fertilisers**, for example, **ammonium nitrate**.

The production takes place in Arklow, where the ammonia arrives from Cork Harbour by rail. A river runs beside the plant to supply water. (The site was originally close to mines in Co. Wicklow as a supply of sulfite ores, which was once used to make sulfuric acid.) The products can be exported from Arklow Harbour or by rail.

The production of nitric acid takes place in a number of steps (see Figure 13.2):

1. The **ammonia and oxygen (air) are heated to 900°C** and pressurised slightly and passed over a **catalyst of platinum-rhodium** to form nitrogen monoxide.

HIGHER LEVEL

$$4NH_3 + 5O_2 \rightleftharpoons 4NO + 6H_2O$$

This is an exothermic reaction, so the formation of NO is favoured by low temperatures. The equilibrium is also richer in NO at low pressure. However those

Figure 13.2   Nitric acid manufacture.

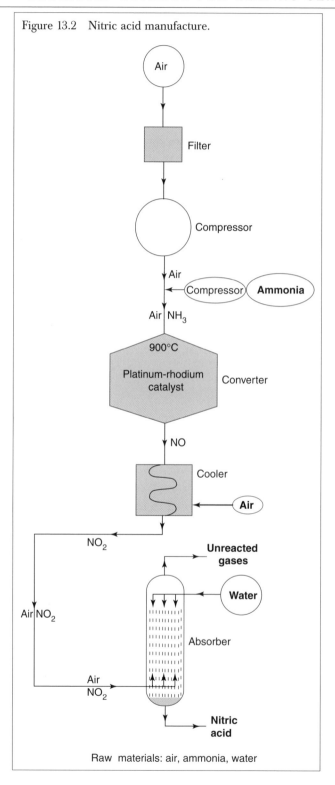

Raw materials: air, ammonia, water

conditions are unsuitable – low temperatures are too slow, and low pressure allows for the formation of nitrogen gas by another reaction between ammonia and oxygen.

2. **The gases are cooled and air is added** to oxidise the nitrogen monoxide.

$$2NO + O_2 \rightarrow 2NO_2$$

3. The **NO_2 is dissolved in water** to form nitric acid.

HIGHER LEVEL

$$3NO_2 + H_2O \rightarrow 2HNO_3 + NO$$

Ammonium nitrate manufacture

Ammonium nitrate is a fertiliser with a high percentage of nitrogen and which is very soluble. It is produced by the reaction of ammonia gas and nitric acid.

HIGHER LEVEL

$$NH_3 + HNO_3 \rightarrow NH_4NO_3$$

Magnesium oxide manufacture

Magnesium oxide (periclase) is manufactured by Premier Periclase in Drogheda. The product has a high melting point, so it is used to make refractory bricks to line furnaces and smelters.

The feedstock includes the following:

- limestone
- fresh water
- sea water.

The site is close to limestone quarries, the Boyne river, and the sea, to supply the raw materials. Drogheda harbour allows for export of the product by shipping.

The product is made via a number of steps (see Figure 13.3):

1. Roasting of limestone to lime (quicklime). The limestone is heated at a high temperature in a kiln:

HIGHER LEVEL

$$CaCO_3 \rightarrow CaO + CO_2$$

2. Lime is added to water (it is first degassed to remove CO_2) to form slaked lime:

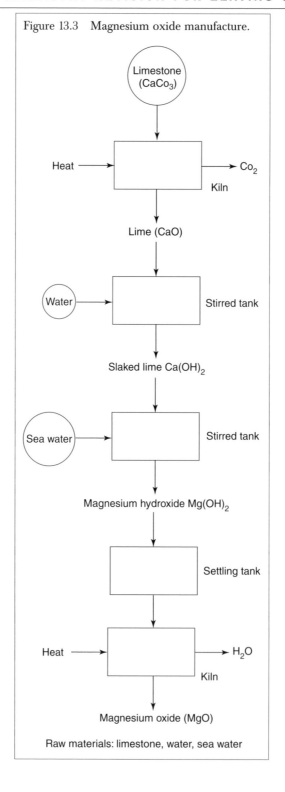

Figure 13.3   Magnesium oxide manufacture.

Raw materials: limestone, water, sea water

HIGHER LEVEL

$$CaO + H_2O \rightarrow Ca(OH)_2$$

3. Sea water (cleared of sand and degassed of CO_2) is added and magnesium hydroxide precipitates out:

HIGHER LEVEL

$$MgCl_2 + Ca(OH)_2 \rightarrow Mg(OH)_2 + CaCl_2$$

4. The precipitate settles and is thickened. It is roasted in a kiln to form magnesium oxide, which is pelleted:

$$Mg(OH)_2 \rightarrow MgO + H_2O$$

13.3 OPTION 1B: ATMOSPHERIC CHEMISTRY

Oxygen (O₂)

Oxygen gas constitutes about 20% of the atmosphere. It stays at a fairly constant level as the rate at which it is used in respiration and burning is matched by the rate that it is replaced by the photosynthesis of plants on land and in the sea.

The industrial manufacture of oxygen

Oxygen is prepared from air in two stages:

- **Liquefaction**. Filtered air is, cooled, pressurised and allowed to expand until it condenses to a liquid at a temperature of around $-200°C$.
- **Fractional distillation**. The liquid air is fed into the bottom of a cold fractionation tower. The liquid is introduced near the bottom and is heated to boil it. The gases rise up and oxygen condenses at $-183°C$ and is removed off, while nitrogen continues up to condense at $-196°C$. (Thus the separation is due to their different boiling points. Oxygen has a higher boiling point due to the larger van der Waals forces because of the larger M_r.)

Uses of oxygen

Oxygen is used:

- in hospitals for patients with breathing problems
- to make steel
- to burn ethyne in the oxy-acetylene flame.

Nitrogen (N₂)

Molecular structure

N_2 molecules consist of two nitrogen atoms held together very strongly by a triple covalent bond, $N\equiv N$. Thus, nitrogen gas is unreactive (inert).

Atmospheric nitrogen

The amount of nitrogen gas in the air is about 78–80%.

Nitrogen is a component of **proteins** in plants and animals. Due to the inertness of nitrogen gas at room temperatures, plants cannot use it to make proteins. Instead, plants absorb nitrate ions and use them in protein synthesis.

Nitrogen fixation converts nitrogen gas into nitrates. Natural fixation takes place in two ways:

- by nitrogen-fixing bacteria, either living in the soil or in the roots of peas and beans
- in lightning flashes, in which the high temperature causes the reaction between nitrogen and oxygen to form nitrogen oxides:

$$N_2 + O_2 \rightarrow 2NO$$

$$2NO + O_2 \rightarrow 2NO_2.$$

The oxides of nitrogen (NOx) dissolve in the rain to form acids, HNO_2 and HNO_3.

$$2NO_2 + H_2O \rightarrow HNO_2 + HNO_3$$

Uses of nitrogen

Liquid nitrogen is used:

- to freeze and store semen and animal embryos
- to quick-freeze foods.

Nitrogen gas is used:

- to keep foods fresh inside packaging
- to make ammonia
- to flush out flammable vapours from oil tankers.

The nitrogen cycle

See Figure 13.4.

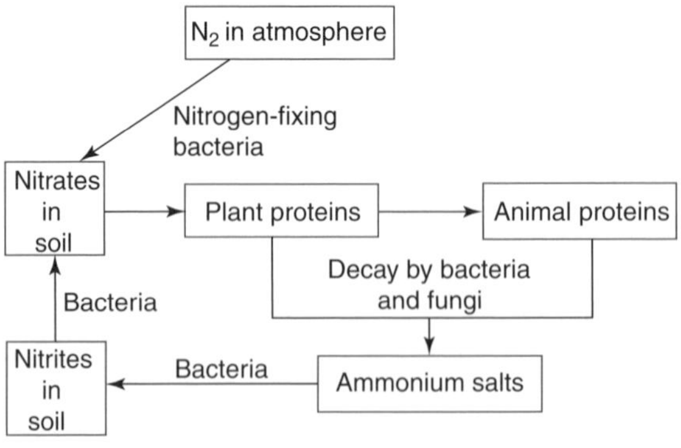

Carbon dioxide

The combustion of carbon in coal, and of hydrocarbons, produces carbon monoxide CO and carbon dioxide CO_2.

Carbon monoxide (CO) is:

- a product of incomplete combustion in car engines, faulty heating systems and cigarettes
- a toxic gas that blocks the haemoglobin from carrying oxygen
- a neutral gas when it dissolves in water.

Carbon dioxide (CO_2) is an acidic gas (it colours universal indicator pink).

Figure 13.4   The nitrogen cycle.

HIGHER LEVEL

CO_2 reacts with water to form a weak acid, carbonic acid:

$$CO_2 + H_2O \rightarrow H_2CO_3$$

This causes normal rain to be weakly acidic (about pH 5.5). Thus rain reacts with limestone to form calcium hydrogencarbonate:

$$CaCO_3 + H_2O + CO_2 \rightarrow Ca(HCO_3)_2$$

Carbon dioxide is found in water in three states:

- free (dissolved) CO_2
- carbonate ions CO_3^-
- hydrogencarbonate ions HCO_3^{2-}.

$$H_2O + CO_2 \rightleftharpoons H_2CO_3$$

$$H_2CO_3 \rightleftharpoons H^+ + HCO_3^-$$

$$H_2CO_3 \rightleftharpoons 2H^+ + CO_3^{2-}$$

Industrial production of CO$_2$ and its uses

Fermentation of beer and wine produces CO_2 (and ethanol). Excess CO_2 is sold as a useful by-product. It is added to mineral water to produce carbonated (fizzy) drinks. It is also used in fire extinguishers.

The carbon cycle

Carbon is circulated through nature through the atmosphere, oceans, plants, animals, decomposers, rocks and fuels (see Figure 13.5).

- CO_2 is **produced** by burning fuels, roasting limestone to make cement and through the respiration of plants, animals and decomposers.
- CO_2 is **absorbed** through photosynthesis and through dissolving in water, where over long periods it is converted into limestone.

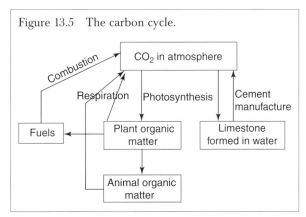

Figure 13.5   The carbon cycle.

The greenhouse effect

The greenhouse gases in the atmosphere allow the sun's heat (short wavelengths of UV light) to pass through, but they absorb the earth's heat (long wavelengths of infra-red) as it is radiated out, and they radiate it back to earth. Without them the earth would be too cold for life, with similar cold temperatures ($-18°C$) as the moon, which has no atmosphere.

Atmospheric gases in order of their greenhouse effect (assigning a value of 1 to CO_2):

- H_2O vapour: 0.1
- CO_2: 1
- CH_4: 30
- N_2O: 160
- CFCs: 25,000.

CH_4, methane, comes from cattle, landfills and paddy fields. N_2O comes from car exhausts. CFCs come from aerosols, refrigeration units, etc.

The amount of CO_2 in the atmosphere has been rising since the industrial revolution, but in recent times the rise has accelerated. Since the 1950s the level has increased from 0.03% to 0.036%. This has been due to **human activity**, principally from the **burning of vast amounts of fuels** in transport and in electricity production. Allied to this is the reduction in tropical forests and the loss of photosynthesis.

Consequently, global temperatures are rising and the climate is changing. Because of the relatively large amounts of CO_2, it contributes almost 50% to global warming.

Possible implications of **global warming** include:

- melting of polar ice caps leading to a rise in sea levels and flooding
- more storms and with more force
- change in the ocean circulation and the end of the Gulf Stream, bringing very cold winter conditions to northern Europe, including Ireland
- growth of deserts
- spread of tropical pests and disease such as malaria.

Atmospheric pollution

Acid rain

Acid rain (see Figure 13.6) **has a pH less than 5.5**. It corrodes stonework, kills aquatic life and releases plant toxins such as aluminium from the soil, resulting in the death of trees.

Acid rain is principally caused by the oxides of two elements – nitrogen and sulfur.

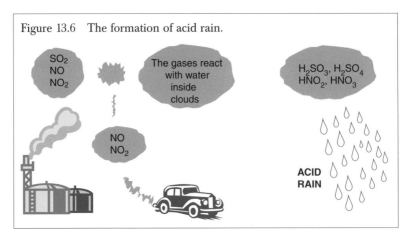

Figure 13.6   The formation of acid rain.

Oxides of nitrogen

At high temperatures, in car engines, power stations, and lightning flashes, nitrogen reacts with oxygen to form NO and NO_2. The NO is quickly oxidised to NO_2, which dissolves in rain to form HNO_2 and HNO_3.

Oxides of sulfur

Some fossil fuels, especially coals and oil, contain sulfur, and when the fuel is burned, SO_2 is released. Some SO_2 dissolves in rain to form H_2SO_3. SO_2 is also oxidised to SO_3, which dissolves in rain to form H_2SO_4.

Scrubbing of waste gases at power stations

To reduce the emission of SO_2, limestone can be added to the coal in power stations. The $CaCO_3$ decomposes to form CaO and CO_2. The CaO reacts with the SO_2 to form $CaSO_3$ in the ash. In addition, the flue gases can be sprayed with dissolved CaO.

The ozone layer

Ozone, O_3, at ground level is harmful to human health, but a layer of ozone in the stratosphere (15 km to 50 km above the earth) protects the earth from the harmful effects of the sun's ultraviolet radiation. UV light can cause skin cancer, eye cataracts and genetic damage to plants and animals.

Ozone is formed by the reaction of oxygen molecules and oxygen atoms.

Ozone depletion is due mainly to the action of CFCs, which were used in fridges and in aerosols.

HIGHER LEVEL

Ozone is formed by the reaction of oxygen molecules with oxygen radicals:

$$O_2 + UV \rightarrow O^* + O^* \quad \text{(photodissociation of oxygen)}$$

$$O_2 + O^* \rightarrow O_3$$

Ozone is broken down by photodissociation when it absorbs UV light:

$$O_3 + UV \rightarrow O_2 + O^*$$

Chlorofluorocarbons (CFCs)

CFCs are substituted hydrocarbons, such as CCl_2F_2, CCl_3F, etc. They are inert, stable, non-flammable, non-corrosive, low in toxicity and are (were) used as refrigerants, propellants, fire extinguishers, solvents and to form plastic foams. Their use has now been severely reduced, but due to their stability they have a **long residency period** in the atmosphere.

Ozone depletion

Ozone is destroyed by O atoms, NO molecules, but **mainly by CFCs** through their production of Cl atoms:

- The **photodissociation of O_2** forms oxygen radicals. They react with ozone:

$$O_2 + UV \rightarrow O^* + O^*$$

$$O_3 + O^* \rightarrow 2O_2$$

- NO is formed when N_2O reaches the stratosphere and reacts with O_2. NO reacts with ozone:

$$O_3 + NO \rightarrow NO_2 + O_2$$

- **CFCs**

  CFCs absorb UV and dissociate as follows:

$$CCl_3F + UV \rightarrow CCl_2F^* + Cl^*$$

  The chlorine radical destroys the ozone molecules:

$$Cl^* + O_3 \rightarrow ClO^* + O_2$$

  The chlorine radical is reformed in the following reaction:

$$ClO^* + O^* \rightarrow Cl^* + O_2$$

This is the start of a chain reaction in which one CFC molecule can destroy 100,000 ozone molecules.

However, the presence of CH_4 is beneficial as it mops up the chlorine atoms:

$$CH_4 + Cl^* \rightarrow CH_3^* + HCl$$

Replacements for CFCs

Hydrochlorofluorocarbons (HCFCs), for example, $C_2H_3Cl_2F$, and hydrofluorocarbons (HFCs), for example, $C_2H_2F_4$, are used instead of CFCs because their C–H bonds are broken down in the troposphere and so they do not reach the stratosphere. However, they are still greenhouse gases and they still deplete the ozone, though at a greatly reduced level.

TEST YOURSELF

1. (a) Distinguish between a batch production process and a continuous production process.
   (b) State two advantages of each method.
   (c) Which production method is likely to have these characteristics:
       (i) lower capital cost
       (ii) more automation
       (iii) more labour-intensive
       (iv) less risk of contamination
       (v) can be more easily changed to make another product.

2. A chemical plant needs the right location and must be run as economically as possible. Answer the following questions with regards to the chemical industry in general:
  (i) List three factors that affect the suitability of a chemical plant's location.
  (ii) State three factors that increase the speed of a chemical process.
  (iii) List four fixed costs that apply to a chemical plant.
  (iv) List two ways of achieving a high product yield.
  (v) Suggest one way of reducing costs.

3. With regard to any one of the following manufacturing industries in Ireland – ammonia, nitric acid, magnesium oxide:
  (a) State the feedstock.
  (b) Describe the preparation of the feedstock.
  (c) Outline the chemical reactions involved.
  (d) Describe any conditions that increase the yield of product.
  (e) Outline the use of the product.
  (f) Give a reason for the location of the manufacturing plant.
  (g) Outline the waste disposal and effluent control carried out.

4. (a) State two uses for oxygen.
  (b) Outline how oxygen is extracted from air.

5. (a) State two uses for:
    (i) liquid nitrogen
    (ii) nitrogen gas.
  (b) Explain why nitrogen gas is relatively inert.
  (c) Explain 'nitrogen fixation'. Outline two natural processes that fix nitrogen.
  (d) Outline the nitrogen cycle in nature.

6. The combustion of carbon compounds produces carbon monoxide and carbon dioxide.
  (a) Under what conditions is carbon monoxide produced?
  (b) Why is carbon monoxide poisonous?
  (c) What effect on a solution of universal indicator do the following have?
    (i) carbon monoxide
    (ii) carbon dioxide.

7. (a) Outline the carbon cycle in nature.
  (b) Why is the level of carbon dioxide in the atmosphere increasing in recent times?
  (c) What effect has a rising level of atmospheric carbon dioxide and what are the possible implications?
  (d) Name one industrial source of carbon dioxide.
  (e) Name one industrial use for carbon dioxide.

8. (a) Explain what is meant by the 'greenhouse effect'.
  (b) List the atmospheric gases in order of their relative effect as greenhouse gases and state a source of each gas.

9. (a) Define 'acid rain'.
  (b) What are the effects of acid rain on the environment?
  (c) Two of the gases that cause acid rain are nitrogen dioxide and sulfur dioxide. State two sources for each gas and outline how they are produced.
  (d) Explain the role of limestone in reducing acid rain.

10. (a) Describe how ozone is formed in the stratosphere and outline its beneficial effects.
    (b) What do the following abbreviations stand for? Give an example of each.
        (i) CFC
        (ii) HCFC.
    (c) State:
        (i) two useful properties of CFCs
        (ii) two uses for CFCs.
    (d) What are two harmful effects of ozone depletion and what is its main cause?

*11. (a) What happens to the ozone molecule when it absorbs UV light? Use an equation to explain how ozone is formed in the stratosphere.
     (b) Explain, with equations, how oxygen gas can cause ozone depletion.
     (c) Explain, with an equation, how NO can cause ozone depletion. What is the source of NO?
     (d) Explain, with equations how CCl_3F breaks down ozone.
     (e) Explain why one CFC molecule can result in the destruction of many thousands of ozone molecules.
     (f) Why does the presence of methane help to conserve ozone?
     (g) Name a suitable substitute for CFCs.

Chapter 14 – Option 2A: Materials.
Option 2B: Electrochemistry

14.1   OPTION 2A: MATERIALS

Crystals

Crystals are solids with a regular shape and smooth sides and with an internal orderly array of their particles.

The particles in a crystal may be ions, atoms, or molecules, and they are positioned in a regular array, called a lattice. The particles occupy the lattice points.

X-ray crystallography

The regular array within crystals was first determined by **William and Lawrence Bragg** in the early 1900s by examining the diffraction patterns from beaming X-rays through crystals. Biological material was also found to have crystalline structure. **Dorothy Hodgkin** used X-rays to determine the structure of vitamin B_{12}, and the structure of penicillin was also found. X-ray crystallography was also used to elucidate the double-helix structure of DNA.

In 1985 a new allotrope of carbon was discovered, which consisted of 60 carbon atoms held in a regular array by three covalent bonds, and which resembles a football. It was named **buckminsterfullerene** in honour of a US architect, **Buckminster Fuller**, who also designed similar structures.

Crystal particles and their properties

The particles that occupy the lattice points in a crystal are held in position by different kinds of forces, and the nature of the forces affects the properties of the crystal.

Ionic crystals
Examples: NaCl (see Figure 14.1), KI.

Ions occupy the lattice points, so that there is an orderly array of positive and negative ions. The crystal of sodium chloride is cubic, but other crystal shapes are possible. The binding force is the ionic bond, which is electrostatic in nature and is very strong.

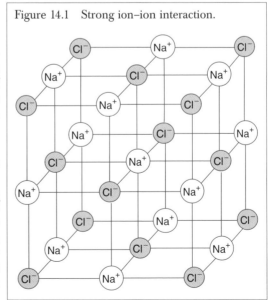

Figure 14.1   Strong ion–ion interaction.

Ionic crystals:

- have **high melting points**.
- do not conduct electricity as solids, but **they conduct electricity when dissolved or melted**.
- in general, **dissolve in water and not in non-polar solvents**.

Molecular crystals

Examples: water, iodine (see Figure 14.2), dry ice (CO_2), sugar.

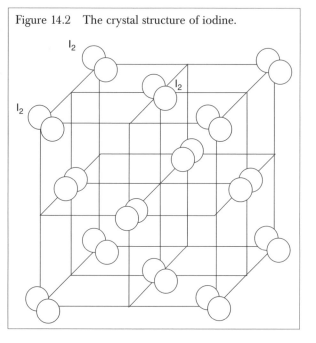

Figure 14.2   The crystal structure of iodine.

The molecules occupy the lattice points. There are three kinds of binding force and thus their physical properties vary:

- **Van der Waals** forces. The molecules are non-polar, for example, iodine (I_2), dry ice (CO_2). This is the weakest force, thus they have **low melting points**. They are **insoluble in water**.
- **Dipole–dipole**, for example, HCl. They have **moderately high melting points and they dissolve in water**.
- **Hydrogen bonds**. The molecules have an O–H bond, for example, water (ice), sugar, ethanoic acid. This is the strongest of the three forces. The **melting point is relatively high**, but much lower than for an ionic crystal. **They dissolve in water**.

    Properties of molecular crystals:
    - They have **relatively low melting points**.
    - They **do not conduct electricity** as solids or when melted or dissolved.
    - They **may dissolve in water** if the binding force is due to a dipole or to hydrogen bonds, but they **do not dissolve in water** if it is due to van der Waals force.

Metallic crystals

Examples: sodium, iron etc.

Positive metal ions occupy the lattice points, but between the ions there is a **'sea of electrons'**, consisting of the delocalised outer electrons which move throughout the crystal. The binding force is the attraction between the ions and the sea of electrons (see Figure 14.3).

When connected to an electrical supply, electrons can enter the electron sea at one end and leave it at the other. Thus, metals are **good conductors** of electricity (and heat). The ions pack together as closely as possible, but they can be relatively easily pushed around. Thus, metals are **malleable and ductile**.

Metals are **not soluble in water or in non-polar solvents**.

Figure 14.3   The structure of a metallic crystal.

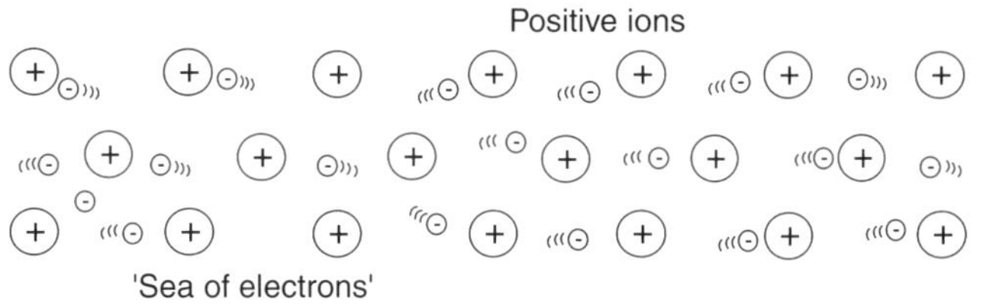

Positive ions

'Sea of electrons'

Macromolecular crystals

Examples: diamond (see Figure 14.4) and graphite (see Figure 14.5)(both are allotropes of carbon), silica (SiO_2).

The lattice points are occupied by atoms that are held in position by covalent bonds. The covalent bonds are very strong, thus the crystals have **very high melting points**.

In **diamond**, each carbon atom uses its four outer electrons to **bond to four** other atoms, and these are bonded to four other atoms, forming one giant molecule. Diamond is therefore **very hard** and it **does not conduct electricity**.

In **graphite**, the carbon atoms are **bonded to three other atoms**, forming planes of atoms that lie parallel. The delocalised electrons from each atom lie between the planes. The planes can be easily pushed over each other and thus graphite is **soft**. Also, the delocalised electrons can flow through the crystal, allowing graphite to **conduct electricity**.

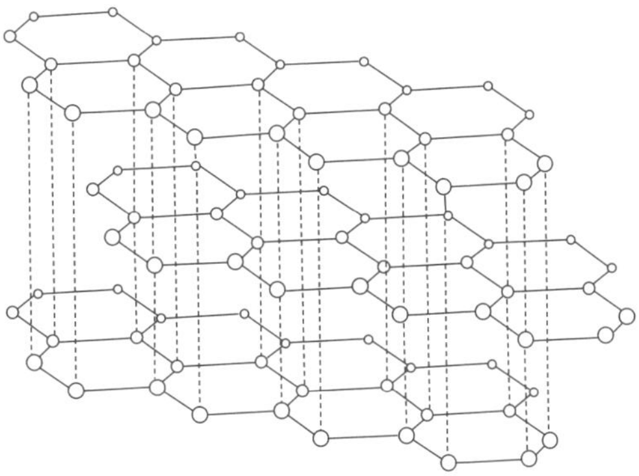

Addition polymers

An addition polymer is made by addition reactions between very many monomers (with double bonds) to form long

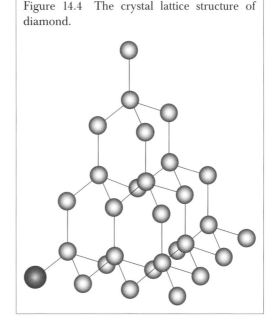

Figure 14.4   The crystal lattice structure of diamond.

Figure 14.5   The structure of graphite.

molecules. (Another group of polymers, such as polyester and nylon, are formed by condensation reactions between the monomers. Their monomers do not have double bonds.)

Monomers are small molecules with double bonds that join together in large numbers by addition reactions to make large molecules.

Examples of addition polymers include:

- poly(ethene)
- poly(chloroethene)
- poly(phenylethene)
- poly(tetrafluoroethene)
- poly(propene).

Low-density and high-density poly(ethene) (LDPE)

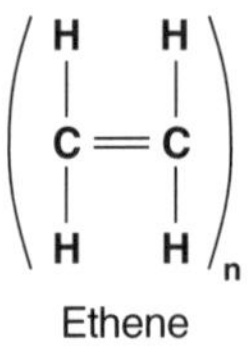

LDPE (see Figure 14.6) was discovered by accident in 1933 in England, when chemists were investigating the effect of high pressure and temperature on reactions. At the end of one experiment using ethene they found a white waxy solid. It was chemically inert and **unreactive**, and was an **electrical insulator**. Its first use was as a replacement of rubber as insulation on electrical wires.

LDPE consists of branched chains that do not pack closely together. Thus it is **soft and flexible** and is used for bags and clingfilm.

Figure 14.6   Monomer for poly(ethene).

Ethene

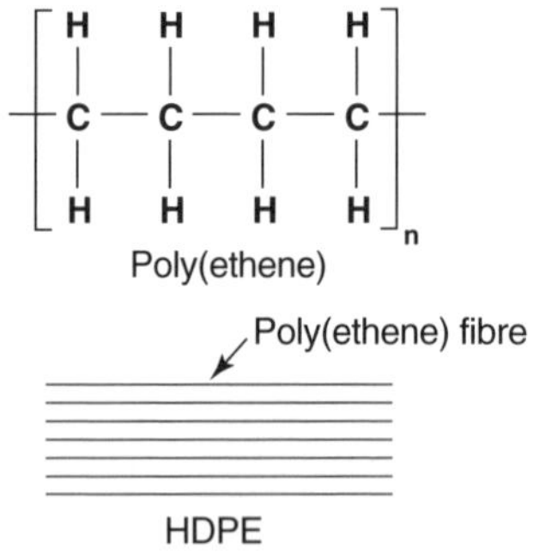

HIGHER LEVEL

In 1953, a German chemist, **Ziegler**, found catalysts (metal-organics) for the polymerisation reaction, so that the reaction could be done at lower pressures. He also found that the chains had few branches, and so they could pack together more closely, forming high-density poly(ethene) – HDPE (see Figure 14.7). Compared with the LDPE, it is heavier, **harder and less flexible**, and has a **higher melting point**. It is therefore suitable for making bowls, buckets and baskets.

Figure 14.7   High-density poly(ethene).

Poly(ethene)

Poly(ethene) fibre

HDPE

Poly(chloroethene)

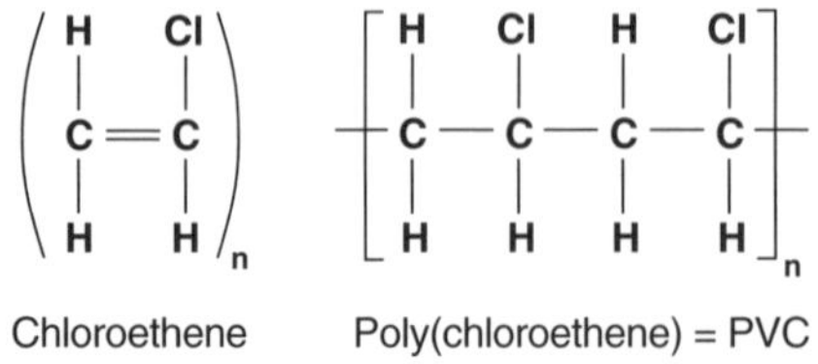

The traditional name for this is **polyvinyl chloride** (**PVC**) (see Figure 14.8). It is a rigid plastic that is used to make window frames, gutters, etc. When plasticers are added, it becomes more flexible and it is used to make rain coats, floor tiles, cable insulation, hoses, handbags, for example.

Figure 14.8   Chloroethene and poly-(chloroethene).

Chloroethene   Poly(chloroethene) = PVC

Poly(phenylethene)

This is traditionally known as **poly-styrene** (see Figure 14.9). It is another rigid plastic that is used to make yoghurt cartons, biros, disposable cups, etc. Expanded polystyrene is made by adding an inert gas (formerly a CFC, but nowadays hexane) to the melted polymer. It is very light and it is used for insulation between walls of houses, egg boxes, food trays, packaging, and so on.

Figure 14.9   Phenylethene and poly(phenylethene).

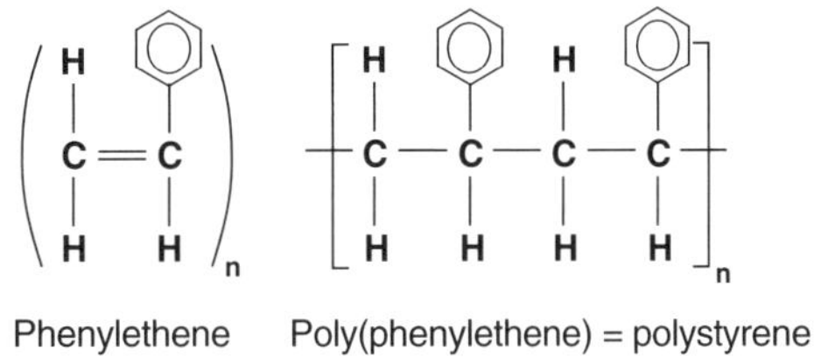

Phenylethene   Poly(phenylethene) = polystyrene

HIGHER LEVEL

Poly(propene)

This is known as **polypropelene** (see Figure 14.10). Its molecules pack closely together, similar to HDPE, making it strong and flexible, and it is used to make bowls, buckets, beakers, chairs etc. Its fibres are used to make rope.

Figure 14.10   Propene and poly(propene).

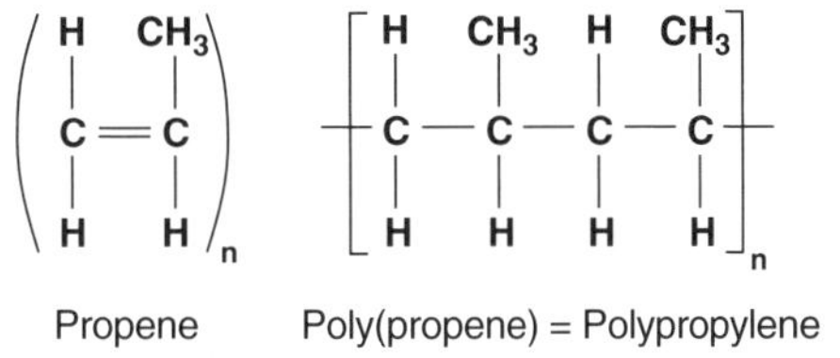

Propene   Poly(propene) = Polypropylene

Poly(tetrafluoroethene)

The traditional name for this is **Teflon** (see Figure 14.11). This polymer was discovered in 1938 when an American chemist, Roy Plunkett, pressurised tetrafluoroethene in a search for a refrigerant. He found a white slippery solid that was inert to acids and bases and was insoluble. These properties make it useful as a non-stick coating on pans, as plumbers tape, and for organ implants. When it has been spun into fibres it forms 'Gore-Tex'.

Figure 14.11   Tetrafluoroethene and poly(tetrafluoroethene).

Tetrafluoroethene   Poly(tetrafluoroethene) = teflon

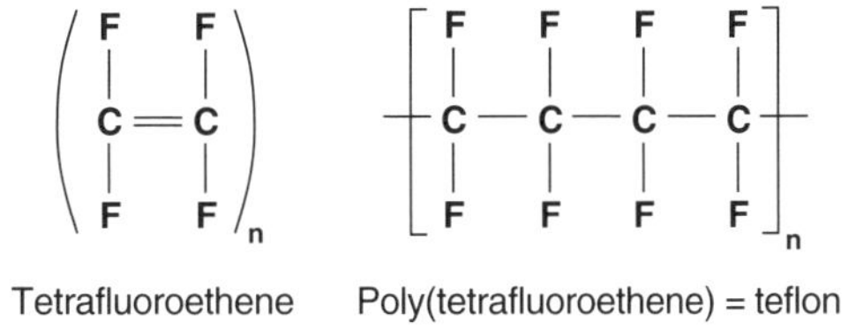

Advantages of polymers

Polymers are used as plastics and as fibres.

A **plastic material** is one that can be forced to take up a **different shape** and hold the new shape (an elastic material reverts to its original shape when the force is removed).

Polymers are used to make a large variety of plastic objects by melting them and either **injecting them** into a mould in the shape of a basin or bucket, etc., or by **extruding them through a die** to make sheets, from which bags are made.

Fibres are also made by extruding the melted polymer through fine nozzles to form threads. The fibres can later be woven to make **fabrics**.

Polymers as materials have the advantage of being:

- good insulators of electricity and heat
- inert to acids and alkalis
- non-biodegradable
- recyclable.

Recycling of plastics

To facilitate the sorting of plastics, each is given a recycling number; for example, polystyrene is 6. This allows them to be kept pure. The plastic objects are then shredded, washed and dried. The material can then be sent to a factory that makes plastic objects. There it is heated to melt it and then injected into a mould or extruded through a die.

Metals

The properties of metals

Compared with non-metals, metals have the following properties:

- lustre
- malleability
- ductility
- electricity and heat conduction.

Alloys

An alloy is a mixture of metals, or of a metal and a non-metal. An alloy can combine the useful properties of different metals. Common alloys include **brass** (copper and zinc), and **steel** (iron and carbon).

In steel the carbon atoms are mixed among the iron atoms and this stops the iron atoms from easily sliding when a force is applied. Thus, steel is harder than pure iron. The percentage of carbon in steels is varied, according to the use each one is to serve. As the amount of carbon is increased the steel becomes harder but more brittle.

14.2   OPTION 2B: ELECTROCHEMISTRY

The electrochemical series

Metal atoms react by donating electrons. The more reactive metals donate electrons more readily.

A **simple cell consists of two different metals immersed in a solution of ions** (salt or acid or alkali). It sends a current of electrons from the more active metal to the other metal, where the electrons reduce the ions of the solution (see Figure 14.12).

The **voltage of the cell depends on the difference in activity of the two metals** – a large voltage results when there is large difference in the activity of the metals.

The **standard electrode potential** of each metal is measured when the other electrode is a **hydrogen electrode** (hydrogen gas bubbling over a platinum electrode at s.t.p. and in a solution of $1M$ H^+). The higher the voltage the more active the metal is.

The **electrochemical series** is a series of metals with the most active metal first, based on their standard electrode potentials:

- potassium
- sodium
- calcium
- magnesium
- aluminium
- zinc
- iron
- lead
- hydrogen
- copper
- silver
- gold.

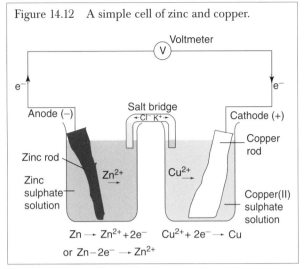

Figure 14.12 A simple cell of zinc and copper.

$$Zn \longrightarrow Zn^{2+} + 2e^-$$

$$Cu^{2+} + 2e^- \longrightarrow Cu$$

$$\text{or } Zn - 2e^- \longrightarrow Zn^{2+}$$

Major discoveries in electrochemistry

Galvani (in 1791) was the first to note a muscular reaction in dissected frogs' legs when they were in contact with two different metals.

Three years later **Volta** produced the explanation: the muscles of the legs had reacted to the electric current that the metals had produced. Volta produced cells and batteries (combinations of cells) by separating copper and zinc plates with salt solutions.

Using batteries **Humphry Davy** (in the early 1800s) passed electric current into molten salts and electrolysed them. He discovered new elements, including sodium, potassium, calcium, magnesium, barium, and strontium.

Michael Faraday worked for Davy. He discovered the electric motor and generator. He furthered the understanding of electrolysis and discovered two laws of electrolysis (Faraday's laws) that relate the amount of a substance that is produced by electrolysis to the amount of current that is used.

Electrolysis of molten salts

If a positive and a negative electrode are held in a melted salt, its ions separate and are attracted to the electrode of opposite charge. Reduction and oxidation take place at the electrodes – at the cathode **reduction** of the cations takes place. At the **a**node **o**xidation of the anions takes place. (Remember the mnemonic CRAO from Chapter 2?)

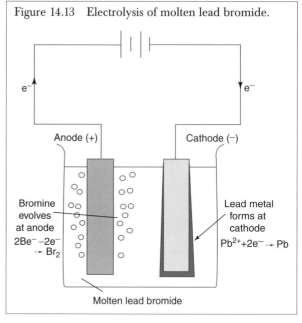

Figure 14.13   Electrolysis of molten lead bromide.

Example

In the electrolysis of molten lead bromide, lead is formed at the cathode and at the anode bromine is formed (see Figure 14.13).

HIGHER LEVEL

At the cathode:

$$Pb^{2+} + 2e^- \rightarrow Pb(s)$$

At the anode:

$$2Br^- - 2e^- \rightarrow Br_2(g)$$

Corrosion

Metals corrode by reacting with their environment, principally with oxygen gas and with water, to form **oxides** and **hydroxides**.

- The metals higher on the electrochemical series corrode faster and more readily.
- Gold, at the bottom of the series, is very resistant to corrosion.
- Iron corrodes rapidly in damp air, though the addition of about 20% chromium converts steel to stainless steel.

Corrosion is an electrochemical reaction. For example, in the corrosion of iron the following reactions occur.

- anode reaction:

$$Fe - 2e^- \rightarrow Fe^{2+}$$

- cathode reaction:

$$\tfrac{1}{2}O_2 + H_2O + 2e^- \rightarrow 2OH^-$$

Overall, the iron reacts with oxygen and water to form $Fe(OH)_2$

Corrosion prevention

Apply a **protective layer** over the metal to prevent it coming in contact with the air. Protective coats include paints, oils, phosphates and zinc (galvanising).

HIGHER LEVEL

- Attach a **sacrificial anode** to the metal that needs protecting. The sacrificial anode is a more reactive metal, and the environment reacts with it instead. Magnesium and zinc are more active than iron so they protect iron objects when they are in contact with it. (The sacrificial anode does not need to cover all of the metal.)
- Aluminium and chromium are resistant to corrosion because they form **a very thin impenetrable layer of oxide** that protects the underlying metal.

Extraction of metals by electrochemical methods

Sodium and aluminium are examples of metals that are extracted from their ores by electrochemical means.

Uses

- Sodium is used in orange street lamps and as a coolant in nuclear reactors.
- Aluminium is used in drinks cans, in window frames and doors, in aircraft, etc.

HIGHER LEVEL

Extraction of sodium

The **Down's cell** (see Figure 14.14) consists of a **graphite anode** surmounted by a hood to remove chlorine gas (a useful by-product), and a **circular steel cathode**, behind a protective gauze. Molten sodium chloride, to which calcium chloride is added to reduce the melting point enters and a large current is passed through the cell.

- at the anode (oxidation):

  $$Cl^- - e^- \rightarrow \tfrac{1}{2}Cl_2$$

- at the cathode (reduction)

  $$Na^+ + e^- \rightarrow Na$$

Extraction of aluminium

Aluminium is produced in two stages:

- Aluminium oxide (alumina) is extracted from **bauxite**.
- Aluminium oxide undergoes **electrolysis** in a country with cheap supplies of electricity (mainly hydroelectricity).

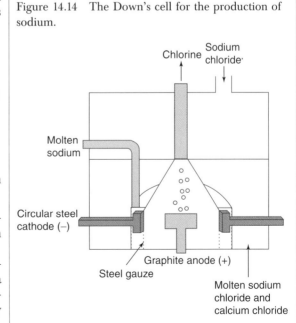

Figure 14.14 The Down's cell for the production of sodium.

The production of aluminium oxide (alumina) from bauxite

One of the world's largest plants is in Aughinish, Co. Limerick. Ships bring in the bauxite from tropical countries, such as Jamaica and Guinea, and the purified alumina is shipped to Canada, or Norway, for example, which have cheap electricity.

What happens in the extraction process?

1. The bauxite is **crushed** and added to a hot solution of **sodium hydroxide**, where the aluminium oxide dissolves by reacting with it, but the impurities (mainly iron oxide) do not.

$$Al_2O_3 + 2NaOH \rightarrow 2NaAlO_2 + H_2O$$

2. The impurities are **filtered out** and stored on the site (red mud).
3. The solution of sodium aluminate is cooled and **seeded** with pure crystals of alumina to precipitate it out.

$$2NaAlO_2 + H_2O \rightarrow Al_2O_3 + 2NaOH$$

4. The alumina is **heated** to dry it and remove its water of crystallisation.

The production of aluminium from alumina

In an aluminium smelter the alumina is heated with **cryolite**, which lowers its melting point, and the melt is passed into steel containers that are **lined with graphite as the cathode**. **Graphite anodes** are lowered into the melt and a large current is passed through (see Figure 14.15).

What happens?

- at the cathode (reduction):

$$Al^{3+} + 3e^- \rightarrow Al$$

- at the anode (oxidation):

$$O^{2-} - 2e^- \rightarrow \frac{1}{2}O_2$$

The aluminium metal sinks to the bottom of the cell and is tapped off. The oxygen slowly burns away the anode, which must be periodically replaced.

Figure 14.15   Extraction of aluminium by electrolysis.

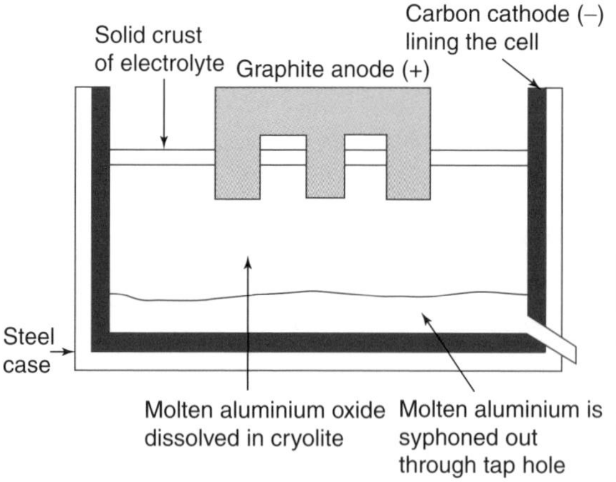

Carbon cathode (–) lining the cell

Solid crust of electrolyte   Graphite anode (+)

Steel case

Molten aluminium oxide dissolved in cryolite

Molten aluminium is syphoned out through tap hole

Anodising aluminium

The aluminium is coated with a **thicker layer of aluminium oxide to protect it from the environment**. It may also be **coloured**, for example, brown. This is because the oxide layer formed in the anodising process is porous.

The aluminium is made the anode of a simple cell by connecting it to the negative electrode of the power supply. The cathode is also aluminium and the **electrolyte is dilute H_2SO_4** (see Figure 14.16).

What happens?

- at the anode:

  $$2Al + 3H_2O - 6e^- \rightarrow Al_2O_3 + 6H^+$$

- at the cathode:

  $$6H^+ + 6e^- \rightarrow 3H_2$$

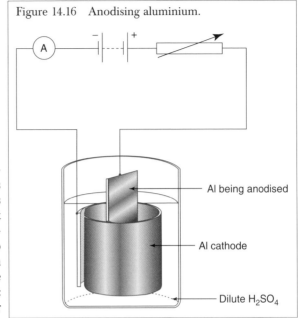

Figure 14.16   Anodising aluminium.

Al being anodised

Al cathode

Dilute H_2SO_4

Recycling aluminium

The energy consumed in producing aluminium from its ore is so expensive that it is economically more efficient to recycle it. One of the common uses of aluminium is to make drinks cans. These can be easily separated from the commercial and domestic waste streams and sent for melting and reuse.

The d-block metals

What are the transition metals?

The transition metals are the **d-block elements, except for the first (Sc) and last (Zn) in each row**. They include copper, iron, chromium, etc.

   They have the following properties in common:

- They have variable valency.
- They have coloured compounds.
- They are catalysts.

Manufacture of iron

Iron is extracted from its ores in a blast furnace. The raw materials are:

- iron ore, mainly **haematite**, iron(III) oxide, Fe_2O_3
- coke, a form of carbon
- limestone, $CaCO_3$.

Hot air is blasted through it to burn the coke and to form carbon monoxide (see Figure 14.17).

   The reactions that take place are:

1. The **coke burns** to heat the furnace to melt the iron and it makes carbon monoxide:

   $$C + O_2 \rightarrow CO_2$$

   $$C + \tfrac{1}{2}O_2 \rightarrow CO$$

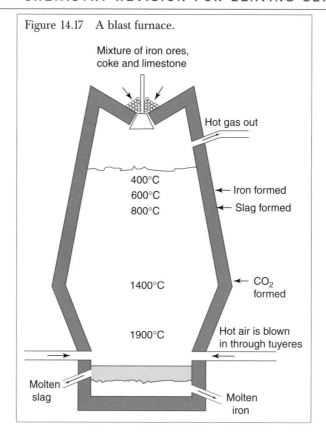

Figure 14.17   A blast furnace.

2. The **coke reduces the iron oxide**:

$$3C + Fe_2O_3 \rightarrow 2Fe + 3CO$$

3. The **carbon monoxide also reduces the iron oxide**:

$$3CO + Fe_2O_3 \rightarrow 2Fe + 3CO_2$$

4. The limestone decomposes to lime, which **reacts with impurities** in the ore, mainly silica SiO_2 to form a **slag**, which floats on the liquid iron and is removed:

$$CaCO_3 \rightarrow CaO + CO_2$$

$$CaO + SiO_2 \rightarrow CaSiO_3$$

The manufacture of steel

The iron from the blast furnace is called **pig iron** or **cast iron**. It is brittle but it is used to make manhole covers, car engines, etc. Cast iron contains about 4% carbon and other impurities.

Pig iron is changed to steel by:

- removing the impurities
- adjusting the amount of carbon.

There are many different kinds of steel, depending on the % carbon and on the presence of other metals. Most steels have less than 1.7% carbon. **Stainless steel** has about **20% chromium**. It is used to make domestic appliances such as cutlery, as well as chemical reactors that are resistant to acids.

Manganese and **tungsten harden** the steel.

There are thousands of everyday objects that are made of steel, from anchors to needles.

The electric arc method of manufacturing steel

Pig iron, scrap iron and **lime** CaO are added to the furnace. They are melted with an electric arc. **Oxygen** is blown through to oxidise the impurities to gases that are removed. The lime removes other impurities. Other metals are added according to the type of steel that is required. The main stages and the reactions in the process are as follows.

1. **Charging the furnace**. The iron, scrap iron and lime are added from the top.
2. **Melting**. A large current is passed through carbon electrodes to melt the charge.
3. **Refining**. Oxygen is blown through the melted charge. It oxidises carbon to CO_2, silicon to SiO_2, (and phosphorus to P_4O_{10}). The lime reacts with the SiO_2 (and P_4O_{10}) to form slag, which floats on top and is removed later on.

$$Si + O_2 \rightarrow SiO_2$$

$$CaO + SiO_2 \rightarrow CaSiO_3$$

   The steel is sampled and the process is continued until the desired composition for the steel is achieved.
4. **Tapping**. The furnace is tilted to remove the slag. The steel is poured into a ladle and other metals are added as required.
5. **Casting**. The liquid steel is poured on to a caster where it is cooled in a mould, using water. It is rolled and cut into the required lengths.

Environmental aspects of iron and steel production

Formerly, steel production caused a lot of air pollution, especially from the release of SO_2. This can be removed from chimneys through scrubbing with lime. Dust is also removed before the gases are released.

The slag was formerly dumped, but it is now used in road-building and to make insulating material.

Steel-making uses water for cooling. The used water is cleaned and reused, rather than discharging it into a polluted river.

Quarrying used to leave the landscape spoiled. Quarries must now reduce dust and noise pollution and landscape the quarry when it is finished.

TEST YOURSELF

1. (a) What are the properties of a crystalline substance?
   (b) Outline the contributions of William and Lawrence Bragg to the understanding of crystal structure.
   (c) What kind of substances did Dorothy Hodgkin investigate for crystal structure?
   (d) What is buckminsterfullerene?
2. Give an example of an ionic crystal. Describe three physical properties of ionic crystals.
3. Molecular crystals can have three kinds of intermolecular forces:
   (a) van der Waals
   (b) dipole–dipole
   (c) hydrogen bonds.
   Give an example of each kind of molecular crystal and describe two of its physical properties.
4. Describe the internal structure of a metallic crystal.
5. (a) Give two examples of substances with macromolecular crystals and describe their internal structure.
   (b) Compare their properties.
6. (a) Define:
      (i) monomer
      (ii) polymer.
   (b) What is the nature of the bonding in monomers that polymerise by addition reactions?
   (c) Draw the molecular structure in two repeating units of these polymers:
      (i) poly(ethene)
      (ii) poly(chloroethene)
      (iii) poly(phenylethene).
   *(d) Draw the molecular structure of:
      (i) poly(tetrafluoroethene)
      (ii) poly(propene).
7. Describe the useful properties and outline the uses for these polymers:
   (a) (i) poly(ethene)
      (ii) poly(chloroethene)
      (iii) poly(phenylethene).
   *(b) (i) poly(tetrafluoroethene).
      (ii) poly(propene).
*8. (a) Compare the structure and properties of high-density and low-density poly(ethene).
   (b) Outline the conditions that make HDPE and name the chemist who discovered the process.
9. (a) What is a plastic material?
   (b) Outline how plastic polymers are used to make objects such as bowls.
   (c) Outline how fibres are made of polymers.
   (d) What are three advantages of using polymers as materials?
   (e) What happens to plastics that are recycled?

10. (a) List four properties of metals as materials.
    (b) What is an alloy?
    (c) Steel is an alloy of iron. Describe how the composition of steel affects its properties.
11. (a) Make a diagram of a simple cell.
    (b) Outline how standard electrode potential of a metal is measured.
    (c) Describe the electrochemical series of metals.
12. Name these scientists:
    (a) He developed laws that relate the amount of an element produced during electrolysis to the amount of current.
    (b) He discovered muscles could contract when metals were in contact with them.
    (c) He discovered new elements by electrolysis of molten salts.
    (d) He produced the first electric cells.
14. (a) Outline what happens in the electrolysis of molten lead bromide.
    *(b) Explain with equations the reactions that take place in the electrolysis of molten lead bromide.
15. (a) Define 'corrosion'. Explain why metals corrode at the anode.
    (b) Outline two methods that prevent corrosion by use of protective layers.
    *(c) Explain, with an example, how a sacrificial anode prevents corrosion.
    *(d) Explain why aluminium and chromium do not normally corrode.
16. (a) Name two metals that are extracted from their ores by electrochemical means and state two uses for each metal.
    *(b) Make a labelled diagram of a Down's cell and outline what happens.
*17. (a) Outline how alumina is extracted from an aluminium ore.
    (b) Describe the production of aluminium from alumina.
    (c) Describe the process of anodising aluminium. State two reasons for anodising aluminium.
18. (a) What are transition metals?
    (b) What are the characteristic properties of transition metals?
19. (a) Name an iron ore.
    (b) (i) Name two other substances that are used in iron smelting and state their functions.
        (ii) Describe the process of reducing the iron ore to iron.
    (c) Describe the process of making steel.

State Examinations Commission

LEAVING CERTIFICATE EXAMINATION, 2007

CHEMISTRY – HIGHER LEVEL

TUESDAY, 19 JUNE - AFTERNOON 2.00 to 5.00

---

400 MARKS

Answer **eight** questions in all

These **must** include at least **two** questions from **Section A**

All questions carry equal marks (50)

Information

Relative atomic masses: H = 1, He = 4, C = 12, O = 16, Na = 23, S = 32,
Cr = 52, Fe = 56,

Avogadro constant = 6×10^{23} mol^{-1}

Universal gas constant, $R = 8.3$ J K^{-1} mol^{-1}

Section A

Answer at least <u>two</u> questions from this section [see page 1 for full instructions].

1. A solution of sodium thiosulfate was prepared by weighing out a certain mass of crystalline sodium thiosulfate ($Na_2S_2O_3.5H_2O$) on a clock glass, dissolving it in deionised water and making the solution up carefully to 500 cm^3 in a volumetric flask. A burette was filled with this solution and it was then titrated against 25.0 cm^3 portions of previously standardised 0.05 M iodine solution in a conical flask. The average titre was 20.0 cm^3.

   The equation for the titration reaction is

   $$2S_2O_3^{2-} \; + \; I_2 \; \rightarrow \; 2I^- \; + \; S_4O_6^{2-}$$

   (a) Sodium thiosulfate is not a <u>primary standard</u>. Explain fully the underlined term. (8)

   (b) Describe how the crystalline thiosulfate was dissolved, and how the solution was transferred to the volumetric flask and made up to exactly 500 cm^3. (15)

   (c) Pure iodine is almost completely insoluble in water. What must be added to bring iodine into aqueous solution? (3)

   (d) A few drops of freshly prepared starch solution were added near the end point as the indicator for this titration. What sequence of colours was observed in the conical flask from the start of the titration until the end point was reached? (12)

   (e) Calculate the molarity of the sodium thiosulfate solution and its concentration in grams of crystalline sodium thiosulfate ($Na_2S_2O_3.5H_2O$) per litre. (12)

   _____

2. A sample of ethanoic acid (CH_3COOH) was prepared by the oxidation of ethanol using the apparatus shown. The reaction is exothermic and is represented by the following equation:

   $$3C_2H_5OH + Cr_2O_7^{2-} + 16H^+ \rightarrow 3CH_3COOH + 4Cr^{3+} + 11H_2O$$

   (a) Before heating the reaction flask, the ethanol and water were added from the tap funnel.
   State **two** precautions which should be taken when carrying out this addition in order to avoid excessive heat production. (8)

   (b) Describe and explain the colour change observed in the reaction flask as the ethanol was oxidised. (9)

(c) What was the purpose of heating the reaction mixture under reflux after the addition from the tap funnel was complete? (6)

(d) Show clearly that the ethanol was the limiting reagent when 8.0 cm^3 of ethanol (density 0.80 g cm^{-3}) was added to 29.8 g of sodium dichromate, $Na_2Cr_2O_7.2H_2O$. There was excess sulfuric acid present. (12)

(e) Describe how the ethanoic acid product was isolated from the reaction mixture. (6)

(f) Describe your observations when a small quantity of solid sodium carbonate was added to a sample of the ethanoic acid produced. Write a balanced chemical equation for the reaction which occurred. (9)

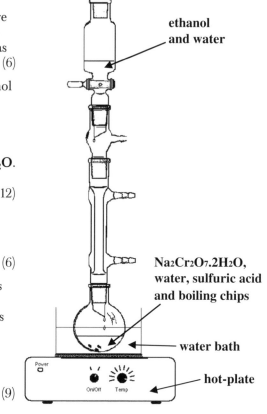

ethanol and water

$Na_2Cr_2O_7.2H_2O$, water, sulfuric acid and boiling chips

water bath

hot-plate

3. In an experiment to measure the heat of reaction for the reaction between sodium hydroxide with hydrochloric acid, a student added 50 cm^3 of 1.0 M **HCl** solution to the same volume of 1.0 M **NaOH** solution in a polystyrene foam cup.

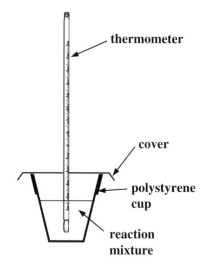

thermometer

cover

polystyrene cup

reaction mixture

(a) To achieve an appreciable temperature rise during the reaction, quite concentrated solutions of acid and base, carrying the label illustrated, were used. What word describes the chemical hazard illustrated in this label? State **one** precaution the student should take when using these solutions. (8)

(b) The student had a choice of using either a graduated cylinder or a burette to measure out the solutions used in this experiment. Which piece of apparatus should have been used to achieve the more accurate result? (3)

(c) If the hydrochloric acid and sodium hydroxide solutions had been stored at slightly different temperatures, explain how the initial temperature of the reaction mixture could have been obtained. (6)

(d) List **three** precautions which should have been taken in order to obtain an accurate value for the highest temperature reached by the reaction mixture. (9)

(e) What was the advantage of mixing the solutions in a polystyrene foam cup rather than in a glass beaker or in a metal calorimeter? (3)

(f) Calculate the number of moles of acid neutralised in this experiment. Taking the total heat capacity of the reaction mixture used in this experiment as $420\,J\,K^{-1}$, calculate the heat released in the experiment if a temperature rise of 6.7 °C was recorded. Hence calculate the heat of reaction for

$$NaOH\ +\ HCl\quad \rightarrow \quad NaCl\ +\ H_2O \qquad (18)$$

(g) Name the piece of apparatus used in industry to accurately measure the heats of combustion of foods and fuels. (3)

Section B

[See page 1 for instructions regarding the number of questions to be answered].

4.   Answer **eight** of the following items (a), (b), (c), etc. (50)

(a) Define *atomic (covalent) radius.*

(b) What is the principal use made of oxygenates such as methyl *tert*-butyl ether, MTBE, in the petrochemicals industry?

(c) Distinguish between sigma (σ) and pi (π) covalent bonding.

(d) What is meant by *heterogeneous* catalysis?

(e) How many iron atoms should be consumed daily to meet the recommended daily intake of iron in the diet of 0.014 g?

(*f*) Name the two reagents used in the brown ring test for the nitrate ion.

(*g*) Name and draw the structure of a carboxylic acid that is widely used as a food preservative.

(*h*) A 500 cm^3 can of beer contains 21.5 cm^3 of ethanol. Calculate its % alcohol, i.e. the concentration of alcohol in the beer as a % (v/v).

(*i*) Explain in terms of bonding why it is more correct to represent the benzene molecule as

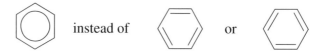

(*j*) Ultraviolet absorption spectroscopy can be used in the quantitative analysis of some organic compounds (e.g. drug metabolites and plant pigments). What is the underlying principle of this analytical technique?

(*k*) Answer part **A** <u>or</u> **B**.

A   The use of CFCs as refrigerant gases has been discontinued. Name a group of substances used to replace CFCs as refrigerant gases.

or

B   Name the electrochemist who was the first to isolate the elements sodium and potassium in 1807 by passing electricity through sodium hydroxide and potassium hydroxide, respectively.

---

5. (*a*) Define *energy level*.   (5)

Write the electron configuration (*s*, *p*) for the sulfur atom in its ground state, showing the arrangement in atomic orbitals of the highest energy electrons.   (6)

State how many (*i*) energy levels, (*ii*) orbitals, are occupied in a sulfur atom in its ground state.   (6)

(*b*) Use electronegativity values (Mathematical Tables p 46) to predict the type of bond expected between hydrogen and sulfur.

Write the chemical formula for hydrogen sulfide.

Use clear dot and cross diagrams to show the bonding in hydrogen sulfide.   (15)

Would you expect the hydrogen sulfide molecule to be *linear* or *non-linear* in shape? Justify your answer.   (6)

(c) Hydrogen sulfide has a boiling point of 212.3 K and water has a boiling point of 373 K.

Account for the difference in the boiling points of these substances.   (6)

Would you expect hydrogen sulfide to be soluble in water?
Explain your answer.   (6)

_____

6. Useful hydrocarbons are obtained by the fractional distillation of crude oil, which itself has little or no direct use. Hydrocarbons are excellent fuels.

(a) In which fraction of crude oil do pentane and its isomers occur?   (5)

Give the systematic (IUPAC) name of each of the structural isomers of pentane shown below.   (9)

Which of these isomers would you predict to have the lowest octane number?

Justify your choice in terms of the structural features of the molecules.   (9)

Write a balanced equation for the combustion of pentane (C_5H_{12}) in excess oxygen.   (6)

(b) Naphtha and gas oil are two of the hydrocarbon fractions obtained from the fractional distillation of crude oil. How do the molecules of the naphtha fraction differ from the molecules of the gas oil fraction?   (3)

Explain with the aid of a labelled diagram how naphtha (b.p. approximately 100 °C) is separated from gas oil (b.p. approximately 300 °C) in the fractional distillation of crude oil.   (9)

Bitumen is a residue fraction obtained from crude oil. Give **one** use for bitumen.   (3)

(c) What is catalytic cracking? What is its economic importance in oil refining?   (6)

_____

7. (*a*) Define (*i*) *acid*, (*ii*) *conjugate pair*, according to the Brønsted-Lowry
theory.   (8)

Identify the two conjugate pairs in the following dissociation of nitrous
acid (HNO_2):

$$HNO_2 \quad + \quad H_2O \quad \rightleftharpoons \quad NO_2^- \quad + \quad H_3O^+ \qquad (6)$$

Distinguish between a strong acid and a weak acid.   (6)

(*b*) Calculate the pH of 0.1 M nitrous acid (HNO_2); the value of the acid
dissociation constant (K_a) for nitrous acid is 5.0×10^{-4}.

What is the pH of a nitric acid (HNO_3) solution of the same
concentration?   (15)

(*c*) *Eutrophication* in water may result from the addition of large quantities of
nitrate fertilizers to it.

Describe the processes occurring in the water leading to eutrophication. (9)

(*d*) Explain how heavy metal ions are removed from large quantities of
water.   (6)

————————

8.   Study the reaction scheme and answer the questions which follow.

$$C_2H_4 \quad \underset{\longleftarrow}{\overset{\longrightarrow}{}} \quad C_2H_5OH \quad \underset{\longleftarrow}{\overset{\longrightarrow}{}} \quad CH_3CHO$$

A   B   C

(*a*) Name the homologous series (*i*) to which **A** belongs, (*ii*) to which
C belongs.   (8)

(*b*) The conversion of **B** to **A** is an elimination reaction. What two
features of elimination reactions are illustrated by this conversion?   (6)

(*c*) Name the reagent and the catalyst required to convert **C** to **B**.   (6)

(*d*) Draw full structural formulas for **B** and **C**. Indicate any carbon
atom in either structure that has planar geometry. List the bonds
broken in **B** and the bond made in **C** in the synthesis of **C** from **B**.   (18)

(*e*) After carrying out a laboratory conversion of **B** to **C**, how could you
test the product to confirm the formation of **C**?   (9)

(*f*) Compound **C** is formed as a metabolite of compound **B** in the human
body. How does compound B come to be present in the body?   (3)

————————

9. (*a*) Define the *rate of a chemical reaction.*

Why does the rate of chemical reactions generally decrease with time? (8)

(*b*) The rate of reaction between an excess of marble chips ($CaCO_3$) (diameter 11 – 15 mm) and 50 cm^3 of 2.0 M hydrochloric acid was monitored by measuring the mass of carbon dioxide produced.

The table shows the total mass of carbon dioxide gas produced at stated intervals over 9 minutes.

Time/minutes	0.0	1.0	2.0	3.0	4.0	5.5	7.0	8.0	9.0
Mass of CO_2/g	0.00	0.66	1.20	1.60	1.90	2.10	2.18	2.20	2.20

Plot a graph of the mass of carbon dioxide produced *versus* time. (12)

Use the graph to determine
(*i*) the instantaneous rate of reaction in grams per minute at 4.0 minutes,
(*ii*) the instantaneous rate of reaction at this time in moles per minute. (9)

(*c*) Describe and explain the effect on the rate of reaction of repeating the experiment using 50 cm^3 of 1.0 M hydrochloric acid and the same mass of the same size marble chips. (6)

(*d*) Particle size has a critical effect on the rate of a chemical reaction.

(*i*) Mark clearly on your graph the approximate curve you would expect to plot if the experiment were repeated using 50 cm^3 of 2.0 M HCl and using the same mass of marble chips but this time with a diameter range of 1 – 5 mm. (6)

(*ii*) Dust explosions present a risk in industry. Give **three** conditions necessary for a dust explosion to occur. (9)

---

10. Answer any **two** of the parts (*a*), (*b*) and (*c*). (2 × 25)

(*a*) (*i*) Write the equilibrium constant (K_c) expression for the reaction (7)

$$N_{2(g)} \quad + \quad 3H_{2(g)} \quad \rightleftharpoons \quad 2NH_{3(g)}$$

(*ii*) Three moles of nitrogen gas and nine moles of hydrogen gas were mixed in a 1 litre vessel at a temperature *T*. There were two moles of ammonia in the vessel at equilibrium. Calculate the value of K_c for this reaction at this temperature. (12)

(*iii*) Henri Le Chatelier studied equilibrium reactions in industry in the late 19th century. According to Le Chatelier's principle, what effect would an increase in pressure have on the yield of ammonia at equilibrium? Explain. (6)

(b) (i)   State *Avogadro's law*.   (7)

(ii) Carbon dioxide is stored under pressure in liquid form in a fire
      extinguisher. Two kilograms of carbon dioxide are released
      into the air as a gas on the discharge of the fire extinguisher.
      What volume does this gas occupy at a pressure of 1.01×10^5 Pa
      and a temperature of 290 K?   (9)

      What mass of helium gas would occupy the same volume at the
      same temperature and pressure?   (6)

(iii) Give **one** reason why carbon dioxide is more easily liquefied
      than helium.   (3)

(c) The halogens are good oxidising agents.

(i)   How does the oxidation number of the oxidising agent change
      during a redox reaction?   (4)

(ii) Assign oxidation numbers in each of the following equations
      to show clearly that the halogen is the oxidising agent in
      each case.   (12)

$$\mathbf{Br_2} \quad + \quad \mathbf{2Fe^{2+}} \quad \rightarrow \quad \mathbf{2Br^-} \quad + \quad \mathbf{2Fe^{3+}}$$

$$\mathbf{Cl_2} \quad + \quad \mathbf{SO_3^{2-}} \quad + \quad \mathbf{H_2O} \quad \rightarrow \quad \mathbf{Cl^-} \quad + \quad \mathbf{SO_4^{2-}} \quad + \quad \mathbf{H^+}$$

      Hence or otherwise balance the second equation.   (6)

(iii) Why does the oxidising ability of the halogens decrease down
      the group?   (3)

———————

11. Answer any **two** of the parts (*a*), (*b*) and (*c*).   (2 × 25)

(a) In 1910 Rutherford and his co-workers carried out an experiment in
     which thin sheets of gold foil were bombarded with alpha particles.
     The observations made during the experiment led to the discovery of
     the atomic nucleus.

(i)   Describe the model of atomic structure which existed immediately
      prior to this experiment.   (7)

(ii) In this experiment it was observed that most of the alpha particles
      went straight through the gold foil. Two other observations were
      made. State these other observations and explain how each helped
      Rutherford deduce that the atom has a nucleus.   (12)

In November 2006 former Soviet agent, Alexander Litvinenko, died in
London. The cause of his death was identified as radiation poisoning by
polonium-210.

(*iii*) Polonium-210 decays emitting an alpha particle.

Copy and complete the equation for the alpha-decay of polonium-210, filling in the values of *x* (atomic number), *y* (mass number) and **Z** (elemental symbol). (6)

$$\underset{84}{\overset{210}{}}\text{Po} \quad \rightarrow \quad \underset{x}{\overset{y}{}}\text{Z} \quad + \quad \underset{2}{\overset{4}{}}\text{He}$$

(*b*) An equimolar mixture of chlorine and methane react together at room temperature only when ultraviolet light is present.

(*i*) Explain clearly the role of the ultraviolet light in the reaction between chlorine and methane. (7)

(*ii*) Name the two main products of the reaction between chlorine and methane. (6)

(*iii*) Account for traces of ethane found in the product mixture. (6)

Chlorine reacts with ethene at room temperature even in the dark.

(*iv*) Name the type of mechanism which occurs in the reaction between chlorine and ethene. (3)

(*v*) Give a use for chloroalkanes. (3)

(*c*) Answer either part **A** *or* part **B**.

A

Environmentalists are concerned about the increasing abundance of carbon dioxide in the atmosphere.

(*i*) State one important way carbon dioxide is constantly added to the atmosphere. (4)

(*ii*) Carbon dioxide is a greenhouse gas. It has been assigned a greenhouse factor of 1.

What use is made of the *"greenhouse factor"* of a gas? (6)

(*iii*) Name **two** other greenhouse gases. (6)

(*iv*) Carbon dioxide is removed from the atmosphere when it dissolves in rainwater, seas, lakes, etc.

What **three** chemical species arise in water as a result of carbon dioxide gas dissolving in it? (9)

or

B

Aluminium, sodium chloride and graphite are all crystalline solids.

For each of these substances, name the type of crystal formed. (7)

Explain clearly, in terms of bonding, why

(*i*)   aluminium is a good conductor of electricity,

(*ii*)   sodium chloride is soluble in water,

(*iii*) graphite is soft and slippery.   (18)

———————

State Examinations Commission

LEAVING CERTIFICATE EXAMINATIONS, 2007

CHEMISTRY – HIGHER LEVEL

MARKING SCHEME

Introduction

In considering the marking scheme the following should be noted.

1. In many cases only key phrases are given which contain the information and ideas that must appear in the candidate's answer in order to merit the assigned marks.

2. The descriptions, methods and definitions in the scheme are not exhaustive and alternative valid answers are acceptable.

3. The detail required in any answer is determined by the context and the manner in which the question is asked, and by the number of marks assigned to the answer in the examination paper and, in any instance, therefore, may vary from year to year.

4. The bold text indicates the essential points required in the candidate's answer. A double solidus (//) separates points for which separate marks are allocated in a part of the question. Words, expressions or statements separated by a solidus (/) are alternatives which are equally acceptable for a particular point. A word or phrase in bold, given in brackets, is an acceptable alternative to the preceding word or phrase. Note, however, that words, expressions or phrases must be correctly used in context and not contradicted, and where there is evidence of incorrect use or contradiction, the marks may not be awarded.

5. In general, names and formulas of elements and compounds are equally acceptable except in cases where either the name or the formula is specifically asked for in the question. However, in some cases where the name is asked for, the formula may be accepted as an alternative.

6. Partial marks for incorrectly completed, or uncompleted, calculations may only be awarded where the significance of the numbers used is clearly indicated in the candidate's work. There is a deduction of one mark for each arithmetical slip made by a candidate in a calculation.

Outline Marking Scheme

Eight questions to be answered in all. These *must* include at **least two** questions from **Section A**.

Section A

1. (a) Primary, Standard $5 + 3$; (b) Describe 5×3; (c) What 3; (d) Colours 4×3;
    (e) Molarity 6, Grams per litre 6.

2. (a) State 2×4; (b) Describe 2×3, Explain 3; (c) Purpose 2×3; (d) Show 4×3;
    (e) Describe 6; (f) Describe 3, Write 2×3.

3. (a) What 4, State 4; (b) Which 3; (c) Explain 6; (d) List 3×3; (e) What 3;
    (f) Calculate 6, Taking 6, Hence 6; (g) Name 3.

Section B

4. (a) Define 2×3; (b) What 6; (c) Distinguish 2×3; (d) What 6; (e) Intake 6;
    (f) Name 2×3; (g) Used 2×3; (h) Calculate 6; (i) Explain 6; (j) What 2×3;
    (k) **A** 6; (k) **B** 6.

5. (a) Define 5, Write 3, Show 3, State (i) 3, (ii) 3; (b) Use 6, Write 3, Show 6,
    Would 3, Justify 3; (c) Account 6, Would 3, Explain 3.

6. (a) Which 5, Give 3×3, Which 3, Justify 6, Write 2×3; (b) How 3, Explain
    3×3, Give 3; (c) What 3, Economic 3.

7. (a) (i) 4, (ii) 4, Identify 2×3, Distinguish 3, 3; (b) Calculate 9, What 6;
    (c) Describe 3×3; (d) Explain 6.

8. (a) Name (i) 4, (ii) 4; (b) What 2×3; (c) Reagent 3, Catalyst 3; (d) Draw
    2×3, Indicate 3, List 3×3; (e) How 3×3, (f) How 3.

9. (a) Define 4, Why 4; (b) Plot 3, 6, 3, Use (i) 6, (ii) 3; (c) Describe 3,
    Explain 3; (d) (i) Mark 6, (ii) Dust 3×3.

10. (a) (i) Write 7, (ii) Calculate 12, (iii) What 3, Explain 3. (b) (i) State 4, 3,
    (ii) What 9, What 6, (iii) Give 3. (c) (i) How 4, (ii) Assign 4×3, Balance 6,
    (iii) Why 3.

11. (a) (i) Describe $4 + 3$, (ii) State 3, 3, Explain 3, 3, (iii) Copy 6. (b) (i) State
    $4 + 3$, (ii) Name 2×3, (iii) Account 6, (iv) Name 3, (v) Give 3. (c) **A** (i) State 4,
    (ii) What 6, (iii) Name 2×3, (iv) What 3×3. (c) **B** Name $3 + 2 + 2$, Explain
    (i) 2×3, (ii) 2×3, (iii) 2×3.

Section A

At least *two* questions must be answered from this section.

QUESTION 1

(a) PRIMARY: **pure / stable / anhydrous (not hydrated) / no water loss (no efflorescence) / not deliquescent / not hygroscopic /does not sublime / high molecular (molar) mass (M_r)** //

from which solutions **of known concentration (molarity)** can be made / **no need to standardise by titration** / water **soluble** (5 + 3)

(b) DESCRIBE: **rinse** from clock glass **into beaker** containing deionised water // **stir** // **dissolve** //
pour (add) through funnel into volumetric flask //
add rinsings of beaker //
add deionised water until bottom of meniscus on (level with) mark /
read at eye level //
stopper and **invert*** several times   ANY FIVE: (5 × 3)
[* Do not allow "shake" for "invert"]

(c) WHAT: source of **iodide (I^-)** ions (potassium **iodide**, KI) (3)

(d) COLOURS: **red / brown / reddish brown / golden-brown / yellow-brown** (3)
orange / yellow / light yellow / straw coloured (3)
blue-black / blue (3)
colourless   [Do not accept 'clear'] (3)
Give marks if order is correct even if one or more omitted.
Can also be marked divided into first two and last two.

(e) MOLARITY: **0.125** mol l^{-1} (6)

$$\frac{20 \times M}{2} = \frac{25 \times 0.05}{1} \quad (3) \quad M = 0.125 \quad (3)$$

GRAMS l^{-1}: **31** g l^{-1} (6)

$$0.125 \times 248^* \quad (3) \quad = \quad 31 \text{ g } l^{-1} \quad (3)$$

addition must be shown for error to be treated as slip.

QUESTION 2

(a) STATE: **add in small quantities (add dropwise)** [Allow "add slowly".] //
shake (stir) after each addition / **wait till reaction ceases (subsides)** // **cool reaction vessel**   ANY TWO: (2×4)

(b) DESCRIBE: **orange** (3)
to green (3)

EXPLAIN: **dichromate** $(Cr^{6+}, Cr_2O_7^{2-}, Na_2Cr_2O_7)$ **reduced to chromium (III)** (Cr^{3+}) (3)
[Accept use of oxidation numbers.]

(c) PURPOSE: to **speed up reaction (oxidation)** //
to ensure complete oxidation (reaction) / to ensure oxidation **does not stop at ethanal** (CH_3CHO) / but **goes on to ethanoic acid** (CH_3COOH) //
to heat **without loss of vapour (product)**   ANY TWO: (2×3)

(d) SHOW: mass of ethanol $=$ 8.0×0.80 $=$ **6.4 g** (3)

moles of ethanol $=$ $6.4 \div 46^*$ $=$ **0.139 (0.14) mol** (3)

moles dichromate $=$ $29.8 \div 298^* =$ **0.1 mol** (3)

0.139 ethanol $(\times\,^2/_3) \equiv$ **0.09** mol dichromate /
0.1 mol dichromate $(\times\,^3/_2) \equiv$ **0.15** mol ethanol (3)

[*addition must be shown for error to be treated as slip.*]

(e) DESCRIBE: isolated by **distillation (or distillation diagram)** (6)

(f) DESCRIBE: **effervescence / fizzing / bubbling / gas** (CO_2)
given off (3)

WRITE: $Na_2CO_3 + 2CH_3COOH \rightarrow 2CH_3COONa + H_2O + CO_2$ /

$Na_2CO_3 + 2CH_3COOH \rightarrow 2CH_3COONa + H_2CO_3$
FORMULAS: (3) BALANCING: (3)

QUESTION 3

(a) WHAT: **corrosive (corrosiveness, corrosion)**   (4)

   STATE: **do not allow contact with skin (eyes) /
             protective clothing (gloves, lab. coat) / eye protection
             (glasses, screen)**   (4)

(b) WHICH: **burette**   (3)

(c) EXPLAIN: **get average (mean) temperatures of the two solutions /
             wait until both solutions at same (room) temperature /
             using plot of temp. v time for both solutions**   (6)

(d) LIST: **thermometer to 0.2°C or better (temperature sensor,
             "sensitive", "accurate") // add quickly // add without
             splashing // replace cover quickly (immediately) // stir**
             constantly // after addition **plot temperature at intervals
             and get highest temperature by extrapolating** back to
             time of mixing // **prevent heat loss (use of suitable
             insulation)**   ANY THREE: (3×3)
             [Do not accept "digital thermometer".]

(e) WHAT: polystyrene a good **insulator / glass & metal poor**er
             insulators   (3)
             [Accept "prevents heat loss" or "not a conductor" for "insulator"]

(f) CALCULATE: **0.05** mol   (6)

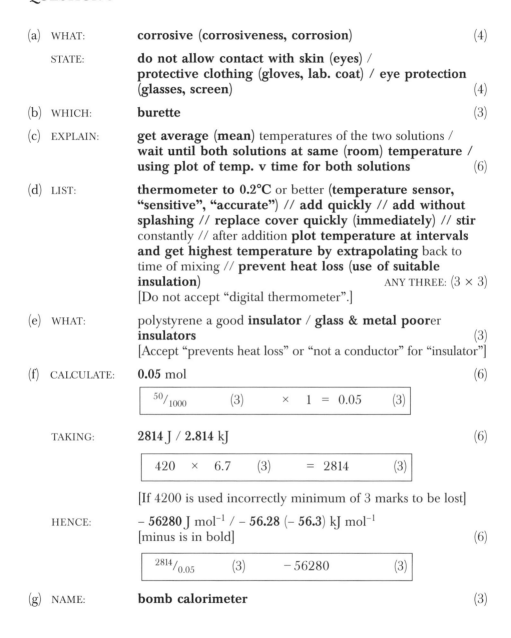

$^{50}/_{1000}$ (3) $\times$ 1   =   0.05   (3)

   TAKING: **2814 J / 2.814 kJ**   (6)

             420   $\times$ 6.7   (3)   =   2814   (3)

             [If 4200 is used incorrectly minimum of 3 marks to be lost]

   HENCE: **– 56280** J mol^{-1} / **– 56.28 (– 56.3)** kJ mol^{-1}
             [minus is in bold]   (6)

             $^{2814}/_{0.05}$ (3)   **– 56280**   (3)

(g) NAME: **bomb calorimeter**   (3)

Section B

QUESTION 4

Eight items to be answered. Six marks to be allocated to each item and one additional mark to be added to each of the first two items for which the highest marks are awarded.

[If only two are attempted and neither is awarded marks: (2×1)]

(a) DEFINE: **half the internuclear distance / half the distance between the centres** (3)
in a single homonuclear bond / of singly-bonded atoms of the same element (3)
[For a diagram to be awarded the marks, all the information must be clearly shown.]

(b) WHAT: **raise octane number / prevent auto-ignition (pre-ignition, knocking, pinking) / cleaner emissions / less pollution / less carbon monoxide (CO) produced** (6)
[allow 3 marks for *"as additives"*]

(c) DISTING: *sigma*: **head-on (end-on) overlap of orbitals** (3)
pi: **lateral (sideways) overlap orbitals** (3)
[Marks can be got from clearly labelled diagrams]
[allow max. of 3 marks if either "orbitals" not stated above *or* if "orbitals" are not labelled in diagram.]

(d) WHAT: **reactants & catalyst in different phases / boundary between reactants & catalyst** (6)
[Allow (3) if "states" used for "phases"; no marks for an example]

(e) INTAKE: $\mathbf{1.5 \times 10^{20}}$ (6)

$0.014 \div 56 = 0.00025$ (3)	$\times 6 \times 10^{23} = 1.5 \times 10^{20}$ (3)	$\times 2(-3)$

(f) NAME: **iron(II) sulfate / ferrous sulphate / FeSO$_4$** [Accept ammonium iron(II) sulfate] //
concentrated **sulphuric acid / H$_2$SO$_4$** (2×3)

(g) USED: **name // structure** (2×3)

ethanoic (acetic) acid // CH_3COOH
propanoic (propionic) acid // CH_3CH_2COOH (C_2H_5COOH)
benzenecarboxylic (benzoic) acid // C_6H_5COOH ($\langle\bigcirc\rangle COOH$)
methanoic acid // $HCOOH$
sorbic acid* // $CH_3(CH)_4COOH$ [* 2,4-hexadienoic acid]

(h) CALC: **4.3**   (6)

$$\frac{21.5}{500} \quad (3) \quad \times 100 \quad = \quad 4.3 \quad (3)$$

(i) EXPL: **all the carbon-to-carbon bonds** in benzene **are identical (same length) /
                 resonance (delocalised)** structure / **bonds intermediate between single and double /
                 six valence (bonding) electrons belong to whole molecule**   (6)
                 [Accept: "double bonds moving" or "double bonds not fixed"]
                 [Allow (3) for: intermediate **between the two** (shown or stated) Kekule **structures**]

(j) WHAT: **absorbance** is //
                 directly **proportional to (varies** directly **with) concentration** of substance (2×3)

(k) **A:**   **hydrochlorofluorocarbons (HCFCs) / hydrofluorocarbons (HFCs) / perfluorocarbons (PFCs)**   (6)
     B: Sir Humphry **Davy**   (6)

QUESTION 5

(a) DEFINE: **discrete (fixed, restricted, definite, specific) energy of electron /**
energy of electron in orbit /
orbit (shell) which electrons of equal energy can occupy   (5)

WRITE: $1s^2 2s^2 2p^6 3s^2 3p^4$ / **[Ne] $3s^2 3p^4$** [Accept if written with subscripts]   (3)

[Do not accept "$3p_x^2 3p_y^2$" for "$3p^4$"]

SHOW: $3p_x^2 3p_y^1 3p_z^1$ / 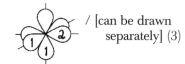   / [can be drawn separately] (3)

[Note: $1s^2 2s^2 2p^6 3s^2 3p_x^2 3p_y^1 3p_z^1$ (6)]

[The electron pair can be shown in the p_x, the p_y or the p_z orbital with the other two orbitals having one electron each]

STATE: (i) **3**   (3)
(ii) **9**   (3)

(b) USE: **weakly polar //** almost **non-polar // covalent** bond   (6)
[Allow 3 marks for *"polar covalent"*]

WRITE: **H_2S** [Accept SH_2]   (3)

SHOW:

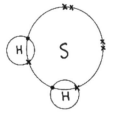      

(6)

[Accept all dots or all crosses, also ● − **x** or ● − ● for bonds. Correct shape not required.]

WOULD: **non-linear**   (3)

JUSTIFY: **there are non-bonding (lone) pair(s) /** [Allow l.p. for lone pair.]
four (> two) electron pairs in valence (outer) shell of central (S) atom   (3)
[Linked answers]

(c) ACC: **hydrogen bonds in water** //
                **weak dipole-dipole* forces in H_2S / London dispersion
                forces in H_2S /**
                weaker **intermolecular forces in H_2S** [*Accept Van der
                Waals' forces]   (6)
                [Accept "big electroneg. diff. between O and H but small
                between S and H for (3)]

     WOULD: only **slightly (sparingly, weakly)** soluble / **no**   (3)

     EXPL: **does not form hydrogen bonds** with water / **H_2S weakly
                (non-) polar**   (3)
                [Linked answers]

QUESTION 6

(a) WHICH: light **gasoline (petrol)** [Accept "petroleum"]   (5)
                 [Allow "second highest fraction" or "from C_5 to $C_{10}(C_{11})$"]

    GIVE: **pentane // 2-methylbutane // 2,2-dimethylpropane** (3×3)
                 [If the names are not given in the same order as the formulas,
                 there must be some way of identifying which formula the
                 candidate is naming. Numbers are not required as the
                 structures are unambiguous but no marks should be awarded
                 if incorrect numbers are used]

    WHICH: **pentane / the first one / the one on the left / pentane
                 structure**   (3)

    JUSTIFY: **pentane is a straight (unbranched)** chain molecule   (6)
                 ["longest chain" or "not highly branched" are <u>not</u> acceptable.]

    WRITE: C_5H_{12} + $8O_2$ → $5CO_2$ + $6H_2O$
                                        FORMULAS: (3) BALANCING: (3)

(b) HOW: **naphtha (they) have shorter (smaller, less carbon atoms,
                 smaller mass, lighter) chains / gas oil have longer
                 (bigger, more carbon atoms, bigger mass, heavier)**
                 chains   (3)

    EXPL: **diagram with one correct label** (3)

                 [layers <u>or</u> outlets must be <u>shown</u>; out-
                 lets may be shown by tubes (pipes),
                 holes, gaps, lines, arrows (→)]

                 heat (boil) / pass vapour **up tower
                 (column) / temperature gradient
                 shown**   (3)

                 **naphtha condenses (comes off) higher up / gas oil comes
                 off lower down**   (3)

    GIVE: **road surfacing (tarring) / roofing / waterproofing**   (3)

(c) WHAT: **splitting (breaking) of long chain molecules** by heat and
                 catalyst(s)   (3)
                 [Accept "hydrocarbons" for "molecules"]

    ECON: **gives useful products (more demand for products) /
                 products needed for petrol / products used as feedstock
                 for chemical industry (source of alkenes) / gives higher
                 octane numbers**   (3)

QUESTION 7

(a) (i) *acid*:   **proton (hydrogen ion, H^+) donor**   (4)

(ii) *conjugate
     pair*:   acid & base that **differ by a proton (hydrogen ion, H^+)** (4)

IDENTIFY: **HNO_2 & NO_2^- // H_2O & H_3O^+** (2×3)

DISTING: *strong*: **good proton donor / completely (high) dissoc.**
            into ions in dil. aq.soln.   (3)

            weak: **poor proton donor / slightly (low) dissoc.**
                     into ions in dil. aq. soln.   (3)
                     [Accept "does not readily dissoc." but <u>not</u>
                     "does not completely (fully) dissoc."]

(b) CALC: $pH = $**2.15** [or answers that give 2.15 when corrected to two
             decimal places.]   (9)

$$pH = -\log \sqrt{K_a \times M} \qquad (3)$$
$$= -\log \sqrt{5 \times 10^{-4} \times 0.1} \quad (3)$$
$$= 2.15 \qquad (3)$$

$$K_a = \frac{[H^\pm][NO_2^-]}{[HNO_2]} = \frac{[H^\pm]^2}{0.1} = 5 \times 10^{-4}$$

$$[H^+]^2 = 5 \times 10^{-5} \qquad (3)$$
$$[H^+] = 0.007 \qquad (3)$$
$$pH = 2.15 \qquad (3)$$

WHAT: **1**   (6)

$$pH = -\log [H^+] = -\log [0.1 \qquad (3)$$
$$= 1 \qquad (3)$$

(c) DESCR: **enrichment with nutrients (fertilisers / nitrates / phos-
             phates) // due to run off from land (erosion from land) /
             due to pollution / dispersion in water / absorption by
             plants**
             // rapid **growth of plants (algae)** on surface / **algal blooms**
             formed

// **light blocked from (photosynthesis reduced in) plants
below surface** / **decay by micro-organisms (bacteria)**
of surface **plants (algae, algal blooms)** / **increase in
micro-organisms (bacteria)** / **increased activity by** aerobic
micro-organisms (bacteria) //
dissolved **oxygen depleted (lowered, used up)** /
oxygen level falls / deoxygenation

ANY THREE: (3×3)

(d) EXPL: **precipitation / adsorption / absorption / ion exchange
(deionising) / complexation**   (6)
[Allow (3) for "flocculation". Give no marks for "distillation"]

QUESTION 8

(a) NAME: (i) **alkenes (olefins)**   (4)
    (ii) **aldehydes (alkanals)**   (4)

(b) WHAT: **loss of (removal of) small molecule (water, hydrogen chloride, H_2O, HCl)**   (3)
[Accept "dehydration"]

    change to (formation of) unsaturated compound **(double bond, planar carbon / planar geometry)**   (3)
[Note: equation not sufficient on its own; the features must be stated.]

(c) REAGENT: **hydrogen**   [Accept: 'hydrogenation']   (3)
[Reagent-catalyst order not required]

    CATALYST: **nickel (Ni) / palladium (Pd) / platinum (Pt)**   (3)
[Accept: **lithium aluminium hydride (LiAlH$_4$, lithium tetrahydroaluminate) / sodium borohydride (NaBH$_4$, sodium tetrahydroborate)** for 6 marks]

(d) DRAW: (2 × 3)

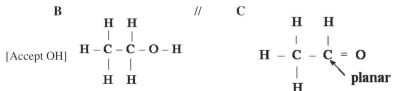

    INDICATE: **correct indication of planar carbon atom**   (3)

    LIST: *bonds broken in B*:   **C – H // O – H**   (2 × 3)
    bond made in C: **C = O**   [Accept "carbon (C) to oxygen (O) bond"]   (3)
    [cancelling applies]

(e) HOW: **heat / warm / boil //** with **specified reagent // observation**   (3 × 3)

reagent	observation
Fehling's solution	red (orange, etc.) ppt.
Tollens' reagent (ammoniacal silver nitrate, ammoniacal silver oxide, ammoniacal silver ions)	silver
2,4-dinitrophenylhydrazine (6 marks)	orange (red, yellow) ppt.

["silver mirror test" on its own gets (3)]

(f) HOW: **ingestion (drink, food, medicine)**   (3)

QUESTION 9

(a) DEFINE: **change* in concentration per unit time /
rate of change* of concentration /
change* in concentration**
    time   (4)
[* "increase" or "decrease" not acceptable for "change"]
[Accept 'mass' or 'amount', but not 'volume' or 'quantity',
for 'concentration']

WHY: **concentration(s) decrease [reactant(s) used up]**   (4)

(b) PLOT: **labelled and scaled axes** [Accept 'time' or 'minutes';
'mass' or 'grams']   (3)

all points plotted correctly   (6)
[Allow (3) if six points are correctly plotted;
assume (0, 0) is plotted correctly]

curve drawn [has to be drawn to (0, 0)]   (3)

Note: award (6) for *plotted correctly* only if graph paper is used,
otherwise 0.
[Allow if the axes are reversed.]

USE: (i)   **0.20 – 0.26 g min^{-1}**   (6)
[allow 3 marks for good tangent *or* 3 marks for calculation
based on data points from candidate's tangent]

(ii)   **0.004 – 0.006 mol min^{-1}**   (3)

(c) DESCRIBE: **slower rate**   (3)

EXPLAIN: acid **less concentrated / rate decreases with
concentration / fewer collisions at lower
concentration**   (3)

(d) (i) MARK: **see** candidate's **graph*** [steeper at start; levels off sooner;
reaches same height]   (6)
[Allow (3) if description is fully correct but not shown on the
graph]
[Allow (3) if two of the three conditions above are shown on
the graph]
* not necessarily on graph paper.

(ii) DUST: **combustible** dust particles // **dryness // above certain
concentration // source of ignition (light, spark, flame,**

**static electricity) // oxygen (air, atmosphere)* //
enclosed space**

ANY THREE: (3×3)

[*Can be picked out of description if clear that it is a
condition.]

[Allow "build up" or "enough of dust" or "spread out" for
"certain concentration".]

[Allow "lack of ventilation" for "enclosed space".]

[Do not accept "heat" for "ignition source"]

QUESTION 10

(a) (i) WRITE: $\dfrac{[\textbf{NH}_3]^2}{[\textbf{N}_2][\textbf{H}_2]^3}$ [Square brackets essential]

                                                                               (7)

     (ii) CALC: **0.009 (1/108)** $\textbf{M}^{-2}$ (12)
                      [or answers that give 0.009 correct to one
                      significant figure]

$$
\begin{array}{lllll}
& N_2 & + & 3H_2 & \rightleftharpoons & 2NH_3 \\
\text{start:} & 3 \text{ mol/M} & & 9 \text{ mol/M} & & \\
\text{equil:} & 2 \text{ mol/M} & & 6 \text{ mol/M} & & 2 \text{ mol/M} \quad (6)
\end{array}
$$

$$
K_c = \frac{2^2}{2 \times 6^3} \quad (3)
$$

$$
= 0.009 \ (1/108) \quad (3)
$$

     (iii) WHAT: it would **increase** the yield of ammonia   (3)
                        [The increase in yield of ammonia must
                        be mentioned; no marks for "reaction shifts
                        forward" or "reaction shifts to the
                        right".]

        EXPL: **reaction shifts in direction (to side) of fewer
                        molecules (moles) (smaller volume)** to decrease
                        the pressure   (3)

(b) (i) STATE: **equal (same) volumes of gases contain equal
                        (same) numbers of molecules (particles,
                        moles)**   (4)
                        under same conditions* of temperature and
                        pressure   (3)
                        [* Do not accept "under all conditions".]
                        [Do not accept "at s.t.p."]
                        [Allow (3) for "the molar volume at s.t.p.
                        is 22.4 litres.]

     (ii) WHAT: **1.069 – 1.10** m^3 [Accept 1.1 but not greater]   (9)

$$
2000 \div 44^* = 45.4 \ / \ 45.5 \text{ mol} \quad (3)
$$
[*addition must be shown for error to be treated as slip.]

$$
V = \frac{nRT}{P} = \frac{45.4/45.5 \times 8.3 \times 290}{1.01 \times 10^5} \quad \text{[or other correct form]} \quad (3)
$$

$$
= 1.069 - 1.10 \quad (3)
$$

$2000 \div 44^* = 45.4 \; / \; 45.5 \; \text{mol} \times 22.4 = 1017 \; / \; 1019 \; \text{litres}$ (3)
[*addition must be shown for error to be treated as slip.]

$$V = \frac{1.01325/1.013/1.01/1.0 \times 10^5 \times 1017/1019 \times 290}{1.01 \times 10^5 \times 273}$$ (3)

[or other correct form]

$= 1069 - 1100 \; \text{litres} \; (1.069 - 1.10 \; \text{m}^3)$ (3)

WHAT: **0.182** kg / **182** g [or answers rounding off to these figures] (6)

$45.4 \; / \; 45.5 \times 4 \; (3) = 182 \; \text{g} \; / \; 0.182 \; \text{kg}$ (3)

(iii) GIVE: **stronger intermolecular (London dispersion, Van der Waals', dipole-dipole) forces (attractions) / higher mass / bigger molecules / polarity of C to O bond / has more electrons** (3)
[To allow opposite points Helium must be mentioned.]

(c) (i) HOW: **it decreases** (4)

(ii) ASSIGN: *1st equation*: oxidation number of Br in $Br_2 = 0$ (3)

oxidation number of Br in $Br^- = -1$ (3)

2nd equation: oxidation number of Cl in $Cl_2 = 0$ (3)

oxidation number of Cl in $Cl^- = -1$ (3)

[The oxidation numbers may be written under the appropriate formulas]

BALANCE: $Cl_2 + SO_3{}^{2-} + H_2O \;\rightarrow\; 2Cl^- + SO_4{}^{2-} + 2H^+$ (6)
[Do not insist on correct formulas (they are given).
(6) or (0) for balancing numbers.
Accept only the *smallest* correct integral balancing numbers (2 & 2) – not multiples.]

(iii) WHY: **increasing atomic radius (size) / increase in number of shells / atoms get bigger / increase in shielding (screening) / decrease in electronegativity (attraction for electrons)** (3)

QUESTION 11

(a) (i) DESCR: **positively charged sphere (ball) // electrons* embedded (scattered, dotted, placed** at random) **in it** $(4 + 3)$
[*The word "electron(s)" required in description or diagram.]
Marks can be got from a labelled diagram such as:
[Allow 3 marks for "plum pudding" unqualified]

electron

+ charge

(ii) STATE: *first observation*: **deflection** of alpha particles   (3)
second observation: alpha particles **reflected (rebounded, bounced back, came straight back)**   (3)

EXPL: *first observation*: particles **passed close to** small, **positive mass (charge)**   (3)
second observation: particles **collided with small,** very **dense mass (material, nucleus, point)** (3)
[The explanations for the first and second observations must be given separately, or else it must be absolutely clear from the candidate's answer which observation is being explained.]

(iii) COPY: $^{210}_{84}\text{Po} \rightarrow ^{206}_{82}\text{Pb} \quad ^{4}_{2}\text{He}$ Both Pb and 82: (3)
206: (3)
[Not necessary to write the equation.
Accept x = 82, y = 206, z = Pb *or* 82, 206, Pb].

(b) (i) EXPL: provides (supplies, gives) energy **for splitting (fission) of chlorine** molecules (Cl_2) // in**to free radicals (free atoms, Cl•)** $(4 + 3)$
[If "molecules" is stated for the first part, "free" is not required for the second part.]
or **homolytic fission** (4) **of chlorine (Cl_2) molecules** (3)
or $\text{Cl}_2 \rightarrow \text{Cl•} + \text{Cl•}$ (7) [Equation without dots (4)]

(ii) NAME: **chloromethane / methyl chloride // hydrogen chloride**
(2×3)
[Not hydrochloric acid, but do not treat as a contradiction]

(iii) ACC: **two CH$_3$• combine** to give ethane / $\text{CH}_3• + \text{CH}_3• \rightarrow \text{C}_2\text{H}_6$ (6)
[or the same in words]

(iv) NAME: **ionic addition / electrophilic addition**   (3)

(v) GIVE: **solvents / dry cleaners / paint strippers / anaesthetics / organic synthesis** (making of **plastics**) / **refrigerants / flame retardants**   (3)

(c) **A**

  (i) STATE: **respiration / combustion (burning) / decomposition
            (decay) / melting ice-caps** (4)
            [Accept "exhaling" for "respiration"; accept "car emissions"
            for combustion.]

  (ii) WHAT: assessing (giving, stating) its influence on the greenhouse
            **effect relative to (compared with) carbon dioxide //
            comparing (measuring, giving, stating) the** greenhouse
            effect of different **gases** (6)

  (iii) NAME: **water // methane // CFC(s) // HCFC(s) // HFC(s) //
            chloromethane // chloroethane // dinitrogen oxide
            (nitrogen (I) oxide, nitrous oxide) // PFC(s) // ozone //
            sulphur hexafluoride // sulphur dioxide {sulphur(IV)
            oxide}, // nitrogen dioxide {nitrogen(IV) oxide} //
            nitrogen monoxide {nitric oxide, nitrogen(II) oxide}
            //carbon monoxide** (or formulas)   ANY TWO: (2×3)

  (iv) WHAT: **carbonate* ion ($CO_3{}^{2-}$) // hydrogencarbonate* ion
            ($HCO_3{}^-$) // carbonic acid (H_2CO_3) // hydronium ion
            (H_3O^+) / hydrogen ion (H^+)**   ANY THREE: (3×3)
                        caution – single solidus!
            [* Do not accept salts such as "sodium carbonate" or "calcium
            hydrogencarbonate".]

  B

  NAME: *aluminium*:   **metallic** crystal
          sodium chloride: **ionic** crystal
          graphite: covalent **macromolecular** crystal $(3 + 2 + 2)$

  EXPLAIN: (i) **outer (valence, highest energy) electrons delocalised
               (form cloud)** (3)
               which **are free to move** when a potential difference is
               applied (3)

          (ii) **ions attracted to polar water molecules / ion-dipole
               interactions (forces, attractions) / ions become
               hydrated** (6)
               [Marks could be got from a good diagram]

          (iii) **forces between layers** of carbon atoms **weak (Van der
               Waals', London)** (3)
               because of distance between them / allowing **layers to
               slide over one another** (3)

State Examinations Commission

———

LEAVING CERTIFICATE EXAMINATION, 2006

———

CHEMISTRY – HIGHER LEVEL

———

TUESDAY, 20 JUNE - AFTERNOON 2.00 to 5.00

———

400 MARKS

———

Answer **eight** questions in all

These **must** include at least **two** questions from **Section A**

All questions carry equal marks (50)

———

Information

Relative atomic masses: H $=$ 1, C $=$ 12, O $=$ 16, Na $=$ 23, Ca $=$ 40.

Universal gas constant, $R = 8.3 \, \text{J K}^{-1} \, \text{mol}^{-1}$

Molar volume at s.t.p. $= 22.4$ litres

Avogadro constant $= 6 \times 10^{23} \, \text{mol}^{-1}$

Section A

Answer at least *two* questions from this section [see page 1 for full instructions]

1. An experiment was carried out to determine the percentage water of crystallisation and the degree of water of crystallisation, **x**, in a sample of hydrated sodium carbonate crystals ($Na_2CO_3.xH_2O$). An 8.20 g sample of the crystals was weighed accurately on a clock glass and then made up to 500 cm^3 of solution in a volumetric flask. A pipette was used to transfer 25.0 cm^3 portions of this solution to a conical flask. A previously standardised 0.11 M hydrochloric acid (**HCl**) solution was used to titrate each sample. A number of accurate titrations were carried out. The average volume of hydrochloric acid solution required in these titrations was 26.05 cm^3.

    The titration reaction is described by the equation:

    $$Na_2CO_3 + 2HCl \rightarrow 2NaCl + CO_2 + H_2O$$

    (a) Identify a primary standard reagent which could have been used to stan-dardise the hydrochloric acid solution.   (5)

    (b) Name a suitable indicator for the titration and state the colour change observed in the conical flask at the end point. Explain why not more than 1–2 drops of indicator should be used.   (12)

    (c) (i) Describe the correct procedure for rinsing the burette before filling it with the solution it is to deliver.

    (ii) Why is it important to fill the part below the tap of the burette?   (12)

    (d) From the titration figures, calculate the concentration of sodium carbonate (Na_2CO_3) in the solution in

    (i) moles per litre,

    (ii) grams per litre.   (9)

    (e) Calculate the percentage water of crystallisation present in the crystals and the value of **x**, the degree of hydration of the crystals.   (12)

    _____

2. A sample of soap was prepared in the laboratory by refluxing a mixure of approximately 5 g of animal fat, 2 g of sodium hydroxide pellets (an excess) and 25 cm^3 of ethanol in an apparatus like that drawn on the right.

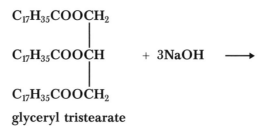

   (a) Why was the reaction mixture refluxed? Name the *type* of reaction which occurs during the reflux stage of the preparation.   (8)

   (b) Complete and balance the equation below for the reaction between glyceryl tristearate, an animal fat, and sodium hydroxide.   (9)

$$C_{17}H_{35}COOCH_2$$
$$|$$
$$C_{17}H_{35}COOCH \quad + \; 3NaOH \quad \longrightarrow$$
$$|$$
$$C_{17}H_{35}COOCH_2$$

glyceryl tristearate

   (c) What is the purpose of the ethanol? Why is it desirable to remove the ethanol after reflux? Describe with the aid of a labelled diagram how you would remove the ethanol after the reflux stage of the experiment.   (12)

   (d) Describe how a pure sample of soap was obtained from the reaction mixture.   (9)

   (e) At the end of the experiment, what is the location

   (i)   of the second product of the reaction,

   (ii) of the excess sodium hydroxide?   (6)

   (f) What would you observe, upon shaking, if a little of the soap prepared in this experiment is added to (*i*) a test tube containing deionised water, (ii) a test tube containing mineral water from a limestone region?   (6)

---

3. A number of tests were carried out on a sample of swimming pool water to test its quality.

   (a) A colorimetric experiment was used to estimate the concentration of free chlorine in the sample.
   What is the general principle of all colorimetric experiments?   (8)

(b) Identify a suitable reagent to test for free chlorine in swimming pool water and state the colour
which develops when this reagent reacts with free chlorine. (6)

(c) Describe briefly how you would estimate the concentration of free chlorine in a sample using either a comparator *or* a colorimeter. (12)

(d) Give the name *or* formula of a *free chlorine* species in the swimming pool water.
Give a reason why the concentration of free chlorine in treated drinking water is usually between 0.2 – 0.5 p.p.m. whereas in swimming pool water it should be between 1 – 5 p.p.m. (9)

(e) When 1200 cm^3 of swimming pool water was filtered, the mass of the filter paper, upon drying, had increased by 0.78 g. When 250 cm^3 of the filtered water was evaporated to dryness the mass of the residue obtained was 0.32 g. Calculate the concentration in p.p.m.

(i) of suspended solids,

(ii) of dissolved solids. (15)

Section B

[See page 1 for instructions regarding the number of questions to be answered]

4. Answer **eight** of the following items (a), (b), (c), etc. (50)

(a) Write the electron configuration (*s, p, etc.*) of a chromium atom in its ground state.

(b) Name the scientist, shown in the photograph, who identified cathode rays as subatomic particles.

(c) Give **two** differences between a nuclear reaction and a chemical reaction.

(d) Calculate the percentage carbon, by mass, in methylbenzene.

(e) What is (i) the conjugate acid and (ii) the conjugate base of H_2O?

(f) What contribution did Newlands make to the systematic arrangement of the elements known to him?

(g) What observation is made when a sample of ethanal is heated with Fehling's reagent?

(h) The concentration of an aqueous solution of sodium hydroxide (**NaOH**) is 0.2 g per litre.
Calculate its pH.

(i) Under what circumstances can ionic compounds conduct electricity?

(j) Which class of organic compound is responsible for the odour associated with fruits such as apples, oranges, pears, bananas and strawberries?

(k) Answer part **A** *or* part **B**.

    A State **two** uses of nitrogen gas based on its chemical stability.

or

    B Name **two** metals, one a main group metal, the other a transition element, both of which are protected from further corrosion by the oxide layer which forms on their surfaces.

_____

5. (a) (i) Describe how you would carry out a flame test on a sample of potassium chloride.   (8)

    (ii) Why do different elements have unique atomic spectra?   (6)

    (iii) What instrumental technique is based on the fact that each element has unique atomic spectra?   (3)

Bohr's model of the atom explained the existence of energy levels on the basis of atomic spectra.
Bohr's theory was later modified to incorporate the idea of *orbitals* in recognition of the wave nature of the electron and Heisenberg's uncertainty principle.

    (iv) Define *atomic orbital.*   (6)

    (v) What does Heisenberg's uncertainty principle say about an electron in an atom?   (6)

(b) (i) Define *electronegativity.*   (6)

    (ii) Explain why there is a general increase in electronegativity values across the periods in the periodic table of the elements.   (6)

    (iii) Explain, in terms of the structures of the atoms, the trend in reactivity down Group I (the alkali metal group) of the periodic table.   (9)

_____

6. (a) The table shows the octane numbers of four hydrocarbons.

Name	Formula	Octane No.
hexane	C_6H_{14}	25
cyclohexane	C_6H_{12}	83
benzene	C_6H_6	100
2,2,4-trimethyl-pentane	C_8H_{18}	100

   (i) What is meant by the octane number of a fuel? (8)

   (ii) Hexane has the lowest octane number of the four compounds listed. What structural feature of the molecule contributes to this? (3)

   (iii) In the case of each of the other three compounds, identify the structural feature of its molecules which contributes to it having a high octane number. (9)

   (iv) Name the process carried out in an oil refinery that converts hexane to compounds such as cyclohexane and benzene. Why is the use of benzene in petrol strictly controlled? (6)

   (b) (i) Give **two** reasons why oxygenates such as MTBE are added to petrol.

   (ii) Give **two** reasons why the addition of lead to petrol has been discontinued. (12)

   (c) The combustion of cyclohexane may be described by the following balanced equation:

$$C_6H_{12(l)} + 9O_{2(g)} \rightarrow 6CO_{2(g)} + 6H_2O_{(l)}$$

   Given that the heats of formation of cyclohexane, carbon dioxide and water are -156, -394 and -286 kJ mol^{-1}, respectively, calculate the heat of combustion of cyclohexane. (12)

---

7. (a) Define the *activation energy* of a chemical reaction. (5)

   (b) Give **two** reasons why the rate of a chemical reaction increases as the temperature rises.
   Which of these is the more significant? Why? (12)

   (c) Describe how you could investigate the effect of temperature on the rate of the reaction between a 0.1 M sodium thiosulfate solution and a 2 M hydrochloric acid solution. (12)
   The reaction is described by the following balanced equation.

$$Na_2S_2O_3 + 2HCl \rightarrow 2NaCl + SO_2 + S + H_2O$$

(d) When silver nitrate and sodium chloride solutions are mixed a precipitate appears immediately.

Explain the speed of this reaction compared to the slower reaction when solutions of sodium thiosulfate and hydrochloric acid are mixed.   (6)

(e) What type of catalysis occurs in the catalytic converter of a modern car?

Give the names *or* formulas of **two** substances entering a car's catalytic converter *and* the names *or* formulas of the substances to which they are converted in the interior of the catalytic converter.   (15)

––––––––––

8. (a) (i) What is *hard water*?   (5)

   (ii) A supply of hard water is treated for domestic use by ion-exchange. You may assume that all the hardness is due to $Ca(HCO_3)_2$. Explain in words *or* using a balanced equation how a cation exchange resin, represented by **RNa**, softens this water supply.   (6)

   (iii) In the treatment of water for drinking, what is meant by the term *flocculation*?
   Name a flocculating agent.   (9)

   (iv) What substance is added to water to adjust the pH if the water is too acidic? Why is it undesirable to have the pH of drinking water below 6?   (6)

   (b) (i) Explain how an acid-base indicator, which is itself a weak acid, and may be represented by **HX**, functions.   (9)

   (ii) Draw a clearly labelled diagram of the titration curve you would expect to obtain when 50 cm^3 of a 0.1 M sodium hydroxide (**NaOH**) solution is added slowly to 25 cm^3 of a 0.1 M ethanoic acid (**CH$_3$COOH**) solution.   (9)

   (iii) Explain with reference to your diagram why phenolphthalein is a suitable indicator for a titration of sodium hydroxide with ethanoic acid.   (6)

––––––––––

9. The alkenes are a homologous series. Ethene (C_2H_4) is the first member of the series.

(a) What is meant by a *homologous series?* (5)

(b) Ethene may be made in a school laboratory using the arrangement of apparatus drawn on the right.

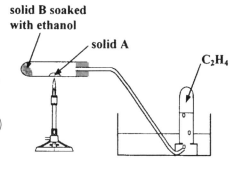

solid B soaked with ethanol

solid A

C_2H_4

    (i) Give the name *and* formula of the solid **A** which is heated using the Bunsen burner. (6)

    (ii) Identify the solid **B** which is used to keep the ethanol at the end of the test tube. (3)

    (iii) What precaution should be observed when heating is stopped? Why is this necessary? (6)

    (iv) Give **one** major use of ethene gas. (3)

(c) Describe the mechanism for the bromination of ethene. (9)
State and explain **one** piece of experimental evidence to support this mechanism. (6)

(d) Draw the structures *and* give the systematic (IUPAC) names for **two** alkene isomers of molecular formula C_4H_8. (12)

_____

10. Answer any **two** of the parts (a), (b) and (c) (2×25)

(a) (i) What are *isotopes?* (4)

    (ii) Define *relative atomic mass, A_r.* (6)

    (iii) What is the principle on which the mass spectrometer is based? (9)

    (iv) Calculate the relative atomic mass of a sample of lithium, given that a mass spectrometer shows that it consists of 7.4 % of ^{6}Li and 92.6 % of ^{7}Li. (6)

(b) Define *oxidation* in terms of change in oxidation number. (4)
What is the oxidation number of (i) chlorine in **NaClO** and (ii) nitrogen in NO_3^-? (6)

State and explain the oxidation number of oxygen in the compound **OF$_2$**. (6)

Using oxidation numbers or otherwise, identify the reducing agent in the reaction between acidified potassium manganate(VII) and potassium iodide solutions represented by the balanced equation below. Use your knowledge of the colours of the reactants and products to predict the colour change you would expect to see if you carried out this reaction. (9)

$$2MnO_4^- + 10I^- + 16H^+ \rightarrow 2Mn^{2+} + 5I_2 + 8H_2O$$

(c) The chart compares the boiling points of alkanes and primary alcohols containing from one to four carbon atoms.

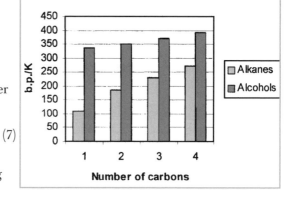

(i) Give **two** reasons why each of these alcohols has a higher boiling point than the corresponding alkane. (7)

(ii) Explain why the difference in boiling points between methane and methanol is 226.5 K while the difference in boiling points between butane and butanol is only 119 K. (6)

(iii) Describe, in general terms, the solubilities of methane, methanol, butane and butanol in water. (12)

———————

11. Answer any **two** of the parts (a), (b) and (c) (2 × 25)

(a) (i) What is an *ideal gas*? (4)

(ii) Give **one** reason why a real gas like carbon dioxide deviates from ideal behaviour. (3)

(iii) Assuming ideal behaviour, how many moles of carbon dioxide are present in 720 cm³ of the gas at 10 °C and a pressure of 1 × 10⁵ Pa? Give your answer correct to one significant figure. (9)

(iv) How many molecules of carbon dioxide are present in this quantity of carbon dioxide? (3)

(v) The reaction between carbon dioxide and limewater is represented by the following balanced equation.

$$Ca(OH)_2 + CO_2 \rightarrow CaCO_3 + H_2O$$

What mass of calcium hydroxide is required to react completely with the quantity of carbon dioxide gas given in (iii) above? (6)

(b) State *Le Châtelier's principle.* (7)

The following equilibrium is set up in solution by dissolving cobalt(II) chloride crystals in water to form the pink species $Co(H_2O)_6^{2+}$ and then adding concentrated hydrochloric acid until the solution becomes blue.

$$Co(H_2O)_6^{2+} + 4Cl^- \rightleftharpoons CoCl4_4^{2-} + 6H_2O$$
$$\text{pink} \qquad\qquad\qquad \text{blue}$$

(i) When the solution becomes blue, has reaction ceased? Explain. (6)

(ii) The forward reaction is endothermic. State and explain the colour change observed on cooling the reaction mixture. (6)

(iii) Other than heating, mention **one** way of reversing the change caused by cooling the reaction mixture. (6)

(c) Answer part **A** *or* part **B**

A

Select **one** of the manufacturing processes below and answer the questions which follow:

ammonia manufacture   nitric acid manufacture   magnesium oxide manufacture

(i) What are the raw materials for the manufacturing process you have chosen? Describe how the raw materials are treated before they become the feedstock for the manufacturing process. (12)

(ii) Name **one** product of the process you have chosen, which, if discharged, could cause pollution. (3)

(iii) State the most important use of the *main* product of the process you have chosen.
What makes this product particularly suitable for this use? (10)

or

B

A blast furnace may be used in the extraction of iron from iron ore.

(i) What materials must be added to a blast furnace in operation? (12)

(ii) Name the principal reducing agent in the blast furnace and write a balanced equation for its reaction with haematite (Fe_2O_3). (9)

(iii) Why is the pig iron produced in a blast furnace further processed into steel? (4)

State Examinations Commission

LEAVING CERTIFICATE EXAMINATIONS 2006

CHEMISTRY – HIGHER LEVEL

MARKING SCHEME

Introduction

In considering the marking scheme the following should be noted.

1. In many cases only key phrases are given which contain the information and ideas that must appear in the candidate's answer in order to merit the assigned marks.

2. The descriptions, methods and definitions in the scheme are not exhaustive and alternative valid answers are acceptable.

3. The detail required in any answer is determined by the context and the manner in which the question is asked, and by the number of marks assigned to the answer in the examination paper and, in any instance, therefore, may vary from year to year.

4. The bold text indicates the essential points required in the candidate's answer. A double solidus (//) separates points for which separate marks are allocated in a part of the question. Words, expressions or statements separated by a solidus (/) are alternatives which are equally acceptable for a particular point. A word or phrase in bold, given in brackets, is an acceptable alternative to the preceding word or phrase. Note, however, that words, expressions or phrases must be correctly used in context and not contradicted, and where there is evidence of incorrect use or contradiction, the marks may not be awarded.

5. In general, names and formulas of elements and compounds are equally acceptable except in cases where either the name or the formula is specifically asked for in the question. However, in some cases where the name is asked for, the formula may be accepted as an alternative.

6. There is a deduction of one mark for each arithmetical slip made by a candidate in a calculation.

Outline Marking Scheme

Section A [At least *two* questions must be answered from this section]

1. (a) Identify 5; (b) Name 3, 2 × 3, Explain 3; (c) (i) Describe 2 × 3, (ii) Why 6; (d) (i) Moles per litre 6, (ii) Grams per litre 3; (e) Calculate (i) 3, (ii) 9.

2. (a) Why 5, Type 3; (b) Complete 2 × 3, Balance 3; (c) What 3, Why 3, Describe 6; (d) Describe 6, 3; (e) Location (i) 3, (ii) 3; (f) Observe (i) 3, (ii) 3.

3. (a) What 2 × 4; (b) Identify 3, Colour 3; (c) Describe 12; (d) Species 6, Give 3; (e) (i) 9, (ii) 6.

Section B

4. *Eight* items to be answered. Six marks are allocated to each item and one additional mark is added to each of the first two items for which the highest marks are awarded.

   (a) 6; (b) 6; (c) 2 × 3; (d) 6; (e) (i) 3, (ii) 3; (f) 6; (g) 2 × 3; (h) 6; (i) 2 × 3; (j) 6; (k) A: 2 × 3, B: 3, 3.

5. (a) (i) Describe 2 × 4, (ii) Why 3, 3, (iii) What 3, (iv) Define 6, (v) What 2 × 3. (b) (i) Define 3, 3, (ii) Explain 2 × 3, (iii) 6, 3.

6. (a) (i) What 8, (ii) What 3, (iii) Identify 3, 3, 3, (iv) Process 3, Why 3. (b) (i) Give 2 × 3, (ii) Give 2 × 3. (c) 12.

7. (a) Define 5; (b) Give 3, 3, Which 3, Why 3; (c) Describe 3, 3, 3, 3; (d) When 6; (e) Type 3, Give 2 × 3, 2 × 3.

8. (a) (i) What 5, (ii) Explain 2 × 3, (iii) What 2 × 3, Name 3, (iv) What 3, Why 3. (b) (i) Explain 3, 3, 3, (ii) Draw 3, 3, 3, (iii) Explain 6.

9. (a) What 5; (b) (i) Name 3, Formula 3, (ii) Identify 3, (iii) What 3, Why 3, (iv) Give 3; (c) Describe 3 × 3, State 3, Explain 3; (d) Draw 4 × 3.

10. (a) (i) What 4, (ii) Define 2 × 3, (iii) What 3 × 3, (4) Calc. 6. (b) Define 4, What (i) 3, (ii) 3, State 3, Explain 3, Identify 3, Colours 3, 3. (c) (i) Give 4 + 3, (ii) Explain 6, (iii) Describe 4 × 3.

11. (a) (i) What 4, (ii) Give 3, (iii) Moles 9, (iv) Molecules 3, (v) Mass 6. (b) State 4 + 3, (i) When 3, Explain 3, (ii) State 3, Explain 3, (iii) How 6. (c) A (i) What 2 × 3, Describe 2 × 3, (ii) Name 3, (iii) State 6, What 4. B (i) What 4 × 3, (ii) Name 3, Equation 2 × 3, (iii) Why 4.

Section A

At least *two* questions must be answered from this section.

QUESTION 1

(a) IDENTITY: **anhydrous sodium carbonate (Na$_2$CO$_3$)**

                                        [Allow (3) for *sodium carbonate*.] (5)

[*OTHER POSSIBILITY*: sodium tetraborate
(disodium tetraborate, Na$_2$B$_4$O$_7$)]

(b) NAME: **indicator**   (3)

                        colour change   (2 × 3)

methyl orange	orange (yellow)	//	to red (pink)
methyl red	yellow	//	to red (pink)
methyl yellow	yellow	//	to red (pink)
bromophenol blue	blue (purple, violet)	//	to yellow
bromocresol green	blue	//	to yellow

[*Colour change must be matched with chosen indicator*]

         EXPLAIN: **indicator is a** weak **acid/indicator is a** weak **base**   (3)

(c) (i) DESCRIBE: **rinse with deionised (distilled) water //
                        rinse with reagent (solution)**   (2 × 3)

     (ii) WHY: **air will be displaced by the solution (reagent)/some
                        of measured volume replaces air/some of measured
                        volume not delivered/some of measured volume
                        goes to fill space/causes (gives) wrong (inaccurate,
                        too high, too low) reading (result, titre)/air will be
                        displaced (removed, got rid of)** during the
                        titration/**will be filled during the titration/affects
                        result**/burette **only works properly when it** (part below
                        tap) **is full**/burette **designed to work properly when it**
                        (part below tap) **is full/distorts result (reading)**
                        [Accept 'air bubbles' for 'air']   (6)

(d) (i) MOL/LITRE: **0.05731/0.0573/0.057 M**   [0.06 (− 1)*]   (6)

$$\frac{25 \times X}{1} = \frac{26.05 \times 0.11}{2} \quad (3)$$

$$X = 0.05731/0.0573/0.057 \text{ M} \quad (3)$$

*Not deducted if more
accurate value also given.
However, lost later if 0.06
used in later calculations.

     (ii) g/LITRE: **6.042 to 6.075 g l^{-1}**   (3)

$$0.0573 \times 106* = 6.075 \quad (3)$$

[*Addition must be shown for error to be treated as a slip.*]

(e) CALCULATE: (i)   **62.9 to 63.2%**   (3)

$$\frac{10.325 \times 100}{16.4} = 62.9 \qquad (3)$$

(ii)   **10**[*Accept answers giving 10 when rounded off to nearest integer*]   (9)

M_r of $Na_2CO_3 = 106$	M_r of $H_2O = 18$

hydrated form $=$ 8.20×2 $=$ 16.4 g l^{-1}
water content $=$ $16.4 - 6.075$ $=$ 10.325 (3)

$\dfrac{6.075}{106}$ $:$ $\dfrac{10.325}{18}$ (3)

0.0573   :   0.573

1   :   10   (3)

OR

anhydrous form $= 6.075 \div 2$ $=$ 3.0375 g/500cm^3
water content $=$ $8.20 - 3.0375$ $=$ 5.1625 (3)

$\dfrac{3.0375}{106}$ $:$ $\dfrac{5.1625}{18}$ (3)

0.0287   :   0.287

1   :   10   (3)

OR

hydrated form $=$ 16.4 g l^{-1} $\Rightarrow$ $M_r = \dfrac{16.4}{0.05731} = 286$ (3)

water content $=$ $286 - 106$ $=$ $\dfrac{180}{286} = 106 + 18x$ (3)

$\Rightarrow$ x $=$ 180 $\div$ 18 $=$ 10 (3)

OR

hydrated form $=$ 16.4 g l^{-1} $\dfrac{M_r}{106} = \dfrac{16.4}{6.075} \Rightarrow M_r = 286$ (3)

water content $=$ $286 - 106 = \dfrac{180}{286} = 106 + 18x$ (3)

$\Rightarrow$ x $=$ 180 $\div$ 18 $=$ 10 (3)

OR

hydrated form $= 16.4 \text{ g l}^{-1} \Rightarrow$ water $= 16.4 - 6.075 = 10.325$g (3)

$\dfrac{\text{water}}{106} = \dfrac{10.325}{6.075} \Rightarrow$ water $= 180$ (3)

$\Rightarrow x = 180 \div 18 = 10$ (3)

OR

anhydrous form $= 3.0375 \text{ g}/500\text{cm}^3$ water $= 8.2 - 3.0375 = 5.1625$ g (3)

$\dfrac{\text{water}}{106} = \dfrac{5.1625}{3.0375} \Rightarrow$ water $= 180$ (3)

$\Rightarrow x = 180 \div 18 = 10$ (3)

[*Note:* If no marks have been got in (e) (ii), 3 marks to be awarded if M_r of Na_2CO_3 (106) appears in the candidate's calculations.]

QUESTION 2

(a) WHY: **to speed up** the reaction/reaction **is slow/to drive** reaction **to completion/to maximise (increase) yield** [Allow even if incorrect reaction specified] [Allow '*to prevent loss of vapour (ethanol, solvent)*]   (5)

    TYPE: base **hydrolysis/saponification** [Accept *substitution*]   (3)

(b) COMPLETE: $\longrightarrow$ **$C_{17}H_{35}COONa$ + $CH_2(OH)CH(OH)CH_2OH$** (2×3)
                             [*Accept without brackets*]

    BALANCE: $\longrightarrow$ $3C_{17}H_{35}COONa$ + $CH_2(OH)CH(OH)CH_2OH$ (3)

[Accept *full structures* (Accept *bonds without Hs*), *also molecular formulas*: $C_{18}H_{35}O_2Na$ *and* $C_3H_8O_3$]

[Give *balancing marks even if both formulas are incorrect.*]

(c) WHAT: **solvent**   (3)

    WHY: **easier to isolate (extract) soap**/some **soap dissolved in ethanol (soap won't precipitate fully)/soap contaminated with ethanol (smells of ethanol, not pure, not got on its own)/more brine needed/avoid waste of ethanol (recover ethanol for further use)/ethanol not needed for end of experiment**   (3)

    DESCRIBE: **diagram showing any *two* from the box and one correct label**   (6)

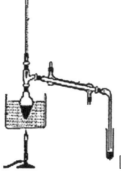

strong heat (Bunsen, hot plate) & thermometer (positioned correctly)/gentle heat (water bath, isomantle)//
still head/distilling flask//
condenser (sloping down, showing inlet & outlet for water)//
collection in vessel (adaptor not required)

[Diagram with any two from the box and no correct label   (3)]

[If no marks got for diagram, (3) may be given for '*heat gently until 20 to 25 cm³ ethanol collected*'. To get this (3) there *must* be a diagram of some sort.]

(d) DESCRIBE: **dissolve residue in minimum of boiling (hot) water/add in a little boiling (hot) water//pour onto brine (salt water, sodium chloride solution)//filter//wash with more brine/wash with** a little **ice-water** POUR INTO BRINE (6) ONE OTHER POINT   (3)

(e) LOCATION: (i)   *second product*: **in the filtrate/in the brine/Buchner flask**   (3)

                           (ii)   *excess sodium hydroxide*: **in the filtrate/in the brine/Buchner flask**   (3)

(f)   OBSERVE: (i)   immediate **lather (suds, bubbles)**   (3)

                           (ii)   **scum/no lather (suds, bubbles)/less lather/does not easily form lather**   (3)

QUESTION 3

(a) WHAT: **intensity (depth) of colour/absorbance/transmittance// proportional to (varies directly with, directly related to, α) concentration**   (2 × 4)

Allow (4) for *colour changes with (depends on) concentration.*

(b) IDENTIFY: **acidified potassium iodide (KI/H$^+$, potassium iodide & ethanoic (sulphuric) acid)/DPD**1 tablet/**DPD** reagent and buffer/**N,N-diethyl-p-phenylenediamine**

        {1-amino-4-diethylamino benzene, (C$_2$H$_5$)$_2$N⟨◯⟩NH$_2$} (3)

COLOUR: *for iodide:* **brown/red/orange/yellow//** *for DPD:* **red/pink** (3)

[*Give the marks for one of these colours even if no reagent or an incorrect reagent is given.*]

(c) DESCRIBE: (12)

Comparator		Colorimeter	
Add reagent to sample	(3)	Prepare (obtain, take) standard solutions	(3)
Colour develops	(3)	Place in colorimeter and note readings (absor/transm)	(3)
Compare with chart (disc, card)*	(3)	Plot readings (results/absor/transm) vs concentration	(3)
Best match gives concentration	(3)	Get it (concentration) from graph (curve)	(3)

[*The (3) for 'colour develops' can also be given, by inference, from this.]

(d) SPECIES: **chlorine (Cl$_2$, dichlorine)/chlorate(I) (hypochlorite, ClO$^-$, OCl$^-$)/chloric(I) acid (hypochlorous acid, HOCl, HClO)/sodium chlorate(I) (sodium hypochlorite, NaClO, NaOCl)/chlorite {chlorate(III), ClO$_2$$^-$}/sodium chlorite {sodium chlorate(III), NaClO$_2$}**   (6)

GIVE: need for greater conc. of chlorine in swimming pool water **to kill pathogens** (harmful **bacteria,** harmful **micro-organisms) added by swimmers/nitrogenous pollutants in swimming pool**/helps disinfection by **forming chloroamines (combined chlorine) in swimming pool/drinking water is less contaminated/drinking water has** much **fewer pathogens** (harmful **bacteria,** harmful **micro-organisms)/ swimming pool water more contaminated**/higher level **would be dangerous (poisonous) to drink**/higher level **would give a bad taste** to drinking water ['to remove' ≠ 'to kill']   (3)

(e) (i):   **650** ppm   (9)

$$\frac{0.78 \times 1000}{1200} \quad = 0.65 \text{ g l}^{-1} \qquad (6)$$

$$0.65 \times 1000 \quad = 650 \text{ ppm} \qquad (3)$$

     (ii):   **1280** ppm   (6)

$$\frac{0.32 \times 1000}{250} \quad = 1.28 \text{ g l}^{-1} \qquad (3)$$

$$1.28 \times 1000 \quad = 1280 \text{ ppm} \qquad (3)$$

Section B

QUESTION 4

Eight items to be answered. Six marks to be allocated to each item and one additional mark to be added to each of the first two items for which the highest marks are awarded.

(a) $1s^2 2s^2 2p^6 3s^2 3p^6 3d^5 4s^1 / 1s^2 2s^2 2p^6 3s^2 3p^6 4s^1 3d^5 / [Ar]3d^5 4s^1 / [Ar]4s^1 3d^5$ (6)

   [Allow 3 marks for $1s^2 2s^2 2p^6 3s^2 3p^6 4s^2 3d^4$] [Accept $p_x^2 {}_y^2 {}_z^2$ for $p_x^2 p_y^2 p_z^2$ or p^6; accept subscripts]

(b) **J J Thomson** (6)

(c) **involves nucleus** of atoms **not electron cloud (electrons)/involves break-up of nucleus/no breaking (forming) of chemical bonds (or named chemical bonds, or molecules)/chemical involves electrons only//involves new elements being generated (made, formed, produced)/transmutation//involves** large scale **release of energy from nucleus//involve the release of nuclear radiation (α, β or γ rays)// mass not conserved in nuclear** (2×3)

(d) **91.3%** (6)

$$\frac{84 \times 100}{92*} \quad (3) = 91.3\% \quad (3)$$

   [*Addition must be shown for error to be treated as a slip but must be based on correct formula]

(e) (i) **H_3O^+** (3)

   (ii) **OH^-** (3)

(f) **identified periodicity of properties/arranged in increasing** rel. **atomic mass (atomic weight)/in his law of octaves/repeat every eighth (after seven)** elements (6)

(g) brick-**red//precipitate (ppt)** produced (2×3)

(h) **11.7** (6)

$$M(OH^-) = 0.2 \backslash 40 = 0.005 \quad (3)$$
$$M(H^+) = 1 \times 10^{-14} \div 0.005 = 2 \times 10^{-12} \Rightarrow pH = -\log 2 \times 10^{-12} = 11.7 \quad (3)$$

OR

$$M(OH^-) = 0.2 \backslash 40 = 0.005 \quad (3)$$
$$pOH = -\log 0.005 = 2.3 \Rightarrow pH = 14 - 2.3 = 11.7 \quad (3)$$

(i) **in solution (in water)//in the molten state (in the liquid state)** (2×3)

(j)   **esters**   (6)
      [Accept *terpenes*]

(k)   **A:**   in **flushing (purging)** oil **tanks**//as **inert atmosphere**//in **preserving
      food**/in **keeping food fresh**/in **packaging food (e.g. crisps)**//over
      gas (oil, flammables) in **tankers (being transported)**//in **glass
      production**//in **semiconductor (microchip) production**//dilutes
      atmospheric oxygen   ANY TWO: (2×3)

      B: *main group*: **aluminium/beryllium/magnesium/calcium**   (3)
      transition: **titanium/nickel/chromium/zirconium/hafnium**
      (Allow *zinc or cadmium*)   (3)

QUESTION 5

(a) (i) DESCRIBE: **place sample of the salt on a nickel** probe {**platinum (nichrome, steel)** wire}//**in (over) a** Bunsen **flame**
[Accept 'in (over) a Bunsen'] (2×4)

(ii) WHY: **each element has a different distribution (set, arrangement) of energy levels/each element has a different electron configuration**   (3)

giving rise to **different electron transitions (jumps)**   (3)

[Allow *due to **different numbers of electrons** and nuclear charge/**different attractions between electrons and nucleus (different electrostatic attractions)** for 3 marks only.*]

Note: the marks here are *not* for how spectra are produced; they are for explaining why different elements have different spectra.]

(iii) WHAT: **atomic absorption spectrometry (AAS)** [Accept the spelling *absorbtion*]   (3)

(iv) DEFINE: **region** around nucleus **in which there is high probability of finding electron/region in which electron likely to be found/wave function of electron got by solution of Schrodinger's equation**   (6)

(v) WHAT: **it is not possible to measure the** exact **position//and energy (momentum, velocity) of an electron** in an atom **simultaneously** (2×3)

(b) (i) DEFINE: **relative (measure of) attraction/number expressing (giving) attraction**   (3)

for shared electrons/for electrons in a covalent bond (3)

(ii) EXPLAIN: **decrease in atomic radius/atoms getting smaller// increase in** effective **nuclear charge** (2×3)

(iii) EXPLAIN: **reactivity increases//**

increase in atomic radius/increase in shells/atoms getting bigger//

effective nuclear charge is the same (effective nuclear charge is +1)/screening (shielding) effect of inner shells cancels the increase in nuclear charge//

outermost electron less tightly held by the nucleus
ANY TWO: $(6 + 3)$

QUESTION 6

(a) (i) WHAT: measure of (indication of, showing, giving) **tendency (likelihood) to auto-ignite (knock, pink, pre-ignite, ignite early, ignite before spark)**/number representing **ability (tendency) of fuel to resist auto-igniting (knocking, pinking, pre-igniting, igniting early, igniting before spark)**   (8)

or

based on a scale where 2, 2, 4-trimethylpentane (*iso*-octane) is assigned a rating of 100 and heptane (*n*-heptane) a value of 0.   (8)

or

percentage by volume of 2, 2, 4-trimethylpentane (*iso*-octane) in a blend (mix) with heptane (*n*-heptane) that matches the behaviour of the fuel in terms of auto-ignition   (8)

[If (8) not given, allow (4) for mention of '*auto-igniting (knocking, etc....see above)*']

(ii) WHAT: **straight chain/unbranched**   (3)

(iii) IDENTIFY: *cyclohexane*:   **ring/cyclic**   (3)
    benzene: **aromatic** [Accept *ring/cyclic*]   (3)
    2, 2, 4-trimethylpentane: **branched**   (3)

(iv) PROCESS: **dehydrocyclisation (cyclodehydrogenation)**   (3)

WHY: benzene **is carcinogenic**/benzene **is toxic (poisonous, harmful to health)**   (3)

(b) (i) GIVE: **high (increase) octane rating (number)/reduces knocking/fuel burns better/improves fuel efficiency**//

produce clean products/produce clean(er) fuel (petrol)/produce environmentally friendly petrol/ reduce pollution/better (more complete) oxidation (oxygenation)/less carbon monoxide produced/do not poison catalyst in **catalytic converter**   (2 × 3)

(ii) GIVE: it **poisons (destroys) the** catalyst in **catalytic converter**// **lead** emission **presents a health hazard/toxic (poisonous)** to living things   (2 × 3)

[Allow for *lead compounds e.g. tetraethyl lead.* Do not accept '*lead is a pollutant*' or '*it damages the environment*']

(c) -3924 kJ mol–1   (12)

C + O$_2$ → CO$_2$ $\Delta H = -394$ kJ mol^{-1}; H$_2$ + ½O$_2$ → H$_2$O $\Delta H = -286$ kJ mol^{-1}

6C + 6H$_2$ → C$_6$H$_{12}$ $\Delta H = -156$ kJ mol^{-1}

C$_6$H$_{12}$ → 6C + 6H2	**156** kJ	(3)	
6C + 6O$_2$ → 6CO$_2$	**–2364** kJ	(3)	[**3924** gets (3) only]
6H$_2$ + 3O$_2$ → 6H$_2$O	**–1716** kJ	(3)	
C$_6$H$_6$ + 9O$_2$ → 6CO$_2$ + 6H$_2$O	**–3924** kJ mol^{-1}	(3)	

Equations not required

$\Delta H = \Sigma \Delta H_{f(products)} - \Sigma \Delta H_{f(reactants)}$

$\Delta H = 6 \times -394 / -2364$ (3) $+ 6 \times -286 / -1716$ (3) $- \{1 \times -156 / -156$ (3) $+ 0\}$

OR $6 \times -394 / -2364$ (3) $+ 6 \times -286 / -1716$ (3) $+ 1 \times 156 / 156$ (3) $- 0$

⇒ $\Delta H_c = -3924$ (3)

QUESTION 7

(a) DEFINE: minimum **energy** required **for colliding particles (molecules) to react**/minimum **energy** required **for effective collisions** between particles (molecules)   (5)
[Accept '*energy needed for colliding particles to initiate reaction*'. Do not accept E_A diagram]
[Allow (3) for '*energy required for reaction to take place*']

(b) GIVE: *first reason*:   **increased energy of collisions (particles, molecules, reactants)**   (3)
[Accept: *more collisions (particles, molecules, reactants) reach activation energy, more collisions are effective*]

    second reason: **increased number of collisions** due to increased velocity (energy) of particles   (3)

WHICH: **first reason above**   (3)

WHY: for same temperature rise **increase in number of collisions** very **small compared with increase in number reaching activation energy (increase in number being effective)/only the high energy collisions lead to reaction (are effective)/** leads to **more (increase in) effective collisions/more collisions reach activation energy/number of collisions reaching (exceeding) activation energy critical for rate** of reaction [Accept '*helps to overcome (exceed) activation energy*'] (3)

(c) DESCRIBE: heat known volumes of **the solutions** separately to a certain temperature   (3)

    mix, note temperature*, and place reaction vessel **over cross (X, mark),** keeping at temperature   (3)
[*Accept a stated temperature]

    record time for cross to become invisible and take rate as $\dfrac{1}{\text{time}}$ (3)

    repeat for other temperature(s)   (3)

[*Note*: could break in different places and still give all the information required.]

(d) WHEN: $AgNO_3$ and $NaCl$ **present as free ions in solution/no bond breaking (dissociation)/**
For $Na_2S_2O_3$ and HCl covalent **bonds must be broken (dissociated)**   (6)

[Accept '*$AgNO_3$ and $NaCl$ are ionic*' or '*$Na_2S_2O_3$ and HCl are covalent*' for (3) only]

(e) TYPE: **heterogeneous** catalysis   (3)

    GIVE: **first entering//first converted to** (2×3)

                     second entering//second converted to (2×3)

[The two substances required can both be hydrocarbons or oxides of nitrogen.]

entering	converted to
carbon monoxide (CO)	**carbon dioxide (CO_2)**
suitable named hydrocarbon (correct formula) Accept the term '*hydrocarbon*' or <u>*any hydrocarbon.*</u>	**carbon dioxide (CO_2) & water (H_2O)**
named oxide of nitrogen (correct formula) Accept NO_x	**nitrogen (N_2) & oxygen (O_2)** [Accept *nitrogen (N_2)* on its own.

QUESTION 8

(a) (i) WHAT: water which **does not** easily **form lather (forms scum instead of lather) with soap**   (5)

[Allow (3) for '*water containing calcium or magnesium ions or their salts*']

(ii) EXPLAIN: **each calcium ion (Ca^{2+})//**
is replaced by 2 sodium ions (Na^+) from the resin (2×3)

or

$$2RNa + Ca^{2+} + 2HCO_3^- \rightarrow 2Na^+ + R_2Ca + 2HCO_3^-$$
$$(2 \times 3)$$

or

$$2RNa + Ca(HCO_3)_2 \rightarrow 2\ NaHCO_3 + R_2Ca$$
[Accept $(R)_2Ca$] (2×3)
FORMULAS: (3)   BALANCING: (3)

(iii) WHAT: **the coming (joining) together (clumping, coagulating)//**
of small (fine) **suspended particles (solids)** in the water
(2×3)

NAME: **aluminium sulfate/aluminium chloride/**
aluminium(III)/ alum/iron(III) sulfate (ferric sulfate)/
iron(III) chloride (ferric chloride)/iron (III)/
polyelectrolytes/lime   (3)
[Accept *a correct formula*]

(iv) WHAT: **lime {calcium hydroxide, $Ca(OH)_2$}/sodium hydroxide**
(caustic soda, NaOH)/sodium carbonate (Na2CO3)/
soda ash   (3)

WHY: causes **corrosion of pipes**   (3)

(b) (i) EXPLAIN: the indicator itself dissociates according to the equation

$$HX \rightleftharpoons H^+ + X^- \quad or \quad HX + H_2O \rightleftharpoons H_3O^+ + X^- \quad (3)$$

in acid (low pH) equilibrium lies on the left (shifts backward) giving colour of molecules (HX)/in acid (low pH) indicator is associated (undissociated) giving colour of molecules (HX)
Associated = present as molecules   (3)

in base (alkali/high pH) equilibrium lies on the right (shifts forward) giving colour of ions (X^-)/in base (alkali/high pH) indicator is dissociated giving colour of ions (X^-) Dissociated = present as ions (ionised)   (3)

(ii) DRAW: **graph with pH axis labelled at 7 and
                    number over 7**   (3)

                    neutralisation point at about 25 cm^3   (3)

                    steep rise at about pH = 6.5 to 10.5   (3)

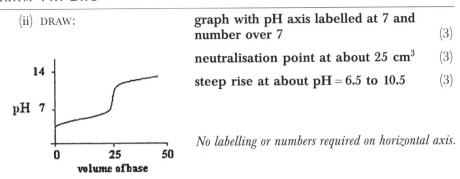

No labelling or numbers required on horizontal axis.

(iii) EXPLAIN: Phenolphthalein has a pH **range from 8.3 – 10 (8 – 10)/
                    phenolphthalein changes colour in steep part of graph** (6)
                    [Allow (3) for *weak acid-strong base* titration]

QUESTION 9

(a)   WHAT: **general formula/differ by CH$_2$/same functional group/similar** chemical **properties/gradation in** physical **properties/similar method of preparation**

ANY ONE: (5)

(b) (i) NAME: **aluminium oxide/alumina**   (3)

FORMULA: **Al$_2$O$_3$**   (3)

(ii) IDENTIFY: **glass wool/roc(k)sil**   (3)

(iii) WHAT: **remove** the delivery **tube from** the trough of **water/ disconnect tube (stopper)** from test tube/**dismantle the apparatus**   (3)

WHY: **to prevent suck-back**   (3)

(iv) GIVE: manufacture of **polythene (polyethene, plastic)**/make **ethane-1,2-diol (ethylene glycol, antifreeze)**/make **polyester (terylene)**/make **PVC**/make **ethanol/ripening fruit**/make **poly(phenylethene) {polystyrene}**   (3)
[*Do not allow general terms e.g. "medicine", "agriculture", "industry", "engineering", but do not cancel them with an acceptable use.*]

(c)   DESCRIBE: **polarisation of Br$_2$/heterolytic fission of the bromine molecule/Br$_2$→ Br$^+$ + Br$^-$//**

addition of bromonium ion (Br$^+$) across the double bond/addition of Br$^+$ forming bridged intermediate (cyclic bromonium ion)//   [Accept *localised carbonium ion*]

attack (addition) of bromide ion (Br$^-$) to the bridged intermediate {cyclic bromonium ion, carbonium ion (C$^+$) } [*Bromide ion (Br$^-$) must be shown or mentioned.*]   (3 × 3)
[*Marks may be got from information given on suitable diagrams.*]

STATE: **other products are formed when the reaction is carried out in the presence of other nucleophiles (anions, negative ions) {e.g. Cl$^-$ (NaCl, HCl)/OH$^-$ (H$_2$O)}** [*May be got from a specific example e.g.2-bromoethanol formed using bromine water (Br$_2$/H$_2$O*]   (3)

EXPLAIN: **these products indicate a positive* (carbonium ion) intermediate/these products support a mechanism with a positive (carbonium ion) intermediate****   (3)

[Accept for 3 marks only: '*reaction works in the dark at room temp. showing that free radicals are not involved.*]

[* For positive, accept also 'ionic', 'Br$^+$'] [**Accept 'intermediate' said in other ways.]

(d) DRAW:

$CH_2=CHCH_2CH_3$
but-1-ene (1-butene)

$CH_3CH=CHCH_3$
but-2-ene (2-butene)

$(CH_3)_2C=CH_2$
2-methylpropene

TWO FORMULAS WITH MATCHING NAMES / TWO NAMES WITH MATCHING
FORMULAS [Note: cis- or trans- or E- or Z- not required]   (4 x 3)

[In expanded structures, bonds without Hs are acceptable. Number not reqd. for
2-methylpropene (allow -1-ene) but award no marks if the number is incorrect.
Apply cancelling if more than two structures are given. Maximum loss is – 3]

QUESTION 10: Answer any *two* of the parts (a), (b) and (c).

(a) (i) WHAT: atoms of **same element (same atomic number, same number of protons)** having **different mass** numbers **(different numbers of neutrons)**   (4)

     (ii) DEFINE: **average mass of atom(s)** of element/**average of isotopes taking abundances into account//relative to (based on)** $\frac{1}{12}$ mass of **carbon-12** atom (2×3)

     (iii) WHAT: positive **ions (particles) separated (deflected, spread out)//based on (according to)** relative **mass(es) {charge/mass ratio}//**when moving **in a magnetic field** (3×3)

     (iv) CALC.:   **6.926** [Accept 6.93 for (6); give (3) for 6.9 if there is nothing else worth marks.]   (6)

$$7.4 \times 6 + 92.6 \times 7 = 692.6 \ (3) \div 100 = 6.926 \quad (3)$$

(b)   DEFINE: **increase**   (4)

             WHAT: (i)   **+1**   [Accept 1]   (3)

                         (ii) **+5**   [Accept 5]   (3)

             STATE: **+2**   [Accept 2]   (3)

             EXPLAIN: oxygen is **more electropositive/less electronegative/ fluorine is more electronegative/fluorine is less electropositive** [*Allow even if ox. no. incorrect.*]   (3)

             IDENTIFY: **potassium iodide (KI) solution/potassium iodide (KI)/iodide (I⁻)/I(** −1 to 0)   (3)

             COLOURS: **purple/violet/maroon**   (3)
                         to brown/red/orange/yellow   (3)

(c) (i) GIVE: alcohols have **higher (bigger)** relative **molecular mass// and polar hydroxyl group (polar OH)/**intermolecular **hydrogen bonds** $(4 + 3)$

     (ii) EXPLAIN: **effect (contrib.) of OH less in butanol/hydrogen bonding weaker in butanol/due to longer carbon chain/due to bigger non-polar part** of molecule   (6)

                         OR

                         effect (contrib.) of OH greater in methanol/hydrogen bonding stronger in methanol/due to shorter carbon chain/due to smaller non-polar part of molecule   (6)

                         [In absence of above 6, allow 3 marks for 'M_r of CH_3OH is double M_r of CH_4 but M_r of C_4H_9OH is only slightly bigger than M_r of C_4H_{10}']

(iii) DESCRIBE: *methane*:   virtually **insoluble**//
                    methanol: completely **soluble (miscible)/miscible in
                                  all proportions**//
                    butane: virtually **insoluble**//
                    butanol: **slightly (sparingly) soluble/less soluble
                                  than methanol** (4×3)

['*All alkanes insoluble*' gets (6); '*All alcohols soluble*' gets (3);
stating the relative solubilities of the four compounds can get (9);
*stating the relative solubilities of the four compounds and giving
the solubility of one of them* can get (12)]

QUESTION 11: Answer any *two* of the parts (a), (b) and (c).

(a) (i) WHAT: perfectly **obeys the gas laws (Boyle's law, kinetic theory, $PV = nRT$)** under all conditions of temperature and pressure   (4)

  (ii) GIVE: **intermolecular forces (attractions between molecules, named correct intermolecular force)/molecules have volume (molecules take up space, volume of molecules not negligible)/collisions not** perfectly **elastic**
                                                                ANY TWO: (3)

  (iii) MOLES: **0.03** mol   (9)

$PV = nRT$ $1 \times 10^5 \times 720 \times 10^{-6} = n \times 8.3 \times 283$ (2×3) $ n = 0.03 (3)$	$\dfrac{P_1 \times V_1}{T_1} = \dfrac{P_2 \times V_2}{T_2}$ $\dfrac{1 \times 10^5 \times 720}{283} = \dfrac{1 \times 10^5 \text{ (or } 1.013 \times 10^5) \times V_2}{273}$ $V_2 = 685 \text{ to } 695 (2 \times 3)$ $\div 22400 = 0.03 (3)$

[Marks in context of correct operations. *Not given correct to one significant figure* (-1)]

  (iv) MOLECULES: **1.8×10^{22}** | $0.03 \times 6 \times 10^{23} = 1.8 \times 10^{22}$ (3) | (3)

  (v) MASS: **2.22 g**   (6)

0.03 mol $CO_2 \equiv 0.03$ mol $Ca(OH)_2$ (3)** $0.03 \times 74* = 2.22$ (3)   [* *Addition must be shown for error to be treated as a slip.*]

  ** *Can be given for 1: 1 ratio or for 0.03 mol Ca(OH)₂*

(b)   STATE: **reactions at equilibrium//oppose (minimise, relieve) applied stress(es)***   (4 + 3)

       [**If the word stress(es) is replaced by particular examples (e.g. pressure), all three (temperature, pressure & concentration) must be given.*]*

  (i) WHEN: **no**   (3)

     EXPLAIN: **forward and reverse reactions continue** at same rate/**reactants changing to products and products changing to reactants**   (3)

  (ii) STATE: **becomes pink**   (3)

     EXPLAIN: equilibrium **shifts (moves, goes) to left/shifts backwards/shifts in reverse/shifts in the exothermic direction/shifts to produce heat/shifts to oppose (minimise) cooling/shifts to minimise (oppose) stress** (3)

(iii) HOW: **add** conc. **hydrochloric acid (HCl)/add chloride ions
(Cl⁻)/add** source of **chloride ions (Cl⁻)** e.g **NaCl/remove
water**   (6)

(c) **A**

AMMONIA:

(i) WHAT: **air//natural gas (methane, CH4)//water**   ANY TWO: (2×3)

DESCRIBE: *air*:   **filter/liquefaction (distillation)/natural gas
(methane, CH₄) burned in it** to get
nitrogen//

natural gas: **desulfurise/steam reform (react with steam)//**

water: **deionised/react with natural gas (steam
reforming)**

TWO MATCHING THE STATED RAW MATERIALS: (2×3)

(ii) NAME: **ammonia/carbon dioxide/oxides of nitrogen (correctly
named)**   (3)
[Accept *formulas*]

(iii) STATE: **fertilisers {urea, CO(NH₂)₂, C.A.N., any sol. amm.
salt}/nylon/nitric acid (HNO₃)**   (6)

WHAT: contains **nitrogen**   (4)

NITRIC ACID:

(i) WHAT: **ammonia/air/water**   ANY TWO: (2×3)

DESCRIBE: *ammonia*:   **no treatment/filter (remove dust)/
vaporise//**

air: **filter (remove dust)//**

water: **deionise**

TWO MATCHING THE STATED RAW MATERIALS: (2×3)

(ii) NAME: **nitric acid/nitrates/oxides of nitrogen (correctly named)**
(3)

[Accept *formulas*]

(iii) STATE: **fertilisers (ammonium nitrate, NH₄NO₃, any soluble
nitrate)/nylon/explosives**   (6)

WHAT: *fertilisers & nylon*: contains **nitrogen**//*explosives*: **unstable
compounds/oxygen rich**   (4)

or

MAGNESIUM OXIDE:

(i) WHAT: **limestone/sea water/fresh (river) water** ANY TWO: (2×3)

   DESCRIBE: *limestone*:   **crushed/washed/calcined {burnt (heated) to quicklime (calcium oxide, CaO)}/slaked [water added to form slaked lime {calcium hydroxide, Ca(OH)2}]**//

   sea water: **acidified (H$_2$SO$_4$ added, pH lowered)/degassed (CO$_2$ removed)/ clarified (solids settle)**//

   fresh water: **acidified (H$_2$SO$_4$ added, pH lowered)/degassed (CO$_2$ removed)**

   TWO MATCHING THE STATED RAW MATERIALS: (2×3)

(ii) NAME: **dust, suspended solids, lime (calcium hydroxide), magnesium oxide, oxides of sulphur (named correctly)**
   (3)

   [Accept *formulas*]

(iii) STATE: **refractory (heat-resistant) materials (ceramics)/furnace linings (walls)** (6)

   WHAT: very **high melting point/melting point > 2000 °C/ insulating** (4)

(c) **B**

(i) WHAT: **iron ore {haematite (Fe$_2$O$_3$), magnetite (Fe$_2$O$_3$), siderite (FeCO$_3$), pyrite (iron pyrites, FeS$_2$)}**//
   coke (C)//
   limestone (calcium carbonate/CaCO$_3$)//
   hot **air** (4×3)

(ii) NAME: **carbon monoxide (CO)** (3)

   EQUATION: **Fe$_2$O$_3$ + 3CO $\rightarrow$ 2Fe + 3CO$_2$**
   FORMULAS: (3) BALANCING: (3)

(iii) WHY: pig iron **brittle (impure, high carbon content)/great(er) demand for steel/small(er) demand for pig iron/steel more useful/pig iron less useful/pig iron cannot be re-worked/pig iron rusts** more easily (4)